# Date Due

*Citizen Hoover*

# Citizen

## A critical study of

# Hoover

*the life and times
of J. Edgar Hoover
and his FBI*

**Jay Robert Nash**

Nelson-Hall nh Chicago

ISBN 0-911012-60-5

Library of Congress Catalog Card No. 72-76266

# Contents

# 1

# The Man Nobody Knows

No man in the last half century of American life has wielded so much awesome and terrifying power as John Edgar Hoover. As head of the FBI since 1924, Hoover has been to generations of Americans a benefactor and bully, protector and oppressor, truth-giver and liar.

Citizen Hoover has outlasted seven presidents and sixteen attorney generals while performing some of the most astounding broken-field running, between Republican and Democrat, liberal and conservative, ever witnessed in this country's politics.

Hoover is—if one looks beyond the bureaucratic labyrinth of the Federal Bureau of Investigation—essentially a politician. At politics he is a master. No one else in Washington today has managed to clutch high power with such tenacious longevity. Should the inscription *Hoover longa, vita brevis* be chiseled on the venerable cornerstone of the new FBI building now under construction, it would surprise few.

The truth about the life of the Director, however, is much less concrete. He is an enigma nervously joked about at Washington teas. There are many "directors" of bureaus and departments in Washington, you will be told over sherry. But when one refers to "The Director," the identity is clear. There is but one "Director" in Washington: Hoover.

He is also known as "The Man," and "The Power." He *is* the FBI. And the FBI under his direction is the most secretive, free-wheeling federally-funded organization in American government. Like Mitsuru Toyama's once all-powerful Black Dragon Society in pre-World War II Japan, the FBI's influence is vast and ominous; the FBI is answerable only to its leader, and its leader is answerable only to the attorney general and the president, two positions of authority Hoover has deftly managed to sidestep whenever he thought best, which, for the past forty-eight years, has been almost always.

Such autonomy has little to do with luck and less to do with authentic achievement; it is more the result of Hoover's astounding political acumen. Imbued with Washington savvy from his earliest days, Hoover cleverly maneuvered his career from the moment he unceremoniously slipped into the FBI's "seat of government," as he calls it, in 1924. Meeting the then newly-appointed attorney general, Harlan Fiske Stone, Hoover played his trump card. He knew his man well. Stone was a stickler for regulations and rabid on reform (and considering the abysmally corrupt FBI at the time of Hoover's takeover, Stone's attitude was not surprising).

Hoover told Stone that he would take over the FBI, but only under certain conditions.

"What are they?" Stone demanded.

"The Bureau must be divorced from politics," Hoover insisted, "and not be a catchall for political hacks. Appointments must be based on merit. Secondly, promotions will be made on proved ability, and the Bureau will be responsible only to the attorney general."

Since Stone was the attorney general, such grand words of stalwart honesty and devotion to duty were more than acceptable. The fact was that Hoover had, in one swoop of rhetoric, established an autonomous base which would be buffered by the attorney general.

From that time to the present, Hoover has been both assailed and supported fanatically, while his personality and operations have quietly receded into an image no bigger nor more expressive than the sharply-stenciled name on his office door. Information concerning the real John Edgar Hoover has become more and more vague—inconsequential tricklings of meaningless gossip, for the most part.

Columnist Jack Anderson vowed he would reveal the real Hoover. Borrowing typical FBI techniques, Anderson burrowed into Hoover's garbage can. What he found and reported to an anxious public was no more than pedestrian rubbish.

Of late, unrevealing trivia seems to be all that can be mustered in telling Hoover's story. The public's curiosity has been weakly appeased with such morsels as:

—Hoover rides about in a chauffeur driven, bulletproof limousine, which, in 1971, cost $30,000; Hoover gets a new bulletproof limousine each year whereas the president gets a new limousine every four years. The prices of Hoover's limousines for the last few years were $21,114 in 1968, $23,241 in 1969, $27,663 in 1970. (Though certain writers have pointed out that Hoover has been given these elegant autos each year in which to wheel about in his pursuit of criminals, Communists, and "The Truth" since 1935, they have neglected to say that this policy was abandoned by the Director in 1936 for one year because he was under severe criticism from certain congressmen sitting on appropriations committees: such personal luxuries during a depression would have been alarming to those from whom he sought an increase in funds for his FBI. (Incidentally, a recent analysis of Hoover's handwriting by an experienced Graphoanalyst indicates that Hoover has "a penchant for things that contribute to his physical comfort and a liking for a variety of luxuries of substantial worth," which might explain, if you are of that mind, Hoover's super cars and expensive vacations paid for by others.)

—Hoover's salary is presently $42,500 a year. (The House approved a raise for Hoover on May 3, 1946, to $14,000 a year, $1,000 less than the attorney general was then receiving. The reason for this raise, according to Majority Leader John J. McCormack (D., Mass.), was friendship—to show support from those who had voted him the raise. McCormack proclaimed the action would "constitute an answer to the unfair critics of this great man, and . . . show that in this body he has friends." Since 1946 Hoover's wages have been increased $1,000 each year, or $20 a week, each and every week, which is one of the best deals any federal employee ever had—once again triumphantly proving that old adage, "It pays to have friends.")

—Hoover's favorite child movie star is Shirley Temple. His favorite adult movie star is Ginger Rogers. (Once, when Hoover was troubled by critics, Ginger's mother referred to him as that "poor child.")

—Hoover is on a strict diet and likes to eat cottage cheese and grapefruit for lunch. He is known to take an occasional drink (Jack Daniels).

—Hoover is the eternal sports fan; he used to enjoy ringside seats at boxing matches, but is now content in his declining years to view sports events via his home TV set.

—Hoover's proudest sports achievement was catching a five-foot-long sailfish near Miami, Florida, in February of

1936; the fish, now stuffed and mounted, is hanging on his office wall. (The alleged death mask of John Dillinger is also mounted and displayed nearby.)

—Hoover likes antiques, clean mystery stories, and *The Reader's Digest*.

—Hoover attends church regularly and is considered to be a religious man.

—Hoover is extremely germ-conscious and has installed special ultra-violet lamps in his W.C. to insure sanitation.

—Hoover has a sense of humor; he once posed for photographers while staring down a bulldog to which unkind critics had likened his countenance.

All in all, these "probes" into Hoover's real character have been less than incisive. Such tidbits of information, however, when coupled with other facets of Hoover's personality, enlarge the puzzle.

Recently, when he was facetiously asked about his sleeping habits by a reporter, Hoover refused to comment. But the FBI did not take the inquiry lightly. Such is the nature of the FBI's concern that almost immediately FBI Assistant Director Thomas Bishop emphatically stated: "The rumors that Hoover sleeps with a night light on are just not true!"

Rumors, after all, are Hoover's business. And the Director has allowed certain rumors about him to go unchallenged, particularly if they serve the image of his all-encompassing authority.

One such story had Hoover methodically reading over the daily reports sent to him from his Bureau chiefs throughout the country. He came to a report that was so jammed with typewritten notes that there was no room for the Director's inevitable hand-written comments. Hoover managed to squeeze onto the memo in tiny printed words the order, "Watch the borders." The following day tense aides sent agents flying to the Canadian and Mexican borders to await further instructions and to guard against the unstated menace.

Ridiculous? Not in the halls of the FBI, where suspicion and constant apprehension over the state of one's job are of foremost concern. Since Hoover has successfully fought off attempts to bring his Bureau under civil service, he can and does fire his federal employees at will and whim without repercussion or regret. Though Hoover and his FBI are sacrosanct, critics are no longer sparsely strewn through Congress and the land at large, laboring under the labels of malcontent and misfit. On the broad plane of public opinion, Hoover's image has all but crashed. New, high-pitched criticism is pointing out that he has outlived the monumental historic image he built for himself in a more gullible time—a time when Steinbeck's Ma Joad was basically concerned with keeping her family on the road to the promised land, and when whatever the G-men did was best for the country.

The general public visiting Washington in the last few years has probably worried Hoover more than his highly vocal critics in Congress. Tourist attendance at his much-vaunted FBI museum has drastically fallen off. It appears that the public is no longer interested in looking at the alleged gun John Dillinger tried to pull on FBI agents outside the Biograph Theater in Chicago on that long-ago July night in 1934, or the necktie an FBI agent used for lack of handcuffs to bind the wrists of "public enemy" Alvin "Old Creepy" Karpis after Hoover "personally" arrested him in New Orleans in 1936.

To the public Hoover's museum must seem akin to the Ripley's Believe-It-Or-Not museums found across the country. Hoover's grisly trophies can only appear to be what they are—curious relics of a barbarous age in which Americans once took "back county" pride.

Yet Hoover can still count a number of important people who not only accept the old myths but are willing to believe in them at all costs, not the least being President Richard M. Nixon.

Mr. Nixon has informed the public that although Hoover has reached an advanced age (seventy-seven), he is still extremely capable of directing America's secret police. Laughable logic or not, Nixon's support of Hoover is understandable, even though Nixon was once turned down for an FBI job.

When Mr. Nixon graduated from Duke University in 1937, he convinced Hoover's friend, Dean H. Claude Horack, to recommend him for an FBI post, which he subsequently did not get. When Mr. Nixon became vice-president, he half-jokingly asked Hoover why he didn't get the job.

Hoover blanched, but quickly recovered. An old hand at political evasion, the Director responded facilely and smoothly. He explained to Mr. Nixon that unexpected appropriation cuts that year compelled the FBI to discontinue the hiring of new men. Had Mr. Nixon thought of this incident as being more than casual ribbing from an old pal, he could have checked the 1937 FBI budget. He would have discovered that Bureau appropriations for 1937 were increased $825,000 over the previous year's appropriations. But Mr. Nixon apparently has never checked that budget.

There has never been a reason for Mr. Nixon to doubt Hoover's word; the Director, for years, had been President Nixon's hero. The two became very friendly in the late 1940s when Congressman Nixon (R., Calif., 1947-50) served on the House Committee on Un-American Activities, which worked closely with Hoover and the FBI.

Mr. Nixon endeared himself to the Director when he played a prominent role in helping to break the Hiss case, which resulted in the conviction and imprisonment of Alger Hiss. In those days, they were both fighting the good fight against Hoover's favorite target—the Red Menace.

Time, political expediency, and unfavorable publicity about Hoover have dimmed Mr. Nixon's once bright image of his FBI hero. Pressure against the Nixon administration to have Hoover ousted became so intense in the fall of 1971 that Mr. Nixon actually rehearsed the firing of the Director.

The plan called for Mr. Nixon to entertain Hoover at the White House. (Such convivial meetings are not unusual since Mr. Nixon has been known to sup with the Director in his home from time to time.) Nixon would praise the Director's illustrious career and then quietly ask for his resignation on a friend-to-friend basis.

When the actual moment came, however, Mr. Nixon could not bring himself to ask the FBI chief to quit. His second thoughts were understandably self-protective. Politically, such an action could not be effectively smoke screened since the Nixon administration had repeatedly stated that Hoover could have his job as long as he wanted it and was physically able to perform his duties. Emotionally, such an action would be difficult in that Mr. Nixon still feels strongly about  the ancient "gangbuster" he has honored for so many decades.

Another good reason for Nixon's stand is the fact that during an election year such as 1972, it would be politically imprudent to dump Hoover and thus arm Muskie, McGovern, McCarthy et al. with another important issue with which to glean votes. Mr. Nixon, who is probably the most energetic political president since FDR, is well aware of the necessity of reducing the potential threat of such issues as Hoover, and does this by allowing noncommittal statements regarding the Director's "retirement" to filter out of the White House without official endorsement.

A good example of this is the rumor which sources close to Mr. Nixon are spreading, in a conspiratorial manner, that Hoover will be dumped *after* the 1972 election—but the plan is not "official," mind you. As a bone thrown to Hoover, such sanctioned gossip unofficially has it that the Director will then be placed in a sort of "chairman of the board" position, whereby he can continue to oversee FBI operations.

Hoover blithely continues to ignore such maneuvering. He has heard all the carping before. More than one president has tried to get rid of him. But his power remains intact.

Not unknown to Hoover is a very active campaign to re-establish his good image and that of the FBI. Ironically, this drive is spearheaded by the very man pondering Hoover's subtle removal, President Nixon. After Congressman Hale Boggs (D., La.) charged that his home phone had been illegally tapped by the FBI, and that the FBI "has adopted the tactics of the Soviet Union and Hitler's Gestapo," Mr. Nixon held a press conference.

The president urged editors and writers "to be fair" when dealing with Hoover. He pointed out that criticism aimed at the Director had been "unfair and malicious" and that Hoover had been taking "a bum rap for a lot of things."

Conservative editor David Lawrence responded to Mr. Nixon's appeal two days later with: "The FBI can be relied upon to carry on inside the United States extensive investigations of subversion, espionage, and any conspiracy against the government. For the FBI is the principal safeguard of the internal security of our country."

Countermoves began. In the same month, the *Washington Post* led a left-handed attack on Hoover by stating: "House Majority Leader Hale Boggs' transparent failure to back up his specific charge that the FBI had tapped his home telephone should not be allowed to obscure the significance of his contribution to an understanding of the grave threat which the Bureau represents to American liberty."

Writer Ken W. Clawson saw a response to this threat being made by an aroused public: "After decades of immunity from public criticism, the Federal Bureau of Investigation and its Director, J. Edgar Hoover, within the last five months have become a punching bag for an ever broadening segment of the nation."

A month later more Hoover testimonials dribbled in from expected sources. One emanated from Congressman Larry Hogan (R., Md.). "As a former FBI agent and ten-year veteran of the Bureau," he announced, "I know from firsthand experience how zealous the FBI and its Director are in protecting the rights of citizens. . . . Even the severest critics of the FBI know that it is a highly professional law enforcement agency, which has been a model for police agencies all over the world."

Congressman Hogan did not take pains to inspect and analyze that model which, for decades, had gone totally against the grain of Hoover's pledge to Harlan Fiske Stone. Hoover, over the years, has consistently skirted the attorney general's office by sending his "alley gossip" memos directly to the president. Presidents Roosevelt and Johnson were particularly delighted by these memos, which gave them considerable political advantage.

The content of such confidential memos was described by Attorney General Francis Biddle. It consisted of "the intimate details of what my associates in the cabinet did and said," Biddle stated, "of their likes and dislikes, their weaknesses and their associations. Edgar was not above relishing a story derogatory to an occupant of one of the seats of the mighty."

Hoover's so-called confidential memos work both ways. While some feel they border on political blackmail, others, no doubt, consider them protective amulets for those who lend their considerable support to Hoover.

In defending the Director against charges of bugging the phones of congressmen, Senator Hugh Scott (R., Pa.) let it be known how convenient it is to be in Hoover's favor. He said, "I know that when one attorney general was busy investigating my income taxes because I was too incisive in my charges against Bobby Baker, I was very much thankful for the FBI, which was prepared to investigate and, I believe, assert my integrity. I was glad the FBI was there when the attorney general was after me."

To be sure. But since the attorney general operates almost solely on information he receives from the FBI, there can be little belief that Scott was in real jeopardy. His announced vulnerability, whether real or imagined, only served to give Hoover heroic stature. Scott's ploy was worthy of Hoover's own genius for snaring favorable publicity.

Senator George McGovern (D., S. Dak.) enjoys no such congenial relationship with Hoover. He, like Senator Muskie (D., Me.), has promised to fire Hoover should he be elected president. McGovern is also Hoover's foremost congressional opponent.

It was McGovern who read aloud a letter (unsigned) which he claimed was written by ten FBI agents from a single Bureau (reported to be the Los Angeles Bureau). The letter stated that Hoover was giving the FBI a bad name and should be removed from office.

McGovern also leapt to the defense of TWA Captain Donald J. Cook, who, the senator claimed, had been viciously attacked by Hoover. McGovern stated that Hoover had tried to pressure TWA into firing Captain Cook after the pilot had criticized FBI agents for mishandling the capture of a would-be sky-jacker.

"It is clear that Mr. Hoover was trying to destroy the career of Captain Donald J. Cook," McGovern charged, "in retribution for Captain Cook's criticism of the FBI. Mr. Hoover informed TWA that Captain Cook had experienced some personal difficulty in the air force prior to his employment with TWA."

Cook's criticism of the FBI was blunt. He stated that the plan put forward by FBI agents to recapture the sky-jacker was "a prescription for getting the entire crew killed and the plane destroyed." This immediately prompted Hoover to take the vendettalike action—far beyond the scope of FBI responsibilities—of informing TWA of Cook's past.

McGovern labeled the plan to capture the sky-jacker, while the plane awaited takeoff at Kennedy Airport, a "wild-west-type FBI raid." A similar type raid by the FBI in Miami resulted in the death of crew members of a sky-jacked plane forced to land there.

When TWA refused to fire Cook, Hoover attempted direct intimidation. McGovern reported: "When the FBI was to supply a contingency force of air marshalls to prevent high-jackings, Mr. Hoover sought to prevent any service by FBI personnel on TWA flights. Hoover also sought to discourage FBI personnel from flying TWA."

Later, McGovern nostalgically related, "As a boy, I, too, regarded J. Edgar Hoover as a great G-man, protector of all virtue, enemy of all vice. This [the incident with TWA] demonstrates the immediate necessity for the end of the Hoover regime."

McGovern's sentiments could be echoed by just about every American over age twenty. Generations were weened on "Junior G-man" badges, secret codes, and rings (inspired by that best-forgotten gangbuster, Special Agent

Melvin Purvis of the FBI, Hoover's personal albatross);
were enthralled by nerve-wracking radio programs drama-
tizing triumphant FBI agents with resonant voices forever
outwitting squeeky-voiced "public rats" of the underworld;
and saluted Hoover's seemingly single-handed extermina-
tion of phalanxes of Nazi fifth columnists.

The FBI of that era was the FBI "in peace and war"; it
stood undaunted, insurmountable and impregnable, against
the forces of evil that challenged the "American Way." One
could be certain in those days that the FBI was always
there, hovering, waiting to pounce upon the wrongdoer.

What happened? Nothing happened. The truth is the
FBI of our collective memory never really existed outside
of the very fertile and imaginative mind of its eternal Director, Citizen John Edgar Hoover. To him, all high adventure was possible in the cause of Right, all moral victories
over obvious evil inevitable, so long as faith in the all-encompassing power of his good office was absolute.

It has been that way with Hoover since the beginning.

# 2

# The Young Years

It is fitting that America's militaristic "March King," John Philip Sousa, and John Edgar Hoover came from the same muddy section of Washington, D.C., known locally as "Pipetown." Sousa immortalized that grubby rut of roads and jumble of little homes in his "Pipetown Sandy." Hoover never speaks of the hardscrabble area of his youth.

Hoover's ancestors were hardy Alpine stock, who moved, contrary to tradition, from Switzerland to the flatlands of Holland; then, in the early 1800s, they immigrated to America, settling in Pipetown's dreary streets. Hoover's grandfather, John Thomas Hoover, worked in Washington for the United States Coast and Geodetic Survey. His son, Dickerson, followed him in the bureaucratic system of civil service jobs, and lived out an unspectacular life without changing employment.

The marriage between Ann Scheitlin and Dickerson Hoover produced three children—Dickerson, Jr., Lillian, and the youngest, John Edgar, who was born in Washington on New Year's Day, 1895. John was anything but a difficult child.

While the Hoovers lived at 413 Seward Square, S.E., John Edgar entered the Brent Public School. Playmates recall that he was a serious-minded youngster who dourly refused to participate in the friendly gang battles between Pipetown boys and those from neighboring areas known as the Foggy Bottom and Cowtown. Young John Edgar minded his own business and read his Bible.

Fundamentalism was at the core of the family's religious beliefs and is still so rock hard in Hoover that he considers any modernization of traditional church teachings tantamount to treason against the American people. This attitude was never more evident than in a recent blast at the National Council of Churches. Hoover was quoted as saying: "Many Communist fronts have operated under the guise of some church commission or religious body. It is ghastly to see the monster atheism being nourished in the churches which it seeks to destroy. . . .

"Any minister who cannot find in his Bible sufficient arguments for the cause of liberty and social justice, who has to borrow the double talk of the Communists, is in the wrong profession, and should be carefully watched by his official superiors and his congregation."

Hoover, it appears, has always felt the need to be on watch—and to do the watching. This feeling, deeply rooted in religion, is much the result of his old-fashioned Bible training and incessant classes in religion.

"I always had to go to Sunday School," he recalled once. "I was given a little Testament for attendance on fifty-two consecutive Sundays and it was one of my treasures. I still have it."

While attending Washington's Central High, John Edgar Hoover pondered the possibility of becoming a minister. Even after graduating from Central in 1913 (he was class valedictorian), Hoover continued with his Bible classes, at times teaching them. On such occasions, Hoover would enter the Bible class with a military bearing, dressed as a captain of the cadets, a military section at Central High which he had voluntarily entered.

Hoover was the silent type at Central. He was reserved. He kept his ambitions close to his chest. He is remembered as having been God-fearing and without any close classmate associations.

The Director's greatest schoolboy love was sports. He was never very good at any single sport, but did manage to play on the baseball team, until his game was cut short by a hard-driven ball that flattened his nose. Since he weighed a scant hundred pounds, Hoover was not allowed onto the football field.

Feeling a need to excel in something, John Edgar joined the school debating team and, to his surprise, helped to win four local championships. This effort, however, did not expand his social life. Hoover remained a "loner."

The only levity Hoover's classmates enjoyed with him was calling him "Speed," a nickname he earned by always being in a hurry to get somewhere. The ultimate destination was unknown then, but it would figure importantly in the United States government.

By the time Hoover entered George Washington University, he had discarded the idea of becoming a minister, filled out to 180 pounds, shot up to five feet, eleven inches, and had taken sharp aim at a law degree. On October 13, 1913, Hoover took a menial paper-shuffling job with the Library of Congress to supplement his income while in college. He graduated an honor student with a Bachelor of Law degree in 1916, getting his master's in 1917. That year he was admitted to the District of Columbia Bar. Also in that year, John Edgar Hoover landed a clerkship in the Department of Justice at a beginning salary of $990 a year.

This was to be his home and subsequently his "seat of government," as he called it, for the next fifty-five years.

But nothing changed in Hoover's personal life on July 26, 1917, when he got his clerkship. At twenty-two, Hoover continued to live at home with his parents in Pipetown. Bible reading went on uninterrupted in the Hoover home, and grace was said before every meal.

While Hoover plodded away in his clerkship, his older brother, Dickerson, Jr., achieved some level of prominence. Dickerson had a federal clerk's job, too, but had finally wangled his way upward until he was appointed supervising inspector general of the U.S. Steamboat Inspection Service. This glorious title and ambiguous position were odd in that Dickerson Hoover, Jr., never went to sea. But at least he hadn't ended up as a clerk stamping endless federal documents.

Shortly after the United States entered the war in 1917, John Edgar's chance came, not as a doughboy, for Hoover never served in the armed forces during World War I (he was listed, however, for years on reserve status as a major and delighted in being called by that rank), but in the Department of Justice.

The department during the war was suddenly understaffed and overworked. The "Hun scare" was at its peak and the department had to contend with approximately two hundred thousand self-styled, self-appointed vigilantes, whose appointments were later casually confirmed by the Justice Department (they wore makeshift badges when the department's "official" identification cards gave out). These vigilantes indiscriminately arrested aliens on "suspicion" of being spies and saboteurs.

Hundreds of hapless immigrants were falsely arrested, beaten, and threatened with deportation simply because they spoke with "suspicious" accents and looked strange.

The voices of certain congressmen and the press brought tremendous pressure against the department to halt such abuses. In desperation, Attorney General Thomas W. Gregory appointed John Lord O'Brien as his special assistant in charge of war work, and gave him a new staff. Hoover was named as one of O'Brien's aides. Though Hoover had had no practical experience to recommend him for the post, he was made unit chief in the enemy alien registration section.

Hoover worked tirelessly at his job. His chance to prove his integrity and ingenuity had arrived. With him it was not a case of "rounding up the usual suspects." He worked day and night rooting out would-be spies, saboteurs, and slackers who had not responded to the draft. Whenever O'Brien, a rock-ribbed Republican from Buffalo, New York, needed a volunteer for any tedious assignment, Hoover was there. He was more than willing to "do his bit" for the boys over there in the Great War.

By 1919, Hoover had accumulated numerous "credits" in his personal government dossier and had acquired a reputation for dedication to duty. Then, on June 2 of that year, an event took place that catapulted him into the Washington limelight. At 11:15 that night, two political activists placed a bomb in front of the home of Attorney General A. Mitchell Palmer.

The resulting blast tore half of Palmer's house away, shattered the glass in almost every neighboring home, and blew the fleeing activists to bits. A large hunk of bloody flesh landed on the front doorstep of the man who lived across the street from Palmer—Secretary of the Navy Franklin Delano Roosevelt.

That night, eight other explosions tore away the facades of government buildings and the homes of political and business leaders. Police stated that at the scene of each bombing, they found the same finely-printed message: "The powers-that-be make no secret of their will to stop here in America the worldwide spread of revolution. The powers that be must reckon that they will have to accept the fight they have provoked. A time has come when the social question's solution can be delayed no longer; class war is on, and cannot cease but with a complete victory for the international proletariat. . . ."

Altogether, thirty-eight bombs were sent out to three cabinet members, a supreme court justice, four senators, two members of the House of Representatives, a U.S. district judge, two governors, and several business tycoons, including J. P. Morgan and John D. Rockefeller. All were intercepted or exploded by police. The servant of Senator Tom Hardwick of Georgia was the only person injured.

The "Red Menace" caused a national panic and created political pandemonium. Attorney General Palmer, shaken and dazed at his close call, reacted swiftly. He gave Hoover, whose work record showed him to be a zealot in this arena, the command of the department's General Intelligence Division. The twenty-four-year-old special assistant to the attorney general was told to study subversives to determine the scope of their activities and how they could be prosecuted.

John Edgar Hoover went to the library.

There he gobbled up the writings of Marx, Engels, Lenin, and Trotsky. He pieced together the Communist blueprint for world revolution and takeover. Having never been steeped in political theory, Hoover developed an enormous fear of the "Red Menace."

While Hoover was writing his report, the so-called "Palmer Red Raids" commenced. Two hundred and fifty officers of the Federation of the Union of Russian Workers were scooped up and jailed.

Hoover was assigned to help prosecute anarchists Emma Goldman and Alexander Berkman, two of the many arrested. There can be no doubt he enjoyed his work. Their conviction and subsequent deportation was a signal victory for him, a triumph.

Berkman and Goldman, along with 247 others, were marched up the gangplank of the old *Buford,* which the press had nicknamed "The Soviet Ark." This ship would carry the deportees to Russia and permanent exile.

The affair had the celebrational air of a military victory, and dozens of congressmen trained to New York from Washington to bid a smug farewell to the activists. Head of the Division of Investigation of the Department of Justice (as the FBI was then known), William J. Flynn, was also on hand with several aides, including Hoover.

As Emma Goldman stood at the rail of the *Buford,* a congressman taunted her with: "Merry Christmas, Emma." She thumbed her nose at him.

Berkman shook his fist at the Washington dignitaries. "We'll come back," he yelled. "And when we do we'll get you bastards!"

William J. Flynn laughed and gave Berkman a cigar.

On this day of momentous personal victory, December 2, 1919, Hoover stood on the gangplank with a prisoner and, his face sternly set, posed for photographers, whose cameras exploded like dull firecrackers.

Eight days later, John Edgar Hoover submitted his report on the Communist conspiracy to Palmer. His was one of the first legal briefs drawn against communism. It charged that a massive conspiracy was afoot aimed at toppling non-Communist governments everywhere.

Attorney General Palmer viewed the briefs as a way of implementing harsh retaliatory methods designed to calm citizens' fears and pacify the nation's press. He ordered another sweep of aliens from both the Communist Party of America and the Communist Labor Party.

Palmer's "Red Raids" began on January 2, 1920. Bureau of Investigation agents, each one of them carrying copies of Hoover's briefs, broke into homes, offices, and stores, haphazardly arresting more than twenty-five hundred aliens. In many instances, the agents took it upon themselves to beat the suspects. Flynn's assistant, Frank Burke, had told them in a memo covering the raid: "I leave it entirely to your discretion as to the methods by which you should gain access to such places."

Burke further ordered the Bureau of Investigation agents to report directly to the twenty-five-year-old mastermind, Hoover, who waited to hear the results of their raids at GID headquarters.

The raids that took place in thirty-three cities may have been edifying to Hoover, but they shocked the nation at large. The expected complaints from Communists (a total of 446 were eventually deported by June 30, 1921) and extremist groups were not upsetting, but when dozens of lawyers, newspapers, and labor leaders responded in anger over the raids, Attorney General Palmer must have wondered whether or not he had jumped the gun, and perhaps he even questioned the feasibility of John Edgar Hoover's instigating briefs.

Palmer fumed as the government was besieged with protests that agents had invaded private homes, meeting places, and offices without warrants; that aliens and citizens had been held without warrants; and that the right of counsel had been denied to prisoners. Complaints charged that agents were guilty of brutal assault, forgery, and perjury.

Assistant Secretary of Labor Louis F. Post said that the nation's press had created a "great terroristic scare in the country." Post's lawyer took another view, saying Palmer had acted in "absolute ignorance of American principles." He then charged the Department of Justice with having organized Communist branches, sought members, and then reported the names of these members for deportation.

In a raging rebuttal speech before the House Rules Committee, Attorney General Palmer exploded: 'I say that I was shouted at from every editorial sanctum in America from sea to sea. I was preached upon from every pulpit; I was urged—I could feel it dinned into my ears—throughout the country to do something and to do it now, and do it quick, and do it in a way that would bring results to stop this sort of thing in the United States. . . . I accept responsibility for everything they [the agents] did. If one or two of them, overzealous or perhaps outraged as patriotic American citizens—and all of them were—by the conduct of these aliens, stepped over the bounds and treated them a little roughly, I forgive them. I do not defend it, but I am not going to raise any row about it."

It was one of the most astounding admissions of misconduct any attorney general had ever been compelled to make. Arch-conservative Harlan Fiske Stone, then dean of the Columbia University School of Law (and, ironically, the man who would name John Edgar Hoover to his directorship of the FBI), was astounded at Palmer's outburst.

"It appears," Stone declared, "by the public admission of the attorney general and otherwise that he has proceeded on the theory that such aliens are not entitled to the constitutional guaranty of due process of law."

But whose theory was it really that had inspired the row? John Edgar Hoover had set up the targets; Palmer had fired the shots. Yet Hoover went unscathed, and all through 1921 he doggedly pursued activities by alleged Communists, anarchists, and random aliens. His GID agents supplied him with volumes of reports. Hoover worked round-the-clock.

He never seemed to tire; one reporter noted that he resembled a "slender bundle of high-charged electric wire." It was Hoover's first press notice, however noncommittal.

The raves and the raspberries came later.

# 3

# *Takeover*

When kindly, pleasant-faced Warren G. Harding was swept with all his "normalcy" into the president's office in 1920, he appointed his poker-playing friend, foxy Harry Daugherty, attorney general. One of Daugherty's first acts was to fire William J. Flynn, chief of the Bureau of Investigation, and replace him with his close crony, William J. Burns, founder of the Burns Detective Agency.

The shake-up brought a change for John Edgar Hoover. On August 22, 1921, he was transferred to the post of assistant director of the Bureau of Investigation, with a $4,000-a-year salary. Hoover was still living at home, reading his Bible, and expanding theories about the Communist conspiracy. The only thing different about him was that he was no longer John Edgar Hoover.

Hoover had learned, while he was special assistant to the attorney general, that there was another man named John Edgar Hoover living in the city of Washington. He discovered that this man owed a large amount of money to a store. Hoover took great pride in paying his bills on time. He found it intolerable that he be confused with a spendthrift.

He changed his name. Now he was simply J. Edgar Hoover.

Hoover's contact with his family at this time involved one person—his mother. He continued to live in the old family house with her (shortly after Hoover's transfer to the Bureau of Investigation his father died.) His brother, Dickerson, Jr., was distantly removed, and Hoover was never close to his sister, Lillian, who had married a man named Robinette.

Years later when Lillian was an invalid, J. Edgar ignored her; he never contributed to her care, leaving the medical expenses totally to his nephew, Fred, who was then an FBI agent. Fred sank heavily into debt, but expected nothing from his uncle, J. Edgar, which is what he got.

Though he refused to help his sister, Hoover went out of his way to pay a $900 hospital bill run up by one of his agents—Cartha "Deke" DeLoach. Later, DeLoach became, as we shall see, one of Hoover's heavy "axemen."

The reason for Hoover's apparent unconcern for his sister may be his inherent distrust of all women, save his mother. As one astute and early Hoover-watcher put it: "No women are among his intimates, for Hoover—and he would have every G-man be likewise—is a woman hater. This may be due to his cardinal creed as a crimefighter, the traditional French directive: *Cherchez la femme* ("Look for the woman").

Hoover directed his agents to look for women associates of criminals—"dirty, filthy diseased women" he once called them—who, he knew, would lead them to the prey. Countless times, Hoover has cautioned his agents in long memos that they should never "be alone" with women suspects picked up for questioning by the FBI.

Hoover's Bureau has been populated solely by carefully-selected male friends—Courtney Ryley Cooper, his future publicist; gun expert Frank Baughman; his ever-faithful assistant Clyde Tolson, who joined him in 1928 and has seldom been away from his side since; and Larry Richey, who was to become an aide to Herbert Hoover when he was secretary of commerce. Richey became the most important friend J. Edgar Hoover ever had.

When Hoover entered the Bureau of Investigation in 1921, it was a cesspool of graft and corruption. Bureau agents, for the most part, were appointed to their posts through political connections. With such immunity, agents felt free to bribe and be bribed. Extortion and blackmail went hand in hand with most agents' jobs. The Bureau had become far removed from the agency Theodore Roosevelt envisioned and inaugurated in 1908.

To combat business monopolies and land trusts, President Roosevelt established a new federal investigation group under the direction of Attorney General Charles Bonaparte. Begun on July 26, 1908, the new agency adopted the title of Bureau of Investigation the following year.

Almost from the beginning, outsiders of considerable influence attempted to erode the ethics and purpose of the infant Bureau. Bonaparte admitted that he was visited regularly by "prominent lawyers representing different corporations or clusters of corporations with which the government was, or expected soon to be, in litigation," who attempted to make deals.

A decade of constant political battering and manipulation finally affected the Bureau under the Harding administration, engulfing it in almost total corruption. Though the Department of Justice in that period was universally termed the "department of easy virtue," graft was rampant throughout the entire administration.

Harding's close friend, Charles Forbes, looted the Veteran's Bureau of its funds; another Harding intimate, Thomas Miller, became wealthy on kickbacks from alien property claims. Albert Fall, secretary of the interior, sold Teapot Dome (from which the Harding administration received its unsavory *sobriquet*) and the Elk Hills government oil preserves to those with the heftiest bribes.

Jesse Smith, Daugherty's fellow poker player and intimate friend, maintained an office in the Justice Department, although he had no official position there. Smith blatantly sold his influence with the department (and subsequently the Bureau of Investigation) to lawbreakers who wanted investigations and litigations quashed. (Smith killed himself in 1923 when his high-level graft was made public.)

One newsman of the era stated that the Bureau had become "a private hole-in-the-corner goon squad for the attorney general. Its arts were the arts of snooping, bribery, and blackmail."

Another writer stated that the Bureau "had become a private secret service for corrupt forces within the Bureau. . . . Included among the special agents were some with criminal records. Bureau badges and property had been issued to persons not employed by the government," and to those who posed "as confidential agents and informers to 'frame' evidence against personal enemies of the Harding administration."

J. Edgar Hoover's own position in this crumbling organization was dubious. One report has it that Burns shunted him into a side office where he handled routine paper work.

Two months after Hoover moved to the Bureau, a man he would grow to hate (but never expose), Gaston B. Means, was appointed by Burns as a special agent. There was much that was special about Mr. Means. First, he made it widely known that he was Burns' favorite investigator and a close personal friend. Secondly, his duties were vague, his hours erratic, and his considerable personal income unexplainable.

From the moment Hoover met Means there was conflict. Hoover classified Means as an opportunist, too well heeled and glib to be on the right side of the law. Hoover went to Burns and demanded that he order Means to stay out of Hoover's office. When Burns asked why he should do such a thing, Hoover replied that Means was distasteful to him. He didn't like the man's spending habits. He didn't like the man's morals.

Means shrugged indifferently when Burns brought up Hoover's complaint. He had a much more interesting office in which to spend his time, the one occupied by mystery-man Jesse Smith. Means was seen constantly going in and out of Smith's unmarked office at the Department of Justice.

When Means could not find Smith in his office, he could contact him at the Wardman Park Hotel in the suite where Attorney General Harry Daugherty lived; Smith lived there, too. Sometimes Smith could be found at the White House playing poker with the president, guzzling illicit hooch with the liquor-loving Harding.

Hoover (and Burns for that matter) later claimed he had no idea of the activities of the Smith-Means combination, but this seems odd, particularly when one considers that Gaston Bullock Means' spectacular criminal career was common knowledge.

In 1916, Means had been a paid secret agent for Germany; his job was to "embarrass" British commerce. Means told everyone in the Bureau (including Hoover) of his colorful background. It was also known that he had actually been a double agent, being paid by both the Allied and Central Powers.

Means stated that he had quit the Germans when America entered the war. This incredible rascal once told a story of how he had captured trunkloads of secret documents vital to America's defense only to have these documents "stolen" by enemy agents before their delivery to army intelligence headquarters. It was only a small annoyance to Means that someone pointed out that the trunks weighed the same when delivered empty to intelligence headquarters as they had when crammed with top-secret documents.

More serious was the fact that Means had been accused of murdering Mrs. Maude A. King, a rich widow. The woman had been shot to death while vacationing with Means in North Carolina in 1917. Though he was acquitted of the murder, Means was exposed in another trial as having filed a forged will, which would have given him the entire estate Mrs. King left at her death.

When these juicy bits of information were revealed, Daugherty and Burns suspended Means as an agent. But, almost immediately, he was put back on the Bureau's payroll as an informant. Hoover was aware of these underhanded dealings, and yet did and said nothing. Perhaps he felt it politically expedient not to act, even though he had an authoritative position in the Bureau as assistant director.

After Jesse Smith blew out his brains rather than face charges of graft and bribery on May 30, 1923, the administration came apart at its rotting seams, but Harding did not live to face criticism. In August of that year, he fell ill and died in San Francisco while on a cross-country goodwill tour. (Gaston B. Means later authored a book which claimed that Mrs. Harding had poisoned the president!)

A Senate investigation of Daugherty's Department of Justice took place in early 1924 (Daugherty was twice tried and each time acquitted of wrongdoing; he refused to testify for fear of incriminating himself). Gaston B. Means was one of the Senate hearing's more spectacular witnesses. Means told the senators that he had conducted espionage-type investigations against those senators and congressmen who had been attacking Daugherty and had delivered any incriminating evidence he found to Jesse Smith. Means admitted that he had opened senators' mail, searched their offices at night, and broken into their files.

The garrulous Means explained to startled senators how, as a super detective, he accomplished his missions: "Oh, search . . . all the mail that comes in, all the papers, anything he [the senator or congressman] has got lying around. Find out in his home. Just like you, senator, when you make a criminal investigation . . . report what you find . . . if it is damaging, why, of course, it is used. If it is fine, why, you cannot use it. It does no damage."

Means' testimony did plenty of damage to Means. He was sent to prison, but he would appear again to cause Hoover embarrassment and headaches.

J. Edgar Hoover watched the entire proceedings, aloof and learning.

Calvin Coolidge took over the presidency vacated by Harding's death. One of his first acts was to fire Harry Daugherty and hire Harlan Fiske Stone as attorney general. Stone was then a New York attorney in practice with J. P. Morgan's son-in-law. He also had been Coolidge's classmate at Amherst College.

When Daugherty was swept out of office, Stone fielded about for a man to replace William J. Burns. He mentioned his quest to Secretary of Commerce Herbert Hoover. Hoover, in turn, mentioned Stone's need for a bright young fellow to head the Bureau of Investigation to his aide, Larry Richey.

Richey didn't hesitate for a moment: "Why should they look around when they have the man they need right over there now—a young, well-educated lawyer named Hoover."

"You think he can do the job?" Herbert Hoover asked.

"I know he can," Richey replied. "He's a good friend of mine."

On the strength of Richey's endorsement, Secretary of Commerce Hoover went to Stone with the suggestion to try J. Edgar Hoover.

Stone followed the secretary's recommendation.

So it was that J. Edgar Hoover, at age twenty-nine, became head of the Bureau of Investigation on May 10, 1924. He immediately called for the setting up of extensive fingerprint files, an idea which has been solely attributed to Hoover. But William J. Burns had tried to establish a comprehensive fingerprint file for the Bureau while he was in office. This was denied to Burns for lack of funds.

By 1927 Burns had his own troubles. A federal judge had ruled that Burns, through his detective agency, had tampered with a jury listening to the case of oilman Harry Sinclair, who was accused of bribing Secretary of Interior Albert Fall. Sinclair had hired Burns detectives to shadow his jurors.

Though his agency was fined $1,000 for jury tampering, Burns declared: "My men didn't do anything for Harry Sinclair that I haven't done for the federal government hundreds of times!" This was a perfect example of Burns' techniques while in the Bureau.

Hoover's idea of barring politics from the Bureau—which he faithfully promised Stone he would do—disappeared completely in 1931-32. The Republicans had been soundly defeated at the polls that year, and Hoover, to curry favor with the New Dealers, fired more than a hundred well-qualified agents, replacing them with men chosen by key Democrats of the new administration. Conservative senators and congressmen, particularly from the South, had no trouble getting men from their districts into the FBI as Hoover's reign continued.

One of these new agents, Melvin Purvis, was hired (though he was too young to satisfy the Bureau's minimum age requirement) soon after Hoover received a call from Purvis' political sponsor, Ed "Cotton" Smith, a New Deal Democrat and senator from South Carolina. Hoover would regret this little deal years later when Purvis created havoc for the FBI.

Soon after Hoover took over the Bureau, he began to weed out those agents who were not up to his "standards." He developed a habit that, in later years, became his full-time occupation in the Bureau—hounding his agents with memos.

Almost all of these terse orders in the early years dealt with proper personal conduct, the kind of conduct that God-fearing Hoover himself practiced. His edicts were rushed out each day to FBI offices across the country.

Because these were the Prohibition years, Hoover would not tolerate any breach of the law, no matter how trivial. One of his memos on the subject read: "I am determined to summarily dismiss from this Bureau any employee who I find indulging in the use of intoxicants to any degree or extent upon any occasion. This, I can appreciate, is a very drastic attitude and I shall probably be looked upon by some elements as a fanatic. . . . I, myself, am refraining from the use of intoxicants . . . and I am not, therefore, expecting any more of the field employees than I am of myself."

Only weeks after special agents in charge of FBI offices received this memo, the Bureau chief in Denver was visited by an agent out of the Washington office. The agent was obviously exhausted from the special assignment he had been working on and asked the Denver chief for a drink. The chief gave him one and two days later he was fired. He had ignored a Hoover mandate.

While Hoover's agents were snitching on each other, the Director was after bigger game. Ferreting out all who might oppose him in his own Bureau led Hoover to the realization that, through his specially empowered organization, he could gain political support on all levels of government using the same methods.

One report has it that Hoover would accumulate a file of embarrassing evidence on a government official through his Bureau. Then he would go to the individual in question and, posing as a friend, state that he had received this information in the mail. It was an adroit way of convincing politicians not to make an enemy out of J. Edgar Hoover.

This period of Hoover's emergence into politics was capped when it was reported that the Director would not even stop his investigations short of the White House, and that he had dug deeply into the background of President Herbert Hoover—the man who had recommended him for his job.

To many Washington wags this seemed to be good politics and a convenient way to protect one's position. Hoover knew better. He was trying not only to preserve his job but to propagate a one-man institution. This required an image the public would never forget.

# 4

# The 'Gangbuster'

When J. Edgar Hoover slipped into the Director's chair of the FBI in 1925, he could easily have entered the "Ten Best-Dressed Men" contest, sedate division. From that moment through the 1930s, Hoover was addicted to gleaming white or pearl gray spats covering mirror-like black shoes. That was the only flamboyant aspect of his attire. His suits were always dark, the crease in his pants razor-sharp. He wore snap-brimmed hats and finely-tailored coats with pinched waists. A conservative striped tie and a meticulously-folded white handkerchief edging from the suitcoat breast pocket completed the ensemble and the image—always the image.

Hoover's office at FBI headquarters in Washington was then, as now, tailored to the same image—all business, stark and efficient. Dominating the spacious office was a giant glass-top desk, clean except for three items—a picture of his dog, a stand-up telephone wrapped with wire, and a framed copy of Rudyard Kipling's *If*.

Entering the office each day was never a triumphal march for Hoover. He always showed up about fifteen minutes before anyone else was in the building—and it is still his habit to do so. That was an essential part of the image, too: All work, all dedication.

Like a conscientious corporate attorney, Hoover was at his mammoth desk by 8:45 A.M. One writer who had several interviews with him during the gangster era described him then as of "medium height, inclined to be chubby, and of dark complexion. His full lips forbid a stern mouth, but he has a piercing glance, which those who have left his service say is the result of practice before a mirror.

"Hoover walks with a rather mincing step, almost feminine. This gait may be a relic of his valedictorian days, for at all times he appears to be making his way as though the caution of a teacher not to race to the rostrum was ringing in his ears."

But once he was seated at the massive desk, Hoover's gangbuster image took over. The phone wrapped with wire was one of the most effective props he employed. Apparently, the wire allowed him to take a firmer grip, or it may have been an early device to prevent wiretapping.

When observers were allowed to enter Hoover's office, and few were, the wire-wrapped phone would begin ringing almost on cue. "Hoover scoops it up like an infielder whips a grounder out of the dust and carries on conversations teasing to the person present, no matter how set he may be against eavesdropping," one visitor remembered.

With the mouthpiece of the phone close up and the receiver against his ear, Hoover, in authoritative, intimate tones, would go into his gangbuster act.

Some examples given went like this:

"You found fingerprints . . . Latent? . . . Yes . . . What's the classification? . . . That sounds like . . . It is? Good . . . Wire Chicago," or "You've got him surrounded? . . . Good . . . Smoke him out . . . Call me when he's under arrest."

The melodrama was thick and unsettling, but it was Hoover on top of crime at all times—sometimes ahead of the crime—an image the Director insisted upon. A significant display of alertness and constant vigilance against the dark powers of crime was mandatory. This putting-up-a-front tactic enlarged itself into a personal obsession with Hoover during the gangster era until it approached the ludicrous.

When Hoover appeared in public in the early 1930s, in the opinion of many observers, he seemed to be imitating Hollywood film sleuths. He could be seen dining alone in Washington restaurants, his table set apart from others, his back to the wall. At such times, the Director would look "about furtively like a G-man."

FBI agents, after leaving Hoover's spartan employ, stated that Hoover's chief recreation, aside from being a "professional" sports spectator, was shadowing innocent persons on the streets of the capital. As one newsman put it: "This, for years, afforded him the only opportunity to play detective. The fact that his unsuspecting victim never gave him the thrill of chase that a criminal, wise to the ways of shaking shadows, might, apparently did not rob the game of pleasure for him."

Essential to Hoover's image and that of his FBI was consistently good press coverage, selling the still-infant Bureau to the public. Then, as now, Hoover was a superb headline hunter. Almost single-handedly he constructed the magnificent fiction of the "G-man." The date from which this heroic image sprang was September 26, 1933. On that day the oversold gangster bumpkin George "Machine Gun" Kelly was captured.

As he did with the Dillinger case, Hoover would often retell the capture of this insignificant hoodlum, heralding it as a milestone of FBI achievement. He has never tired of repeating this canard. In June 1946, he wrote: "In the early morning hours of September 26, 1933, a small group of men surrounded a house in Memphis, Tennessee. In the house was George "Machine Gun" Kelly, late of Leavenworth Penitentiary. He was wanted by the FBI for kidnapping. [Kelly, his wife Kathryn, and Albert Bates had kidnapped wealthy Oklahoma oilman Charles F. Urschel on July 22, 1933, and ransomed him for $200,000.] For two months FBI agents had trailed the gangster and his wife Kathryn Kelly. Quickly the men of the FBI, accompanied by local law enforcement officers, closed in around the house and entered.

" 'We're federal officers! Come out with your hands up!'

" 'Machine Gun' Kelly stood cowering in a corner. His heavy face twitched as he gazed at the men before him. Reaching trembling hands up toward the ceiling he whimpered, 'Don't shoot, G-men; don't shoot!'

"That was the beginning of a new name for FBI agents. By the time Kelly had been convicted and had received his sentence of life imprisonment, the new nickname, an abbreviation of 'Government men,' had taken hold throughout the underworld. Along the grapevine of the powerful empire of crime passed whispered words of warning about the G-men."

Hoover's florid description made for a heady tale and terrific publicity, even though it was utterly false.

On that long-ago night in Memphis, Detective Sergeant W. J. Raney of the Memphis Police Department crept into a small bungalow at 6 A.M. He was the only one to go inside. FBI men mingled with Memphis police outside to provide cover fire. As Raney tiptoed through the front room, a door leading to a bedroom suddenly swung open. Kelly stood there, framed in light and holding an automatic. He never raised the weapon. Quickly, Raney jammed the barrel of a shotgun into Kelly's more-than-ample paunch.

"Drop the gun," the Memphis police officer ordered.

Kelly dropped the weapon, and smiling, he said "I've been waiting all night for you."

"Well," Raney said, "Here we are."

Kelly was marched outside without another word. As far as the "grapevine of the powerful empire of crime" was concerned, the term *G-men* did not exist. Federal agents were referred to then (as now) as *Feds*.

The Kelly caper was a forerunner of the Dillinger case of 1934. That cornerstone FBI case is the grossest fraud ever perpetrated by the FBI, for all the evidence in the case clearly points to the fact that Dillinger was never killed outside the Biograph Theater in July 1934, and that an innocent man was executed in his place.

The entire Dillinger fiasco, ineptly handled by Special Agent Melvin Purvis (who headed the Chicago Bureau at that time), was preceded by the botched Roger Touhy case, also personally handled by the FBI's boy wonder, Purvis, who had entered the FBI politically while underage only a few years previous to his appointment as Chicago chief.

Melvin Purvis was everything an FBI man shouldn't be— reckless, adventure minded, and a hunch player. He was also a publicity hound which probably grated on Hoover more than anything else. This spectacular agent, who was later to head the Junior G-man Club sponsored by Post-Toasties, began his FBI career with a string of dubious achievements.

Once, when searching for the notorious bank robber, Frank Nash, Purvis followed a hunch and employed the services of an Indian named War Eagle, an exconvict who was willing to "finger" the elusive Nash. Purvis led a raid on a would-be Nash hideout, but then discovered that War Eagle had identified the wrong man. Even more embarrassing was the fact that Purvis led the raid in War Eagle's car, which was a stolen car.

After millionaire brewer William A. Hamm, Jr., of St. Paul, Minnesota, was kidnapped on June 15, 1933, Melvin Purvis again swung into action. After Hamm was ransomed days later for $100,000, Purvis proudly announced—subsequent to his whirlwind investigation—to the press: "We have an ironclad case." In effect, Purvis had Roger Touhy and three friends, all charged with putting "the snatch" on Hamm. Touhy, a mild-mannered bootlegger from northern Illinois, suddenly erupted in the press as Roger "The Terrible" Touhy, and his trial by headline (mostly provided by Purvis) began.

Hoover sat mute in Washington as his wonder boy attempted to build a case against Touhy. This consisted of badgering witnesses with Touhy's photograph in an attempt to have him identified as the Hamm kidnapper; Touhy was identified as such by this method. The investigation also consisted of FBI men, who were constantly closeted with Touhy, writing down almost every word he uttered, no matter how inane.

It also included severe beatings. According to Touhy: "I went into the jail in excellent physical shape. When I came out, I was twenty-five pounds lighter, three vertebrae in my upper spine were fractured, and seven of my teeth had been knocked out. Part of the FBI's rehabilitation of prisoners, I supposed. . . .

"They questioned me day and night, abused me, beat me up, and demanded that I confess the Hamm kidnapping. Never was I allowed to rest for more than half an hour. If I was asleep when a team of interrogators arrived at my cell, they would slug me around and bang me against the wall. . . .

"I couldn't have confessed if I had wanted to. I didn't

know what Hamm looked like, how the ransom was paid, where he was held, or anything else. Neither did McFadden, Stevens, or Sharkey [Touhy's co-defendants]. But that seemingly made no difference." Purvis' whole trumped-up case was not important for long to defendant Willie Sharkey. Sharkey "never was a strong-willed fellow and he couldn't endure being beaten," Touhy later stated. Defendant Sharkey hanged himself in his cell.

Purvis' so-called "ironclad case" wilted to nothing for lack of evidence several months later and Touhy, McFadden, Stevens and, posthumously, Sharkey were declared not guilty. (Two years later, it was discovered that the Hamm kidnapping had been conducted by the Barker-Karpis mob.)

One of Touhy's witnesses during the Hamm trial, Edward J. Meany, testified that one of Purvis' agents told him in Chicago: "If you go to St. Paul to testify for Touhy, you'll be sorry, and maybe you won't come back."

This kind of gross intimidation didn't bother Special Agent Melvin Purvis in the least and he went on his way creating headlines and prosecuting cases by his own special methods without so much as a reprimand from Hoover. Purvis went after Touhy again in 1933 for the kidnapping of Jake "The Barber" Factor. After one of the most confused cases in FBI history, Purvis somehow managed to make this charge stick and Touhy got ninety-nine years in Illinois' Stateville Penitentiary.

Almost twenty-five years later, Roger Touhy was set free after Federal Judge John P. Barnes ruled that the Factor kidnapping was a fake. In 1954, Barnes stated that "the Department [of Justice] did evince an astounding disregard for Touhy's rights and indulged in practices which . . . cannot be condoned." He further ruled that the state attorney's office (Illinois) and the Department of Justice "worked and acted in concert to convict Touhy of something, regardless of his guilt or innocence."

To Melvin Purvis of the FBI, thriving on the self-created image of super crimefighter in his dark heyday of the 1930s, the possibility of such future retribution meant nothing. No sooner had he conveniently disposed of Touhy than he was hot on the trail of "public enemy number one," John Herbert Dillinger, the most extraordinary bank robber in American history.

This Indiana-born outlaw, who had spent most of his adult life in prison after an abortive attempt to rob a grocer of fifty dollars when he was twenty-two years old, was paroled on May 22, 1933. For a year, accompanied by the most professional bank robbers at large, Dillinger went on a crime spree that captured the nation's headlines, the public's fancy, and the considerable wrath of J. Edgar Hoover.

To Hoover, Dillinger represented the classic American criminal. He was the boy next door who had gone wrong; he had sneered and snickered at the law all of his life. By early 1934, Dillinger, with a string of impressive bank robberies to his credit, had become Hoover's personal nemesis, a man who eluded capture and jailors alike with incredible ease while disdainfully thumbing his nose at the law.

Hoover's agents, led by the indomitable Purvis, got on to Dillinger's trail "officially" in March of 1934 when he escaped from the Crown Point, Indiana, "escape-proof" jail, bluffing his way out with a wooden gun he had carved from the top of a washboard and blackened with boot polish. Dillinger had made the mistake of driving a stolen car (taken from Crown Point Sheriff Lillian Holley) across the Indiana state line into Illinois, thus committing his first federal offense. (It was not a federal offense to rob a bank at that time.)

Following a tip, Melvin Purvis learned that Dillinger and members of his gang were vacationing at a remote Wisconsin resort. By plane and car, Purvis rushed agents to the Little Bohemia Lodge in northern Wisconsin and there, on the night of April 22, 1934, led a wild frontal attack against the building, machine guns blazing.

Under Purvis' personal command, FBI agents indiscriminately sprayed the lodge with bullets. The raid was a disaster. Neither Dillinger nor any of his gang members were captured. Two innocent men, who had been dining at the lodge that night, were severely wounded by FBI agents. Purvis' men also killed another innocent man— Eugene Boiseneau—that night, riddling him with machine gun bullets. (In later years, several pro-Hoover sources would neatly pin this killing on Dillinger, who, careful research indicates, never personally killed anyone in his life.)

The Little Bohemia failure turned into a nightmare for the FBI in a matter of days. The press screamed for Purvis' dismissal and certain congressmen asked the same for Hoover. Even after he knew of Purvis' shoddy FBI career, Hoover refused to take action against him; to do so would have been an obvious loss of face and would have increased the tempo of bad publicity for Hoover's Bureau, which the Director would attempt to prevent at all costs. Hoover ignored the criticism as usual and kept Purvis on the job. His only directive to Purvis was: "Act first, talk afterward. Shoot straight and get the right man." That was the kind of gun-toter's statement Melvin Purvis understood. Hoover's "Wild West" attitude was endorsed by his patronizing superior Attorney General Homer Cummings, who added, "Shoot to kill, then count to ten."

Bloodthirsty or not, Hoover had decided Dillinger's fate weeks before the Little Bohemia raid. Even though his only federal offense had been to drive across a state line in a stolen car, Dillinger had been made "public enemy number one" by the Director. Hoover also placed a "shoot-to-kill" order on him and offered a $10,000 reward for him, dead or alive. It is not difficult to understand such drastic action on Hoover's part when one realizes the importance the Director placed on the tremendous amount of press coverage Dillinger received; Hoover understood headlines.

Three months after Little Bohemia, on the night of July 22, 1934, Purvis and a host of FBI men and East Chicago (Indiana) policemen shot and killed, outside the Biograph Theater in Chicago, a man the FBI insisted was John Herbert Dillinger. And yet, all the hardcore evidence concerned with this shooting—which conveniently disappeared for thirty-five years—points directly to the fact that the Bureau did not kill John Herbert Dillinger, bank robber, but another person, an innocent man.

The high points of the FBI-Dillinger *debacle* are these:

—Purvis, frantic to get Dillinger to save his reputation and job, was readily duped into allowing a pigeon to be shot down in Dillinger's place by a syndicate madam, Anna Sage, and her crooked-cop lover, Martin Zarkovich, of the East Chicago Police Department, whose motives were obviously rooted in aiding Dillinger's permanent escape. (Purvis never bothered to check on Anna Sage's long history of criminal activities or on Martin Zarkovich.)

—The man who was shot (all evidence indicates that Martin Zarkovich did the shooting, not an FBI man) was known as "James Lawrence," a minor underworld figure, whose physical likeness to Dillinger was as remote as the FBI's trumped-up claim of plastic surgery having altered Dillinger's features.

—"James Lawrence," an autopsy revealed, was not Dillinger's height or weight, and was missing a known birthmark of Dillinger's, a scar from a bullet wound, and a facial scar discernable in mug shots of Dillinger; he possessed teeth Dillinger did not have.

—The dead man had had a rheumatic heart condition since childhood; it probably was terminal (which might explain James Lawrence's willingness, for a price or other motives, to become a decoy). Dillinger, if he had had such a condition, would not have been able to serve in the navy, play semi-professional baseball, or perform his daredevil feats.

—The dead man had brown eyes. John Dillinger's eyes were blue-gray.

—The man killed outside the Biograph was wearing prescription glasses; Dillinger had perfect eyesight.

—Records reveal that the Colt automatic (now on display at the FBI museum in Washington), which the Bureau claimed "Dillinger" pulled on agents at the Biograph, was sold for the first time five months *after* the shooting.

—Fingerprints offered up by the FBI as a way of identifying "Dillinger" were obviously planted.

The irony of the Dillinger episode is that Hoover still insists FBI agents did the shooting in Chicago, when facts show that East Chicago policeman Martin Zarkovich killed "James Lawrence." It is a case not only of ignoring the lawman who performed the execution (regardless of his motive), but of blindly assuming the responsibility for killing the wrong man.

Establishing the identity of a criminal has never been a problem to J. Edgar Hoover. On the testimony of one witness, a much-harassed caseworker for the Traveler's Aid Society, Hoover determined that Charles Arthur "Pretty Boy" Floyd and his bank-robber sidekick, Adam Richetti, were the machine gunners who slaughtered five men in the "Kansas City Massacre."

Floyd, when hearing that the FBI had pinned the killing on him, indignantly wrote to Kansas City's Captain of Detectives Thomas J. Higgins: "Dear Sirs: I—Charles Floyd—want it made known that I did not participate in the massacre of the officers at Kansas City. Charles Floyd."

Added to Floyd's unusual disclaimer was the word of the caseworker, Mrs. Lottie West, who worked a booth in a train station. It was outside of this station that five men (four of whom were police officers, including FBI agent Raymond Caffery, the other being their prisoner, Frank Nash) were slaughtered on June 17, 1933, in broad daylight by parties unknown who were attempting to effect Frank Nash's release. Mrs. West identified Nash as "Pretty Boy" Floyd.

This confused identification made little difference to Hoover's gangbusters. They pursued "Pretty Boy" across the Midwest and finally caught up with him in an Ohio cornfield on October 22, 1934. Among the agents who shot him to death was none other than Melvin Purvis, who had assumed command of the Floyd case.

Purvis ran to the fallen gangster (whose fate seemed justified because of the number of killings he *had* committed) and realized he was dying. Purvis still clamped the cuffs on him, saying, "Are you 'Pretty Boy' Floyd?"

"I'm Charles Arthur Floyd," the outlaw managed.

When Purvis dutifully ran for a phone to tell Hoover of the capture for a quick press announcement, another agent approached Floyd. The FBI man asked Floyd if he had committed the Kansas City Massacre.

With almost his last breath, Floyd hissed a denial. "I didn't do it," he said. "I wasn't in on it." Floyd thought of himself as another Jesse James and attended church regularly. Those who knew him believed that Floyd would not have lied himself into the grave.

Still, Hoover was convinced Floyd and Richetti did the job. Floyd died in the cornfield of gunshot wounds. Richetti, on Mrs. West's doubtful testimony, was executed on October 7, 1938, denying his guilt to the last.

In 1954, a Missouri underworld figure, Blackie Audett, who was present during the shooting at Kansas City, stated: "One of the officers that was killed was a federal agent [Caffery]. The FBI was on the case in a matter of minutes. They got a bum steer somehow or other because later they killed Charlie Floyd and hanged Adam Richetti as being the two men that was in the second car.

"I knowed better because I seen with my own eyes who was in that car. Both of them that was in it got clean away." Then Audett named the real killers—Verne Miller, Maurice Denning, and William "Solly" Weissman, all syndicate professional murderers sent out to "hit" outlaw Frank Nash, who was being taken to a federal prison and who knew too much.

The fact that the Kansas City Massacre was a syndicate-directed operation was supported in the subsequent deaths of the real killers, who were disposed of in typical syndicate fashion to prevent their true mission from being exposed. Verne Miller's naked body was discovered in a culvert on the outskirts of Detroit on November 29, 1933. According to one report, Miller had been "trussed up like a turkey ready for roasting. His tongue and cheeks had been punctured with ice picks. Hot flatirons had left searing burn scars on his body. Some heavy object had finally bashed in the back of his skull."

Weissman's body was found in Chicago shortly after that; he, too, had been horribly tortured. Denning completely disappeared. These kinds of killings, like many other obvious signs jutting from the underworld since the turn of the century, screamed "organized crime" in the early 1930s.

But, like Audett's damaging information, they were handled with the usual Hoover aplomb; he ignored them.

At the dawning of his invented G-man image, Hoover could take some satisfaction from his personal progress. His agents always appeared to be the first on the spot to arrest the mad-dog criminal; that's the way he told it in the 1930s and that's the way it would be, irrespective of the facts. Hoover no longer settled, as he had in 1926 with the escape of the notorious Morris "Red" Rudensky, for second best.

Rudensky, an expert safecracker and escape artist, squeezed his muscular frame into an eight-inch-wide printing materials box and was passed through Leavenworth's gates and onto a freight car for shipment. Unfortunately for Red, train guards ignored the "This Side Up" stamp inmates had printed on Rudensky's escape box and he was packed on the freight car upside down. The train chugged away and, because his head wasn't cushioned, the bumps and jolts caused Red to hemorrhage severely for eight hours. Train guards at a stop up the line noticed the blood seeping from the box, broke into it, and captured Rudensky.

The FBI was not in on the taking of this escaped federal prisoner, but Hoover did the next best thing. He ordered the bloody printing box to be displayed at the Philadelphia Sesquicentennial International Exposition of 1926. Here visitors gaped at the gory box—an FBI trophy—for six months.

In 1932, Charles Augustus Lindbergh, Jr., son of the famed American flyer, was kidnapped from his crib, and a ransom of $70,000 was demanded for his return. The case was a fiasco. When FBI agents visited Lindbergh at his Hopewell (New Jersey) home, the Lone Eagle expressed his distrust of the Bureau's ability to handle the case by ordering the FBI men from his house.

One Bureau man—or ex-Bureau man—would not be put off. Recently released from prison where he had served time for his involvement in the illegal investigations of congressmen during the Harding administration, the amazing Gaston Bullock Means became involved almost immediately. The thoroughly-discredited Means was himself surprised to receive a call from the wealthy socialite and owner of the *Washington Post,* Mrs. Evalyn Walsh McLean.

Mrs. McLean, acting on her own whim, told Means that she knew he had underworld contacts. He admitted he did. Means hatched a cunning scheme as he listened to Mrs. McLean's plea that he help her recover the poor Lindbergh baby.

Means told Mrs. McLean that, coincidentally, he had been in recent contact with a kidnapper he had known in the Atlanta penitentiary. The kidnapper, Means stated, had asked him to go in on a "big caper." Of course, he had refused, and he now believed the job was the Lindbergh abduction.

After several exciting forays into the underworld, Means reported back to Mrs. McLean that he had made contact with the kidnappers, that the baby was well (the Lindbergh child was by then dead, lying in a shallow gully only four miles from the Lindbergh home), and that, for $100,000, he could return the twenty-month-old child. As intermediary in such a desperate situation, Means explained that he would need expenses—$4,000.

Mrs. McLean sold some property, put many of her jewels in hock, and came up with the ransom money and Means' expenses. Following an elaborate series of meetings devised by Means, Mrs. McLean moved through five states while doling out portions of her $100,000 through Means to a mythical kidnapping ring. She was even visited by a member of the kidnapping mob, introduced to her by

Means as "The Fox." After her funds were depleted, Mrs. McLean had yet to recover the stolen baby. She finally decided something was terribly rotten about Means' unproductive arbitrations and called the federal authorities.

Means and his fellow conspirator and swindler, Norman T. Whitaker, an exconvict and disbarred attorney who had played the role of "The Fox," were arrested and tried.

J. Edgar Hoover made it a point to attend the trial of his old acquaintance Means. He sat in court listening to Means rattle off a ridiculous story of how he had desperately attempted to effect the Lindbergh baby's release. After testifying in his own defense, Gaston Means staggered from the witness chair and sat down next to the Director.

"Well, Hoover, what did you think of that?" Means said.

Hoover gave him his sternest look and said, "Every bit of it was a pack of lies."

Means replied, "Well, you've got to admit that it made a whale of a good story!"

Means' story was insignificant when compared to the tale Hoover would tell regarding the FBI's role in solving the Lindbergh kidnapping. In the fall of 1934, Bruno Richard Hauptmann was arrested for the crime, and was tried, convicted, and finally executed in 1936. In the year Hauptmann went to the chair, Hoover told members of Congress that taking the kidnapper was an FBI capture:

"The facts in the case, if I may have them as a matter of record here, were these: Bruno Richard Hauptmann went to the gasoline station and bought some gasoline and paid for it with a gold certificate. The gasoline attendant, having no thought of the Lindbergh case, wrote down on the gold certificate the license number of the car that Hauptmann used, as a precautionary measure to prevent himself from being prosecuted for having gold certificates. [All gold certificates being used as U.S. currency were called in by the government, and it was illegal to possess them after May 1, 1933.]

"That certificate was sent to the bank. The teller in the bank happened to have a list of the Lindbergh ransom bills, and the teller communicated with the office of the Federal Bureau of Investigation in New York City. Our agents then went out and ran down the license number, [and] located and arrested Hauptmann, being assisted by the New York State Police and the New Jersey State Police."

The true events leading up to Hauptmann's capture are these: Bruno Richard Hauptmann drove an old sedan into the Warner-Quinlan gas station at 2115 Lexington Avenue on Saturday afternoon, September 15, 1934.

Attendant Walter Lyle came out to wait on Hauptmann. Lyle knew all about the Lindbergh kidnapping and had posted in his office a flyer, which had been issued by police, asking that all gold certificates be noted. (The Lindbergh kidnapper had been paid $30,000 in regular greenbacks and $20,000 in gold certificates, all marked.)

Lyle recalled later, "When I hooked up the hose, he gave me a five dollar bill. I suddenly remembered the flyer asking us to watch for fives, tens, and twenties. Something told me to take down his license number.

"When I went to get the change, I grabbed a pencil, and when I came out I jotted down his license number— 4U 13-14, New York—on the bill. Then I put the bill into the register. It went to the bank and that's how the case was finally broken."

Teller William R. Strong received the bill at the Mount Morris Branch of the Corn Exchange Bank at 85 East 125th Street a few days later. He saw Lyle's scribble on the bill and checked it against the number of the Lindbergh ransom notes.

Strong *did not* call the FBI; he dialed the Treasury Department's office in New York and got Treasury Agent Thomas H. Sisk on the phone. Sisk had been assigned to the Lindbergh kidnapping case and had been working doggedly on it for months.

Strong told Sisk: "We are holding a five-dollar bill, serial number A73976634A. Our records show that this is one of the Lindbergh ransom bills. Will you please confirm this?"

While Strong held the wire, Sisk checked his records. Back on the phone he said, "It's one of the bills all right. Do you have any idea . . ."

Strong broke in with: "Somebody has written a license number on the bill. Here it is." He read the number and Sisk immediately phoned Lieutenant James J. Finn of the New York Police Department, and Colonel Schwartzkopf, who headed the state police in New Jersey. Finn traced the license number of Hauptmann's car through the New York state motor vehicle records.

On September 18, 1934, Finn and his detectives curbed Hauptmann's car at Tremont and Park avenues in the Bronx. Finn personally made the arrest and supplied the evidence that led to Hauptmann's conviction.

How Hauptmann's identification and arrest became the exclusive property of the FBI is a question that can be answered only by J. Edgar Hoover, who not once mentioned the deciding role played in this case by Lieutenant Finn and the agents of the Treasury Department.

The Treasury Department, as well as the Secret Service, Federal Bureau of Narcotics, and other security branches, were, however, used to this kind of treatment from Hoover. They did the work; Hoover took the credit. At times, Hoover's headline-mania became so acute that it almost converted the Bureau's image to that of strutting, comical Keystone Cops. One story Hoover did not tell Congress in 1936 was of a massive FBI snafu in 1935, which involved the capture of the notorious counterfeiter Victor "The Count" Lustig.

Treasury agents captured Lustig and turned him over to the FBI's detention headquarters in New York. Lustig escaped from Hoover's men on September 1, 1935. The Director, first to call the press about any FBI events he felt significant, never announced Lustig's escape.

Again Treasury agents set out to capture "The Count." They located his hide-out near Pittsburgh. When they appealed for help from the FBI, Hoover's agents replied that they were too busy. The Treasury agents recaptured Lustig on September 29. As they were bringing the counterfeiter by car to Pittsburgh, FBI men, in another car, overtook them. Hoover's men told the Treasury agents that they had changed their minds; they would now take custody of Lustig.

The Treasury agents had had enough of the Bureau's unpredictable antics. They told the FBI men they were too late and drove Lustig to their own headquarters in Pittsburgh. The head of the FBI contingent, following Hoover's mandate to report all captures immediately to him, called the Director. Hoover then called all the press services and announced the taking of Lustig as an FBI capture (or recapture since, by then, Lustig's escape from the FBI had been discovered).

Hoover's bombastic announcement of Lustig's capture pinched a tender nerve in Secretary of the Treasury Henry Morganthau, Jr., whose agents' investigative prowess had been ridiculed and subverted by the FBI for years. Morganthau walked out of a conference when he heard the news and exploded in anger at his agents. After he was informed that they, not the FBI, had captured Lustig, Morganthau ordered the true facts be given to the newspapers.

Hoover's public posturing alarmed many more government leaders than Morganthau. Among them was Senator Kenneth D. McKellar (D., Tenn.), chairman of the Senate Subcommittee for Appropriations. McKellar challenged Hoover's expenditures in advertising the FBI, as well as the performance of his men and the Director's own credentials. The dramatic confrontations took place in 1936 when Hoover was seeking $1,025,000 more than he was allowed by budget to spend in the fiscal year.

For Hoover, it was a disaster.

McKellar wanted to know if Hoover took part in the making of motion pictures based on the activities of G-men. Hoover emphatically denied that he did. McKellar countered by asking if the G-men pictures did not virtually advertise the FBI since Hoover's picture was often displayed in advertisements for the movies. Hoover allowed that this was "indeed true."

The senator hammered away at Hoover's self-styled publicity campaign, stating that such publicity had hurt the Bureau. Hoover replied that official disapproval had been registered and strong objections had been made in every instance. He neglected to tell the committee about his almost daily habit of calling in the press and of the myriad releases he handed out. He also failed to tell McKellar that he had driven to Baltimore to screen a G-man picture only days before it was scheduled to run in Washington.

Then McKellar asked Hoover if any of the money appropriated by Congress for the Bureau's budget was used to promote the FBI's image.

Hoover's response to this was quick. He stated that not a penny had been appropriated to pay writers to build up the image of the Bureau, that the FBI employed no writers, and that he had no knowledge of any writers in or out of government service who were hired to write about the Bureau.

However, the facts of the matter were these:

—In 1933, Attorney General Homer Cummings invited several newsmen for dinner, at which time he asked if the Washington journalists would recommend a top flight promotional writer to build up the FBI's image of invincibility. The group unanimously selected the chief Washington correspondent for the *Brooklyn Eagle,* Henry Soudam, to fill the promotional post. Soudam performed adroitly, getting spectacular news results, which transformed the name of an unknown bureaucrat, Hoover, into a household word within a year.

—Courtney Ryley Cooper, who glorified Hoover and the FBI with the publication of his book *Ten Thousand Public Enemies,* had been rewarded with a propaganda job in the Department of Justice with, as one newsman put it, "the express function of publicizing the division of investigation."

—Hoover had aided a Washington newspaper man who was writing a G-man series for radio shortly before his congressional appearance on April 10, 1936.

—During the time Hoover was testifying before McKellar, he was having conferences with writers to develop a cartoon strip designed to embellish the FBI's heroic image. The strip was to be syndicated in newspapers throughout the country.

Hoover apparently chose to ignore his publicity activities at the Senate hearing. Given enough time, money, and power, he would be able to remember or forget whatever best served his cause.

McKellar's pointed questions to Hoover also concerned the Bureau's bungling in several kidnapping cases. It was pointed out that in one instance, Thomas H. Robinson, Jr., who had kidnapped Mrs. Alice Speed Stoll in Louisville, Kentucky, in 1934, had not only eluded an extensive FBI dragnet, but agents were uselessly pursuing "Mr. Robinson's father and Mr. Robinson's wife" instead of the real kidnapper. (When Robinson was later captured, Hoover took full credit until newsmen tracked down a lunch-counter manager, Lynn Allen, who recognized Robinson in his Pasadena, California, diner and tipped off local police who informed the FBI.)

McKellar struck again at Hoover, saying that, as in the Hauptmann, Kelly, and Dillinger cases, the information leading to the arrest of William Mahan, kidnapper of nine-year-old George Weyerhaeuser of Tacoma, Washington, had been supplied by a citizen, in this case a department store clerk who turned in a ransom note to local police, who again brought in the FBI for the victorious pinch.

Hoover has made it a strict policy never to publicize any of the outside help that the Bureau has had in cracking cases, help they have received in almost every important case to date. Any FBI blunders along the way simply didn't exist. Years later, FBI man Leon Turreau was to confide that his agents recovered the wrong baby in the Lindbergh case. "Naturally," Turreau stated, "all of us on the Lindbergh squad took special pains to keep these blunderings out of reach of the reporters. The FBI was still struggling for recognition and respect and couldn't afford the public's horse laughs."

When Senator McKellar pushed Hoover to admit that the FBI could not have functioned in these sensational cases without direct aid from the public, Hoover stated: "Of course, our men have to have information to solve these cases."

It was a strange statement from a man seeking several million dollars to support less than seven hundred agents plus clerical help in a federal bureau that advertised itself as autonomous in its actions, research, and development, and as being the only significant crime prevention arm in the country.

Hoover, who listed himself in *Who's Who* as a "criminologist," was then asked by McKellar to describe his experience as a crimefighter. Hoover admitted that he had never attended any kind of school for criminologists—not even his own, the National Police Academy. (Hoover's position was also unique in that his mentor, Harlan Fiske Stone, specifically expressed a desire for *a man with police experience* to fill the FBI director's role, experience which Hoover completely lacked.)

From the committee record:

McKELLAR: Did you ever make an arrest?

HOOVER: No, sir; I have made investigations.

McKELLAR: How many arrests [*sic*] have you made and who were they?

HOOVER: I handled the investigation of Emma Goldman and prosecuted the case before the immigration authorities up to the secretary of labor. I also handled the Alexander Berkman case and the case of Ludwig Martens, the former Bolshevik ambassador to the United States. [Hoover was speaking of three cases that had occurred seventeen years prior to the time of his testimony in 1936, more than a decade before he took office as head of the FBI.]

Hoover the criminologist emerged from this senatorial scathing badly bruised and exposed, but Hoover the publicist was a long-distance runner whose claims of successes overshadowed any FBI shortcomings.

As if to prove his capability as the nation's chief lawman, Hoover flew to New Orleans a few weeks after the hearings and there claimed, on May 1, 1936, to have personally arrested "public enemy number one," Alvin "Old Creepy" Karpis. In reality, Karpis was surrounded by squads of FBI men who held several weapons to his head before Hoover was called out from an apartment building where he had been waiting.

"We've got him! We've got him! It's all clear, Chief!" an agent called out.

Hoover walked to Karpis' car with aide Clyde Tolson and ordered the cuffs put on the outlaw. By the time cartoonists McDayter and Drew sent out their version of the episode, Hoover was portrayed as single-handedly approaching Karpis' parked car, dragging the outlaw onto the street with a mighty yank, and subduing him with a hammer lock while breathless agents watched in awe.

In the cartoon, as Karpis is led away, an agent turns with pride and says to Hoover: "After risking your life capturing Alvin Karpis, no senator will dare call you a 'swivel-chair' detective again." Senator McKellar made no comment.

The mock heroics continued. In 1936, Hoover set out again to bolster his shattered image. Harry Brunette, a bank robber, was discovered hiding in a New York apartment building in busy midtown Manhattan. Hoover ignored the appeals of New York City Police Commissioner Lewis J. Valentine to not endanger innocent people. With platoons of FBI agents, Hoover directed a full-scale gun battle with Brunette that lasted for forty-five minutes.

Valentine, who thought it should have been a routine arrest, called Hoover's actions "melodramatic."

But the Brunette capture brought headlines and that's what counted with Hoover. The melodrama was good copy as even an old journalist like Walter Winchell knew when he arranged for the surrender of Louis "Lepke" Buchalter, head of "Murder, Inc.," to Hoover on the sultry night of August 24, 1939, in New York City.

The diminutive Lepke got out of Winchell's car and into Hoover's car, which was parked at Twenty-eighth Street and Fifth Avenue.

"Lepke," Winchell said dramatically, "Meet Mr. Hoover." The columnist then turned to the Director. "Mr. Hoover, this is Lepke."

Nothing spectacular, actually, until Hoover's propagandists got hold of the incident and once again had Hoover emerging as a two-fisted, stern-jawed G-man collaring another vicious criminal.

There was nothing Hoover's PR men could do but grimace, however, when the Director committed some of his more expansive errors in judgment. Once such *faux pas* occurred New Year's Eve, 1936. On that night the carefully selected patrons of the Stork Club—all handpicked by owner Sherman Billingsley—were festive, and were consuming huge quantities of champagne.

Everybody who was anybody in New York was there. Billingsley made sure of that. Of course, the club owner had been meticulously cautious in making out his guest list: no Blacks, only a few Jews of social distinction (Billingsley never allowed more than thirty percent of his guests to be Jewish when he gave a private party), no representatives of labor unions.

That was the way boss Billingsley wanted it. The Stork Club, which the glib gossiper Walter Winchell called "the New Yorkiest place in New York," was Billingsley's kingdom.

Winchell was there that night, holding court in the Cub Room. Next to him sat the only man besides FDR who enjoyed freedom from Winchell's "journalistic" assaults, J. Edgar Hoover.

Billingsley sat next to Hoover, gracious and smiling, ordering his nonunion waiters forward with a stern, single gesture to refill the FBI Chief's champagne glass.

Long before that night, the Stork Club had become Hoover's favorite watering hole when in New York; his

Hoover kisses his favorite movie star, Shirley Temple, after he received honorary membership in the Variety Clubs of America in 1938. (Wide World)

J. Edgar Hoover at age four. (Wide World)

In 1924 at age twenty-nine, Hoover was appointed head of the FBI. (Wide World)

Attorney General A. Mitchell Palmer ordered the
Red Raids of 1920, arming his agents with copies
of Hoover's briefs on communism. (Wide World)

The amazing FBI agent, Gaston Bullock Means (center) who worked for the Germans during World War I, spied on congressmen and senators, charged that Mrs. Harding poisoned the president, and, before he finally went to jail, bilked the wealthy Evalyn Walsh McLean through a wild scheme to recover the Lindbergh baby. (Wide World)

William J. Burns, Hoover's boss, was sacked by the Coolidge administration and replaced by Hoover. (UPI)

Attorney General Harry Daugherty, who first brought Hoover into the Department of Justice, was replaced in 1924 amid charges of corruption that blew the lid off the Teapot Dome. (Wide World)

Hoover told Attorney General Harlan Fiske Stone (shown here on vacation) that he would take over the FBI only if it were free of politics. Later the Director fired more than 100 agents for political reasons of his own. (UPI)

good pal Walter Winchell, who touted the club at every opportunity in his column, saw to that. The gossip-monger and the FBI Chief were lionized by those favored with a nod from Billingsley. They came forth with outstretched hands and words of awe.

No doubt Senator Kenneth McKellar would have given much to have known the backgrounds of those surrounding Hoover at this Stork Club gathering. He would have been intrigued, one can imagine, to know Billingsley, who was twice arrested and convicted of violating liquor laws in Seattle in 1916.

Billingsley, who liked to snarl melodramatically when newsmen inquired into his past: "I killed a man back in Oklahoma," was convicted again in Detroit in 1919 for running bootleg hooch from Ohio to Michigan. This charge got him a sentence of fifteen months (four of which he served) in Leavenworth, plus a $5,000 fine.

The time in jail taught Sherman Billingsley nothing. After his release he made his way to Broadway and opened a speakeasy, which he ran successfully with the help of mob contacts, until repeal of the Volstead Act in 1933.

Hoover, who had admitted under severe crossfire from McKellar that he had never attended any police schools to gain investigational acumen, knew nothing of Billingsley's criminal career or contacts, nor had he bothered to check on him.

But let us return to New Year's Eve at the Stork Club. As the small band swung into "Auld Lang Syne," an enterprising Stork Club photographer, as a joke, produced a toy machine gun. Billingsley and Winchell thought it would be fun if someone in the bubbling Cub Room would hold it on the FBI Director as his picture was snapped.

Hoover went along with the idea with good humor. He wouldn't want to disappoint Winchell, then the mightiest newsman in the nation, whose column was syndicated in over a thousand newspapers and upon whom Hoover depended for gratuitous nationwide publicity. Of course Hoover would pose for the picture, but he insisted that someone who looked like an authentic criminal train the gun on him. He pointed to a tough-looking character in the crowd.

The guest, apprehensive and nervous, walked over in response to Hoover's wave. Billingsley and Winchell broke into a sweat. The tough-looking customer, they knew, was one Terry Reilly.

The photographer explained the gag to Reilly and held out the toy machine gun. Hoover grinned. Reilly shook his head no. It was only a joke, Hoover explained. If he was willing, why not Reilly?

Reilly absolutely refused to take part as Winchell and Billingsley exchanged anxious glances. The FBI Director attempted all manner of persuasion. Suddenly, Reilly bolted for the door. His action puzzled Hoover for a minute before he went back to his champagne.

But Winchell and Billingsley were relieved. They knew that a major crisis had been averted. Terry Reilly was one of the most vicious underworld killers on the syndicate's payroll. He was then on parole after serving time for extortion, as well as for impersonating an FBI agent.

# 5

# The Spyhunter

Almost at the height of Hoover's embarrassing cross-examination by Senator McKellar in 1936, President Roosevelt, perhaps as a way of getting the heat off his top cop, gave the Director overall responsibility for counter-espionage in the United States. Roosevelt was definitely concerned about the expansionist plans of Germany and Japan; Hoover obviously viewed his new duties as a way of bolstering his image.

This new role entailed "a responsibility which Hoover welcomed," one historian recalled, "since it represented a considerable addition to the prestige and influence of the FBI, whose interests its ambitious Director was always most zealous in promoting."

Ten years later, in 1946, Hoover announced to congressmen: "I recall in the prewar years that the FBI was criticized on the ill-founded premise that nothing was being done to meet the Nazi-Fascist-Japanism [sic] threat to our internal security. When the time came to act, the FBI was fully prepared to carry out its responsibilities. There was not one successful enemy-directed act of sabotage during the war and enemy espionage was kept under complete control."

That statement stood like granite for two decades. Backing Hoover's claim was the fact that FBI agents had quickly snared two groups of would-be secret agents (via informers) who boldly blundered onto beaches in Florida and New England from Nazi submarines early in the war.

What really happened between the time of Hoover's counterespionage appointment and his boast to Congress makes it appallingly clear that German and Japanese agents were more than moderately successful in obtaining important U.S. secrets and in effecting disastrous sabotage. Hoover's understanding of the subtleties practiced by Axis spies was pedestrian at best. He apparently reasoned that the greatest espionage threat the enemy could muster was to have agents storm U.S. shores with time bombs ticking in their hands. The FBI's capture of two such raiding parties cemented this thinking.

Hoover believed in the trite portrait of Nazi spies drawn by popular historians of that time. One wrote (comparing German spies to ultrasinister Soviet agents): "Where the Soviet spies carried briefcases, the Nazi agents affected sword canes. The former were often unobtrusive, mild-mannered men. . . . The latter tended to be human tumbleweeds —unstable, flamboyant, and frequently alcoholic."

This stereotyped description neatly justified Hoover's deeper dread of Soviet espionage, a more familiar threat. He continued to hunt Reds.

Almost from the day of his espionage assignment, Hoover moved against Communists and "Communist sympathizers." In 1937, his Detroit office took particular interest in those who recruited volunteers to serve in the Abraham Lincoln Brigade of the Loyalist government in Spain. Hoover's agents kept at these Detroit activities for almost three years. On February 3, 1940—long after the Spanish Civil War had ended—FBI agents, armed with secret indictments against the Abraham Lincoln Brigade recruiters, struck at 5:00 A.M. The fact that those arrested could not be arraigned before a federal judge until 3:00 P.M. that day meant nothing.

Ten persons in Detroit and one in Milwaukee were arrested (two doors were smashed down in the process). FBI Inspector Myron E. Gurnea told agents that "under no circumstances should they mention communism, or accuse any person whom they may encounter as being Communist, or any way affiliated with . . . the Communist movement." And yet this was the underlying motive for the arrests.

Hoover himself had admitted to President Roosevelt in 1936: "Of course, it is not a violation of the law to be a member of the Communist party. . . ."

Hoover's agents, therefore, refrained from mentioning any specific charges against the eleven. The following account emphasizes the drama of the arrests, which Hoover would be sure to appreciate.

An agent of the Milwaukee office called a doctor, one of those to be arrested, at his home at 4 A.M. This brief and incredible conversation ensued:

"This is the FBI," the agent announced on the phone. "We have a warrant for your arrest and there are agents at your door. Go to the door and let them in."

The doctor was understandably startled. "Arrest? What for?"

"That will be explained to you later." The FBI agent hung up.

Agents were outside the man's home listening for the phone to ring. After the phone conversation ended, one announced: "We are agents of the FBI. We have a warrant for your arrest. Open the door." When the doctor refused, the agents broke down the door and promptly arrested him.

The eleven were hustled off to FBI headquarters in Milwaukee and Detroit, where they were fingerprinted, photographed, and grilled. After their arraignment, the suspects were handcuffed to a chain and led to jail. As they filed out of the courtroom, news photographers took their pictures.

In a matter of days, Hoover and the FBI, red faced but unbowed, reaped a whirlwind of criticism. One national magazine stated: "In foreign countries people are forced by their governments to submit to their gestapos. In this country, Hoover has the voluntary support of all those who delight in gangster movies and ten-cent detective magazines. . . ."

Quickly, Attorney General Robert H. Jackson pulled in the FBI's horns. On February 16, 1940, he ordered the dismissal of the indictments in the Spanish Civil War cases, adding lamely, "I can see no good to come from reviving in America at this late date the animosities of the Spanish conflict so long as the struggle has ended and some degree of amnesty at least is being extended in Spain."

This mad-hatter statement all but said that since the dictator of a foreign government, Francisco Franco (whose autographed portrait, incidentally, adorned the office of Admiral Wilhelm Carnaris, chief of the Abwehr, Germany's espionage arm), had forgiven the remnants of the Loyalist armies he had conquered with the aid of Hitler and Mussolini, we in the United States could do no less.

But the matter did not end with Jackson's announcement. Senator George W. Norris (D., Nebr.) attacked the FBI for its action on the floor of the Senate on February 26.

Jackson hurriedly wrote to Norris explaining that the warrants to arrest those suspected of recruiting for the Loyalists "were given to the Bureau for execution under circumstances which warranted the impression that their service was of the utmost importance and immediacy. Being given a warrant for the arrest of these parties, the obvious duty of the Bureau was to effect their arrests promptly, simultaneously, and without escapes. . . ."

Jackson thus vindicated the FBI raids on the basis that Hoover's men were only following orders. The truth was that Hoover and his Bureau chief in Detroit had lobbied for the raids, swamping the Department of Justice's criminal division with memos and reports on the recruiters all through 1938, until the criminal division relented the following year, stating that it felt it was "highly desirable" that the recruiters be investigated.

Hoover could also hide behind the fact that Secretary of State Cordell Hull had asked the Department of Justice to inspect the backgrounds of Communists and would-be Communists. Yet such requests from Hull were neatly engineered and were, to say the least, cavalier.

In 1936, President Roosevelt asked Hoover to gather data on would-be Communists and Fascists. Roosevelt called Hull into his office to meet with Hoover.

"Edgar says he can do this," Roosevelt told Hull, "but the request must come from you to make it legal."

Hull's terse, quixotic "request" came instantly: "Go ahead and investigate the bastards."

In such manner, Hoover received his orders, ironically convenient to his own political convictions, and, being "ordered," he was thus exonerated from any embarrassing situations which might arise from actions he initiated.

Hoover's usual method of transcribing such whimsical directives into apparently carefully thought out, well-researched orders from on high was to issue a staff memorandum, which instantly exculpated him and placed the responsibility clearly and wholly upon his superiors.

Following the meeting with Roosevelt and Hull, and

a subsequent get-together with the attorney general, Hoover issued a "strictly confidential" staff memorandum.

It read: "In talking with the attorney general today concerning the radical situation, I informed him of the conference which I had with the president on September 1, 1936, at which time the secretary of state, at the president's suggestion, requested of me, the representative of the Department of Justice [Hoover's superior, then Attorney General Homer Cummings, was not informed of this meeting until *after* the decision to investigate had been made], to have investigation made of the subversive activities in this country, including communism and fascism. I transmitted this request to the attorney general and the attorney general verbally directed me to proceed with this investigation. . . . This, therefore, is the authority upon which to proceed in the conduct of this investigation. . . ."

The Spanish recruiter raids, authorized or not, continued to rankle Senator Norris and others. Norris charged that "the prisoners were subjected to third-degree methods from the time they were arrested until three o'clock in the afternoon, when they were taken into court, methods which are not only disgraceful and indefensible, but which could have no other object in view except to break down, to intimidate, to frighten them, and to fill their hearts with fear and trepidation." Norris then demanded and got a "quickie" investigation of the FBI.

This investigation, handled by Henry Schweinhaut, chief of the Civil Liberties Unit of the Department of Justice, yielded nothing. Schweinhaut curtly reported, "I am satisfied that . . . the conduct of the agents is not subject to justifiable criticism."

Norris screamed "whitewash" and labeled Hoover the "greatest hound for publicity on the American continent today."

Concerning the incident, Professor Franz Boas of Columbia University wrote in a letter to Teamster boss Daniel J. Tobin: "You are undoubtedly aware of the apprehension with which intelligent people throughout the country have realized the dangerous nature and the scope of the FBI's activities as recently exposed by Senator Norris. . . ."

The furor over this completely mismanaged affair subsided when Roosevelt pooh-poohed the criticism. The president's thinking might have been that Hoover was merely receiving the usual political flak from liberal congressmen. On the other hand, if he had investigated, he would have realized that his super spy-catcher had done little or nothing to combat espionage up to that time.

In fact, only three years after Hoover assumed power over the FBI, German intelligence agents had already infiltrated classified government production areas and had stolen staggering amounts of top secret information for their budding war machine.

One German agent, using the cover name of William Lonkowski, landed at Hoboken, New Jersey, stepping off the liner *Berlin* on March 27, 1927. Lonkowski was described by one historian as "a plain, pale, placid man, he became a face in the crowd," which was anything but the "flamboyant" type of spy Hoover envisioned.

Within a year, Lonkowski and two confederates, working as engineers and designers (which they were) in highly secret areas of aeronautical plants developing equipment for the armed services, supplied the German secret service with complete information, blueprints, and plans of a "fireproof plane," "the world's most powerful air-cooled motor" (being built for the army by the Wright Aeronautical Corporation), and the design of a pursuit plane which could land "either on a ship or on water" from the Curtiss Aeroplane and Motor Company.

By 1935 there wasn't a piece of ordnance or a secret plan being developed by the American armed forces that the Abwehr didn't demand and receive almost overnight from their operatives in the United States.

In the space of six months the Germans obtained the plans of every airplane being built at the Sikorsky Airplane Factory in Farmingdale, Long Island, complete specifications for scout bombers (from Vought Aviation), blueprints of Boeing and Douglas bombers, secret army maps, information on the construction of destroyers, tactical air exercises, classified radio equipment manufactured by the Lear Corporation, and highly secret plans of a special army night bomber.

The Japanese secret service, which Hoover all but ignored, had not been inactive either. By the early 1930s, the Japanese had placed dozens of operatives in West Coast communities, and, with the help of paid American traitors, secured vital information about movements, personnel, and equipment of the U.S. Pacific Fleet.

Between 1933 and 1936, an ex-yeoman, Harry Thompson, provided the Japanese with minute details concerning the personnel, armament, and secret equipment installations of the battleships *Colorado, Mississippi, Texas,* and *Utah,* the latter sunk at Pearl Harbor. Thompson's downfall was not brought about by dogged agents of the FBI, but through an informer and associate, Willard Turntine, who turned Thompson in to naval authorities. Thompson was tried and convicted on Turntine's testimony, and sentenced to fifteen years at McNeil Island Federal Penitentiary.

Thompson's secret service boss, Toshio Miyazaki (code name "Tanni"), whose presence and activities were known to American authorities, was, however, allowed to continue his damaging espionage for quite some time without interference.

Ex-Lieutenant Commander John S. Farnsworth also worked methodically for the Japanese (at a monthly salary of $300), and provided, over a three-year period, priceless information on American war ships and aviation. Besides top secret code books, maps, sketches, photos, and models of new naval equipment, Farnsworth provided the Japanese with a copy of the navy's top-secret manual, *The Service of Information and Security,* material on the effectiveness of almost all types of guns used by the navy, and detailed information on the carriers *Saratoga* and *Ranger.*

Naval intelligence got on to Farnsworth in 1934 and called in the FBI. Hoover's men kept a twenty-four-hour vigil on Farnsworth's activities, and yet he penetrated the Navy Department in Washington and the Naval Academy at Annapolis, obtaining closely-guarded secrets. The FBI allowed Farnsworth to continue his nefarious operations for almost two years.

In July 1936, without ever having been arrested by the FBI, Farnsworth inexplicably went to the Hearst-owned Universal News Service in the National Press Building in Washington and confessed his spying activities to newsmen John Lambert and Fulton Lewis, Jr. After Farnsworth left, Lewis phoned the police, who called the FBI.

Only then did Hoover's agents arrest Farnsworth, who was ultimately sentenced to serve four to twenty years in a federal prison. His immediate superiors, Japanese Commander Akira Yamaki and a Japanese journalist named Sato, were, as in the Thompson case, allowed to continue their espionage work unmolested.

Outside of the atomic bomb (which was also quickly stolen by espionage agents after its first appearance), there was no greater secret in America during the war than the Norden bombsight. In publications and motion pictures throughout the war, it was dinned into the public's ears that whatever else might happen the enemy would never lay hands on the ultrasecret, supereffective Norden bombsight, which, it was claimed, was the only one of its kind ever developed, and which absolutely guaranteed pinpoint bombing accuracy.

Carl Norden's first crude model of 1921 was known to foreign spies at its inception. The bombsight was completed and refined in 1931 and secret patents for it were granted. The navy and the army air corps guarded the bombsight tenaciously. At first the Japanese tried to buy it and were turned down. The Nazis were never so blunt.

By 1937, Germany was mobilized for war and was ready to begin the conquest of Europe. One of the vital pieces of equipment lacking was the much-vaunted Norden bombsight. Chief of Germany's air ordnance, General Ernst Udet, asked the Nazi secret service head, Carnaris, to obtain the plans for the bombsight.

Carnaris dispatched a plain-looking businessman, Nicholaus Ritter, to the United States, where he had previously lived and worked for ten years. Ritter's assignment was to get the Norden bombsight specifications.

Ritter landed in New York on October 17, 1937. After establishing himself under a cover name, Ritter visited a resident German agent, Heinrich Sohn, who lived in Brooklyn. Sohn put Ritter in touch with a German-born assembly line inspector, Hermann Lang, who worked at the Norden plant. Lang, in a piecemeal operation, fed Ritter the plans of the Norden bombsight; these were carefully placed inside an umbrella and carried on board the German liner *Bremen*. Within a week they were in the hands of the Abwehr.

Ritter himself departed for Hamburg on November 11, 1937. It had taken less than a month for three German operatives to steal America's most guarded secret.

Hoover's ignorance of such fantastic successes scored by

enemy espionage agents was further emphasized by the spy career of Dr. Bernard Julius Otto Kuehn and his industrious family, who performed double duty for the Nazis and the Japanese.

In 1935, shortly before Hoover took over his counter-espionage duties, Dr. Kuehn, a personal friend of SS chief Heinrich Himmler, and his family landed in Hawaii, and settled in Honolulu. Dr. Kuehn, his wife, Friedel, and his step-children Ruth and Hans all went immediately to work gathering data for the Axis.

On the surface, Dr. Kuehn appeared to be a harmless professorial type studying the Japanese language and the history of the Hawaiian Islands. He was also well fixed. "And it was no secret to the FBI," one report stated, "that Kuehn had deposited more than seventy thousand dollars in a Honolulu bank from 1936 to 1939. He had become a member of the Nazi Party." It was also known that Ruth Kuehn had been, at one time, the mistress of Nazi propaganda chief Joseph Goebbels.

Yet the Bureau allowed the Kuehns to conduct wholesale spying on the Pacific Fleet. The Kuehns noted the types of vessels—from battleships to destroyers—which entered and anchored in Pearl Harbor, the times of their arrival and departure. They clocked the schedules of the army's reconnaissance flights in and about the naval complex; they freely grilled naval and army personnel, gathering volumes of data on equipment, staffs, and tactics.

This information was passed along in detail to the Japanese consuls in Hawaii and to the German secret service. Friedel Kuehn even made two trips to Toyko to detail the espionage information. In 1939, the Kuehns increased their surveillance of American forces stationed in the islands by moving to Pearl Harbor. There, Ruth Kuehn opened a beauty parlor and successfully pumped information from free-talking officers' wives. She also dated naval and army officers and wormed from them vital secrets. Even little Hans Kuehn worked hard and successfully at espionage. He made friends with several sailors, who invited the eleven-year-old boy on board ships. There he memorized information about the ships' guns and equipment which he related to his father each evening.

All the data collected by the Kuehns was conveyed to the Japanese consul by a series of signal flashes the Kuehns jointly sent out. These signals, flashed from their home high above Honolulu, could be seen easily and recorded by the Japanese super secret-agent Takeo Yoshikawa, who arrived in Honolulu in early 1941, and worked under Consul General Nagao Kita and Vice-Consul Otojiro Okudo. He used the cover name Tadasi Morimura.

The special agent in charge of the Honolulu FBI office, Robert L. Shivers, was well aware of the Japanese conspiracy in Hawaii, as was Hoover, yet Yoshikawa, along with receiving and transcribing all of the Kuehn messages, operated openly in Honolulu as an espionage agent.

One report had it that "barefoot and unshaven, disguised as a Filipino laborer, or, at other times, dressed in the flashy manner of a Japanese playboy fond of Americans, Yoshikawa energetically uncovered an abundance of information himself as he walked the streets of Honolulu, through the red-light district and up the hills overlooking the harbor during fleet exercises. Toward the end, shortly before the attack, he rented a small plane at a local airport and took aerial photographs of the hangers at Wheeler and Hickam fields and the ammunition and fuel depots within the U.S. complex."

Yoshikawa even went to the length of exploring the mouth of Pearl Harbor to determine the depth, and to discover whether or not there were mines which might hinder the submarine that was being sent to take away the Japanese consul staff and the Kuehns after the attack.

A sharp-eyed sentry saw Yoshikawa swimming about and fired a warning shot, whereupon Yoshikawa waded ashore adorned only in a loin cloth, brandishing a string of fish. He pretended not to understand English, conveying the fact that he was only a poor fisherman. Believing him, the sentry chased him out of the restricted area.

When the attack on Pearl Harbor did come, the Japanese and the Kuehns were ready. The Kuehns informed the Imperial Japanese Navy in Toyko that there would never be a better day to attack the American fleet than Sunday, December 7, 1941. On this day the largest number of ships in the Pacific Fleet would be anchored in the harbor.

Ruth Kuehn, positioned in an attic window of the family's hilltop home which afforded an excellent view of Pearl Harbor, held powerful Zeiss binoculars to her eyes, and, at 7:55 A.M., December 7, 1941, spotted the Japanese squadrons piercing the bright blue Hawaiian sky.

"Here they are!" she yelled to Dr. Kuehn, who stood ready at another window with his signal flasher.

Suddenly the earth beneath them trembled as the Japanese bombs struck their targets anchored in Pearl Harbor and the more remote Kaneohe Bay, and Wheeler and Hickam Fields.

Ruth Kuehn precisely noted the damage being done to the shuddering American ships and called out the lethal thrusts made by the 105 attacking Japanese aircraft.

"Direct hit on battleship . . . one destroyer on fire . . ."

Dr. Kuehn repeated what his daughter said and, while clearly pronouncing each word, transcribed the words into light signals from his flasher. Yoshikawa, watching the Kuehn window with binoculars from the Japanese consulate, repeated each word to a clerk, who then flashed the message to the attacking Japanese by wireless. In this way the effectiveness of the bombing was tripled.

The Japanese attack lasted until 9:45, but the Kuehns, much to Yoshikawa's puzzlement, stopped transmitting messages at 9:30. They had been interrupted and taken into custody by two American intelligence officers, not connected with the FBI, who had noticed the flashing lights from the Kuehn home during the bombardment and had investigated.

After the attack, Special Agent Shivers ordered the arrest of all members of the Japanese consulate. The submarine which had come for them and the Kuehns had been sunk. Over forty Japanese planes had been shot down and the incredible spy career of the Kuehn family was at an end. These Japanese losses, however, could not compare with the smoldering carnage of Pearl Harbor: 3,435 casualties, 8 battleships, 3 light cruisers, 3 destroyers, and 4 other vessels were lost, plus 188 American planes. The American Pacific Fleet was all but wiped out and the Kuehns—spies who were apparently not important enough for Hoover's agents to arrest—could claim the dubious honors.

At the height of the Japanese attack, Special Agent Shivers placed a call to J. Edgar Hoover over five thousand miles away in Washington, D.C. He got through to headquarters in a matter of minutes but Hoover wasn't in; he was in New York. Shivers asked for Assistant Director Edward A. Tamm, but he wasn't in either. None of the top men of the FBI were in. It was 2:30 P.M. in Washington, and Tamm and other top FBI officials were at Griffith Stadium watching the pro football game between the Washington Redskins and the Philadelphia Eagles. Shivers got through to the field and Tamm was called from his box.

Hoover had been reached in New York, and, according to an FBI historian, he was somehow switched onto the same line as that connecting Shivers with Griffith Field. Tamm and Hoover listened as Shivers yelled, "The Japanese are bombing Pearl Harbor. There is no doubt about it—those planes are Japanese. It's war. You may be able to hear the explosions yourself. Listen!"

Hoover listened and he heard the bombs exploding on American warships. His reaction was swift. In this instance it was a case of rounding up "the usual suspects"—every American-born Japanese (Nisei) available.

Still, much of the nation thought this a useless gesture. Days later an anonymous press memorandum was circulated in Washington which stated: "The failure of our counterespionage forces to be on the alert was a twenty-six-months failure. . . . The full facts will not be known, however, unless the president's board looks into the adequacy of the FBI . . . to deal with the fifth column in our territory."

Hoover begged off by saying that he had only nine special agents under Shivers and five stenographers with which to combat the entire Japanese intelligence service in Honolulu, consisting primarily of Dr. Keuhn, his wife, a young girl, an eleven-year-old boy, and a Japanese agent.

Everybody wanted to know where Hoover's agents had been, other than watching football games.

Where had they been? One place was South America.

Early in his career as spyhunter, Hoover was convinced, influenced by a book published in 1911, that Germany's main thrust would come through South America. That book stated that one day almost the whole of South America would become a German colony. Since South America was within Hoover's sphere of counterespionage authority, he sent swarms of agents there in 1940.

It was a time of high adventure, full of intrigue, urgent cross-country flights in small, jittery planes (four agents were killed in crashes), and trips in dingy little steamboats, working against the currents of murky jungle streams.

Hoover's agents poured into Argentina, Brazil, Chile, Mexico, and Columbia in search of spies. This group was known as the SIS—Special Intelligence Service—and was Hoover's counterespionage arm abroad, wholly organized by the FBI.

A typical heroic account of this group's activities in South America: "SIS agents penetrated the 'Green Hell' of the Choco jungle in Columbia trailing platinum smugglers. They tramped the rugged coasts looking for submarine hiding places. They traveled by canoe on the headwaters of the Amazon, where the tributaries are infested with piranhas, the vicious little man-eating fish. . . ."

Well, that's where Hoover's agents were, a lot of them.

In such exotic atmospheres, Hoover's men could hardly resist the dramatic. One agent at a mountain resort in Mexico during this period was loudly upbraided by an irate American citizen who demanded to know why he, a perfectly healthy young man, was not in uniform serving his country.

The agent took the tourist aside and whispered menacingly, "I'm wanted for murder. I killed a man in the States. He asked too many questions." Perhaps that was considered the subtle way of avoiding attention.

Dramatic or not, Hoover's South American venture produced only a few arrests of Nazi operatives. Yet the Director hailed these minor successes as important victories. After the war, Hoover was to write that an even greater espionage victory had been achieved by the Bureau in the taking of a German double agent, whom he named Albert van Loop. This man had come to the American consulate in Madrid during 1942 and confessed that he was an agent of the Abwehr; his mission was to go to the United States under the cover of being a Catholic Dutchman (which he was) fleeing Nazi oppression. His real mission, he told the American vice-consul, was to set up a radio station in America and send back to the Abwehr all information regarding troop movements.

By way of proof, the agent showed the vice-consul all of his Abwehr spy apparatus—wireless set manuals, codes, his transmission schedules and personal call letters written in invisible ink, and more than six thousand dollars in currency, checks, gold, and jewels to pay for his mission.

Van Loop, whose real name was Walter Koehler, then proposed that he spy for the Germans on a phony basis, and that his mission be made known to the FBI with whom he would cooperate. He was offering to be a double agent and Hoover, after hearing from the vice-consul, lost no time in accepting this prize. "Send him along," the Director wired Madrid.

Once Koehler was in the United States, the FBI set up his secret radio station on Long Island, and a team of FBI specialists employing Koehler's peculiar sending style began transmitting true but "safe" information to the Germans, who replied that they were elated with the data sent.

Hoover was also elated with his coup. "Week by week we fed the Germans military and industrial information for the most part true," he was later to write. "We wanted to find out whether any other spies were operating in America. Hamburg might tell van Loop to get in touch with them. We wanted to know how the Germans paid their operatives in the Americas. And, most important, we hoped to mislead the High Command by feeding them false information. We succeeded on all scores."

Not quite. More than twenty-five years later, it was learned that Koehler was not a double agent working for Germany but really working for the United States. He was a triple agent and was actually working for the Nazis.

After the FBI set up Koehler's radio station, the middle-aged spy and his wife were allowed to live unharassed in New York with minimum Bureau surveillance. He had managed to smuggle $10,000 past the FBI, by hiding it in his wife's girdle. With this sum, while the FBI was tapping out phony messages to Germany (which the Nazis knew were bogus since they had devised the entire Koehler "cooperation" scheme), Koehler organized his own clandestine radio operation, working with Nazi agents located in Rochester, New York. The Rochester station continued to send real and important information without detection to Abwehr chiefs until Germany's collapse in 1945.

Hoover's boast in 1946 did not include this small detail, nor did he explain how the luxury liner *Normandie* happened to blow up in the Brooklyn naval yards as it was being converted to a troop ship; he failed to say how the Nazis knew that the United States had broken Japan's top diplomatic code before the war. Hoover neglected to announce that sabotage went on regularly in American airplane plants, thanks to German agents working in the plants. The Director never stated how the Nazis knew all the schedules and cargoes of American convoys going to Europe, or that the Nazis had access to almost all the top secret diplomatic messages between President Roosevelt and his ambassador to England, Joseph Kennedy, and, most shocking of all, how Nazi agents had penetrated the highest top secret nerve centers of American defense, and had detailed reports of the president's cabinet meetings, cleverly gleaned from Hoover's own boss, Attorney General Homer Cummings.

But then, all of these espionage and sabotage operations were apparently too arcane for Hoover. He was much more at home—as he had been during Palmer's Red Raids era—

with rounding up suspicious aliens. Though later he was to loudly protest the internment of Nisei (some of whom had been murdered by the Axis while doing undercover work for the FBI on the West Coast) as a gross violation of civil rights, Hoover lost no time in rounding them up.

Only days after Pearl Harbor, he rushed out an order to his agents stating: "Immediately take into custody all Japanese who have been classified in A, B, and C categories in material previously transmitted to you. Take immediate action and advise Bureau frequently by teletype as to exact identity of persons arrested."

Hoover's agents hurriedly supplied lists of those to be arrested to local police on the West Coast and thousands were scooped from their homes. Within three weeks, all Nisei were swept from Los Angeles by a single squad of police working exclusively with lists supplied by the FBI. Housing for these people was nonexistent. For a period, hundreds of Nisei were kept penned up inside the Del Mar racetrack grounds, according to one report.

Eventually, mass housing was thrown up in remote desert areas of southwestern United States, and the unfortunate Nisei were taken there. "That housing was incredibly cheap and barren," one internee was to remember. "Workmen who had never seen Japanese people before in their lives figured we were a race of midgets and the buildings were almost built in miniature. My father had to stoop while going through the door—an opening a lot less than six feet —when entering our 'home.' "

One of those contractors responsible for building housing for the Nisei was Del Webb, athlete, sportsman, millionaire, and close friend of J. Edgar Hoover. Webb built housing for some 10,000 Japanese during the war, one report has it. Yet official statistics state only 1,532 Nisei were interned.

Webb's relationship with Hoover is cloudy. Some say they

became friends because of a mutual interest in sports. (Webb had been a professional baseball player and one-time owner of the New York Yankees, which he purchased with Dan Topping in 1945 for $2.8 million—with $1 million cash deposit—and sold in 1965 to CBS for $7 million.)

Webb, a high roller who always traveled in important company (Howard Hughes and President Eisenhower were among his intimate friends), was one of the first construction impressarios to move into Las Vegas, where he now operates a successful casino.

Hoover once told President Johnson: "The Las Vegas casinos represent the worst element of the Cosa Nostra—except, of course, for Del Webb's." Some years ago Hoover had every casino in Las Vegas wiretapped, except, of course, Del Webb's.

Hoover's intimate association with Webb together with his evaluation of the notorious killer, Benjamin "Bugsy" Siegel, one of the first syndicate bosses to move into Las Vegas (murdered syndicate-style in 1947), is, to say the least, peculiar. After "Bugsy's" violent and bloody death, Hoover remarked: "The circumstances surrounding Bugsy Siegel's career in crime tell the story better than the words. Here was an individual whose life was a constant challenge to common decency. Yet he and his criminal scum were lionized and their favors sought after in so-called respectable social circles."

The Director has never pointed out the fact, however, that his good friend Del Webb was the man who personally supervised the construction of the Flamingo Hotel and Casino in 1946-47, expressly at the orders of its syndicate owner, Benjamin "Bugsy" Siegel, and that Webb's private plane was always at Siegel's disposal and he used it frequently (as did Moe Sedway and other notorious gangsters still in power).

Webb's association with Siegel had been so intimate that Siegel broke a cardinal syndicate rule and told Webb that he had "personally killed twelve men."

The fact that Siegel was a member of the ruling board of a national crime syndicate, which, over the past forty years, has profitably entered every facet of American life, apparently never occurred to Hoover. If it did, he chose to ignore the fact, just as he had ignored the real effectiveness of Axis espionage and sabotage agents in the United States and its territories throughout World War II.

Such indifference would handsomely pay certain people in the future.

# 6

# The Organization That Didn't Exist

Although, in 1939, he had personally handled the surrender of Louis "Lepke" Buchalter, the head of the most deadly arm of the national crime syndicate, Murder, Inc., Hoover pronounced at the end of the decade that "not one organized-crime gang was operating."

Hoover possessed intimate knowledge of Buchalter, Al Capone, Charles "Lucky" Luciano, Bugsy Siegel—the major figures responsible for creating nationwide organized crime in the early 1930s—and yet he insisted that no such organization existed.

Interstate crimes of bootlegging, traffic in narcotics, cross-country "floating" brothels, and gambling by wire were all firmly established by the syndicate as early as 1935.

A year later, while Hoover was personally taking captive Alvin Karpis to jail by plane, the outlaw tried to explain that two distinct criminal societies existed in America: one consisting of the lone outlaw bands, such as the Dillinger and Barker mobs who concentrated on robbing banks; the other, "organized crime."

Hoover called Karpis a "hoodlum" and Karpis yelled

back, "I'm no hood! I don't like to be called a hood. I'm a thief."

"As far as I'm concerned, you're still a hoodlum," Hoover growled.

Karpis emphasized his position in the outlaw world as opposed to the underworld of organized crime: "You don't understand. I was offered a job as a hoodlum and turned it down cold. A thief is anybody who gets out and works for a living, like robbing a bank, breaking into a place and stealing stuff . . . he really gives some sort of effort to it. A hoodlum is a pretty lousy sort of scum. He works for gangsters and bumps guys off after they have been put on the spot. Why, after I made my rep, some of the Chicago syndicate wanted me to work for them as a hood—you know, handling a machine gun. They offered me $250 a week and all the protection I needed, but I wouldn't consider it. 'I'm a thief,' I said. 'I'm no lousy hoodlum.' "

Hoover reacted no more to this bit of instruction than he did to the obvious historical growth of organized crime in the United States. As the country's leading "criminologist," Hoover gave a shabby performance against the syndicate, the roots of which were firmly planted in such early secret societies as the Black Hand and the Mafia.

The Black Hand Society was established in America in the late nineteenth century. One criminal historian knew and stated that the Black Hand was "only a method, a modus operandi. . . . It was used by large and well-organized gangs. . . . It had been employed for generations by bands of the Mafia and Camorra."

The Black Hand, discernible in extortion letters by a picture-signature of a hand, printed with black ink (prior to the development of fingerprint identification), should have stood out like an evil thumb indicating organized crime to any criminologist worth his statistics. Between

1900 and 1918, there were more than eight hundred Black Hand bombings in Chicago alone.

Dozens of Black Handers involved in the Mafia were prosecuted by the federal government in 1910 for illegal use of the mails, and received stiff sentences. This was a matter of record which apparently escaped the ever-watchful eyes of the Director.

Earlier, on October 20, 1890, an incident in New Orleans exploded the Mafia into national headlines as an organized crime cartel that would be stopped by no one who challenged its operations. On that night Police Chief Peter Hennessey, who had been combating the Mafia in New Orleans, stepped from his office at 11:00 P.M. and minutes later was attacked by a band of armed men.

One account states that Hennessey was "hit six times by chunks of lead, but he drew his revolver and returned fire. One of those in ambush ran out into the street, knelt down, and fired at Hennessey again. The stricken man turned and staggered down the street. His assailants followed on the opposite side firing as they walked with sawed-off shotguns."

Before Hennessey died ten hours later in New Orleans, he identified his killers as members of the Mafia. The killing was a sensation. Here, for the first time, was evidence that a powerful, organized crime cartel existed in the United States, a group with ethnic origins clearly traceable to Sicily, with members who operated rackets far beyond the boundaries of Italian communities.

Nineteen Mafia members were arrested and locked up to await trial. At this point the Pinkerton Detective Agency, in cooperation with officials of the Secret Service in Washington and New Orleans, placed an undercover man, Frank Dimaio, in jail with the Mafia prisoners. Dimaio learned the extent of the Mafia, not only in New Orleans, but across the nation; its political influence was vast and it had already taken root in American labor, shipping, and commerce of all kinds.

On March 14, 1891, before Dimaio could testify in the trial of nineteen defendants, W. S. Parkinson, a prominent New Orleans attorney, led several thousand citizens into the New Orleans jail, overpowered the guards, and dragged eleven of the Mafioso from their cells. "All were kicked, beaten, and riddled with bullets as they begged for mercy," one account has it. The bodies were then strung up to lamp posts and left swaying in the warm New Orleans wind.

Parkinson climbed on top of a wagon and said, "I have performed the most painful duty of my life today. Now let us go home and God bless you and our community." The crowd evaporated.

The lynchings touched off an international incident. The Italian ambassador, Baron Fava, demanded an apology and punishment for the lynch mob leaders.

After the federal government chided New Orleans officials, the matter was dropped.

The national press, however, continued to point out the menace of the Mafia. One exhorted immigration authorities to "keep out the refuse of the murder breeds of southern Europe."

The New Orleans incident, coupled with the much publicized Mafia killing on March 12, 1909, of New York Police Lieutenant Joseph Petrosino, who traveled to Palermo, Sicily, to investigate the Mafia and its origins, were important matters of record to the average American. To the head of the FBI they should have been telltale signs of the growth of organized crime in the United States.

There were literally hundreds of much-publicized cases that clearly outlined the existence of a brotherhood of crime flourishing in America. In the year Hoover was chasing draft dodgers—1918—the sensational murder trial of New

York Camorra killer, Pelligrino Morano, again spotlighted the secret society.

Tony Nataro, witness and Camorra member, testified as to his initiation into the brotherhood: "A man named Tony the Shoemaker gave me a penknife . . . [and] extended his arm in this fashion [witness illustrates]. He said to me, 'Strike here.' I did with the penknife and just a little blood came out. Pelligrino bent over the Shoemaker's arm and sucked the blood and a little blood came out. He said to me, 'You have gained.' "

Hoover, however, never took even a cursory look at the historic development of the organization that was to become the syndicate. On the contrary, he chose to blame "the boy down the block" for crime in America, typified by Dillinger and company. One of his arguments for this "fact," written in 1938, was that the biggest percentage of the nation's criminals were native Americans. Each had an "American name" (whatever that means). "The names are monotonously of a type we have come to classify as 'American' against the Latin or north of Europe 'foreigners.' "

It is little wonder then that Hoover refused to look at the records of such syndicate founders as Charles "Lucky" Luciano, who had set up a nationwide brothel and dope empire in the United States by the time Hoover had written down his thoughts on the genealogy of the American criminal.

Months after Hoover took Lepke into custody (he was wanted for violation of federal narcotics laws), he was identified as one of the board members of the nationwide syndicate and head of the organization's execution arm, Murder, Inc.

Hoover's prisoner, Lepke, was also wanted for a number of New York murders. This local probe into Lepke's background unearthed the reality of something Hoover always insisted did not exist—a national syndicate.

"Early in 1940," one account of the day stated, "while digging into the source of local felony, the district attorney's office in Brooklyn ran head on into an unbelieveable industry. This organization was doing business in assassination and general crime across the entire nation, along the same corporate lines as a chain of grocery stores.

"The ensuing investigation exposed a vast network dealing in every known form of rackets and extortion, with murder as a by-product to that 'business'—an incident to the maintenance of trade [Lepke's troop of 'hit men']. The disclosure, in fact, uncovered a national syndicate with coast-to-coast ramifications. It is, moreover, the same national syndicate decried today by all law, up to and including the United States Senate, but far more closely knit than is generally and popularly believed."

Lepke, imprisoned in the Federal House of Detention in New York in 1940, then began legal maneuvers to save his life. It wasn't until October 30, 1942, that the New York State Court of Appeals upheld his conviction for murder. Yet Lepke didn't go to the electric chair.

First, Lepke would have to receive commutation for his federal offenses before he could be executed by the state of New York for murders he had committed there. At this juncture, Lepke's fortunes rose and J. Edgar Hoover, among a select few, certainly must have known why.

From November 9, 1942, to January 17, 1944, New York authorities attempted to get the federal government to release Lepke by granting him a pardon for his federal offenses. Even though the U.S. Supreme Court had ruled seven days earlier that Lepke's execution should take place, the Department of Justice refused to relinquish their prisoner, saying on January 8, 1943, that the Lepke case was "not a proper case" for pardon.

Again on July 10, 1943, the Department of Justice refused to release Lepke to New York custody. Governor Thomas E. Dewey, on November 20, 1943, charged that Lepke "was protected from punishment by failure of the president of the United States to grant the customary unconditional pardon."

The Department of Justice's odd refusal to turn Lepke over to New York was based, one report said, on the fact that Lepke threatened to "blow the roof off the country" if he was handed over to local authorities for execution. Hoover, who worked intimately with this case, knew that Lepke said he would "deliver" a nationally prominent labor leader on a murder charge; a New York City public official, known widely throughout the United States, on a charge of conspiracy; and the close relative of a 'very high public officeholder' on the charge of acting as a "front" for two board directors of the syndicate who controlled crime in the country.

Hoover, who had insisted on a "no politics" credo for the FBI, could hardly be ignorant of the fact that the Department of Justice was shielding Lepke because he might damage the Roosevelt administration.

Attorney General Francis Biddle finally yielded on January 17, 1944, and, in a complex face-saving maneuver, turned Lepke over to New York State officials. The move was obvious. Dewey, running against Roosevelt in 1944, could not then use Lepke's federal "safety" detention as a political issue.

The small, doe-eyed syndicate gangster was executed in the electric chair at Sing Sing, March 4, 1944. Lepke was the only member of the organization's board of directors to receive capital punishment to that date. And that was only brought about by pressure on the highest level of American government, which certainly should have convinced Hoover of the omnipotence of the crime syndicate.

Or, perhaps, this was no revelation at all. Lepke's surrender to Hoover, it turned out, was directed by the syndicate itself. The syndicate board specifically ordered one of its co-rulers to turn himself in to the Director personally. "Buchalter, most hunted man since the Lindbergh kidnapping, was wanted in New York for eighty murders, while J. Edgar Hoover's FBI wanted him for narcotics and income tax cases," one reliable news source stated. "Fischetti [Charles Fischetti, Chicago board member of the syndicate] promised the fugitive gang would see he only did a few years *if he would give up to Hoover* [italics mine], through the latter's friend, Walter Winchell."

The meaning was quite clear. Fischetti was more than implying that either Hoover was too ignorant to recognize Lepke's real criminal role and would possessively keep him under wraps as a federal prisoner, an exclusive FBI prize, or that Hoover or someone above him was reachable by the organization.

This and the fact that Bugsy Siegel, who had once been in Lepke's troop of killers, migrated to the West Coast to set up, with Jack Dragna, the syndicate's early operations (gambling, juice, and a new specialty, blackmailing promiscuous movie stars) in the 1940s didn't phase Hoover. None of his reports throughout that decade mentioned the national crime organization.

By then, the Director was too involved with his favorite enemy, the Reds (an obsession that would never leave him), and with the witch hunts led by Senator Joseph McCarthy (R., Wis.).

While crime commissions in almost every major American city documented the ever-expanding operations of the syndicate in the 1950s, Hoover concentrated on hunting down Communists and spreading alarming reports of the general increase in crime. He concentrated on statistics which he juggled masterfully to show how the FBI had achieved convictions in almost all the cases the agency investigated. However, most of these cases were in the areas of interstate transportation of stolen cars and property. Much of the statistical success Hoover was to boast of in the ensuing two decades was due to work of FBI accountants, who discovered discrepancies in bookkeeping which led to antitrust and embezzlement apprehensions—in short, the capturing of sneak thieves, not leaders of the syndicate.

Anyone closely inspecting Hoover's annual statistical reports on FBI achievements will discover that the FBI's performance was poorest in such categories as racketeering and interstate transportation in aid of racketeering.

Yet Hoover could hardly be uninformed about the syndicate's expansion into all of the gambling in Nevada, particularly in Las Vegas and the interstate crime emanating from there. All of his ex-FBI men, as all ex-FBI men must, kept in close contact with the Bureau and the Director after leaving the FBI, to report anything amiss in the land. Several of these took up watchdog posts in Las Vegas in the 1950s.

In 1955, an ex-FBI agent, William Sinnott, headed the Nevada Gaming Control Board, whose job it was to screen applicants for casino-owner and employee licenses. This vantage point certainly must have given Sinnott, as well as his successor, ex-FBI man Ray J. Abbaticchio, Jr., an eye-opening view of the organization's powerful grip on Las Vegas gambling.

Ex-FBI men or not, the Vegas casinos continued to have syndicate subleaders owning operating licenses, and syndicate henchmen all over their payrolls. For instance, in 1959, the Desert Inn was licensed to Moe Dalitz, onetime bootlegger, Sam Tucker, another bootlegger, and Maurice Kleinman, who had spent three years in prison for tax evasion. Manager of the Desert Inn then was John Drew, ex-Capone payroller.

All of the most important and most unsavory leaders of the syndicate had (and still do have) their piece of the action in Las Vegas from the time the ex-FBI men got onto the Gaming Control Board.

In 1957, an alert New York City detective removed a small slip of paper from the coat of one Frank Costello, who had been shot. Costello, an eastern syndicate kingpin, who vied with Vito Genovese for the top position of the Mafia after Luciano's deportation, was in for a take of the Las Vegas plums. The sheet of paper found in his pocket was a complete accountant's report on the gambling winnings of the Tropicana in which Costello had an interest.

Others who had interests were Tony "Joe Batters" Accardo, co-captain of the Chicago syndicate (with Paul "The Waiter" Ricca), and the most durable syndicate board member of them all, Meyer "Little Meyer" Lansky.

When Howard Hughes stormed into Las Vegas in 1966, a great cry went up that the cryptic billionaire would clear the syndicate out—the one man who had more money than they did; he would simply buy the rascals out. Hughes arrived in his private rail car and promptly purchased $200 million worth of land, hotels, and casinos.

At first, Hughes did clear out several syndicate members from his initial purchase, the Desert Inn Hotel and Casino. Then he brought in an ex-FBI man, Robert Mayheu, as his chief steward.

In an interview with a newspaperman representing a national publication, Mayheu stated in 1969: "No more of this stuff like sending girls up to the rooms of VIPs. We've given this town a massive infusion of legitimacy as well as money."

Minutes later, when the newspaperman was in his room

in the Hughes-owned hotel, the phone rang. He received "a call . . . from a hotel functionary in the Hughes organization. Would the visitor [hardly a VIP] like a girl sent up?"

Hughes bought up five other casinos, but the syndicate was still very much with him. In the Sands Hotel and Casino was Mario Marino, the catering manager, who had worked for Carlos Marcello and had been convicted in 1968 for assaulting an FBI agent. Another Hughes employee at the Sands was Charlie "Babe" Baron, onetime Capone henchman, once prominent enough to be included in a list compiled by agents of the Treasury Department of the forty-two most powerful mobsters in the United States.

Though many of Hoover's ex-Bureau men were acutely aware of the far-reaching syndicate activity in Las Vegas (and across the nation, for that matter), the Director remained mute about its existence for more than thirty-five years after he took command of the FBI, offering no excuse or rationale for such behavior.

What might explain this purposeful neglect? Organized crime, from its birth in the United States to this day, has presented a complex and swiftly moving target. Hoover "likes to concentrate on relatively easy aspects of police work," one newspaper pointed out, "rather than those that are less likely to make FBI records shine.

"Thus it is said that Mr. Hoover emphasizes car thefts and bank robberies because the statistics are good on solutions of these crimes. But for a long time he is said to have resisted bringing the FBI fully into the much more difficult problems of organized crime and civil rights."

FBI critic Tom Wicker also pointed out that "Hoover resisted taking jurisdiction [over organized crime] until recent years. He knew that these were the areas of crime in which lawmen themselves were most often corrupted, and he saw no reason to expose his agents, and the reputation of his masterpiece, the FBI, to that sort of temptation."

One could easily add that this, too, is pure speculation if one is to accept Hoover's statement that his agents are above reproach and corruption (as well as being the highest paid of any federal investigative personnel).

It is a matter of record, however, that Hoover gave only the assistance asked of him (and no more) by the Senate Labor Rackets Committee in its investigation, during the 1950s, of organized crime in labor unions. The committee's chief counsel at that time was Robert Kennedy.

Kennedy felt the sting of Hoover's stubborn "cooperation" even then and attacked the FBI in 1959: "The department still hasn't learned what it is dealing with. They're over there shuffling papers and handing out press releases. They have to do more investigating. They should use the FBI to find out who these racketeers are, whom they meet, where they go, what business they're in, how they operate. . . . The FBI has to be ordered into this job."

The young crimefighter had more than a point. In the year Kennedy made his verbal onslaught against Hoover, only four FBI agents in the New York City office were at work on investigating the operations of the national crime organization; these were accountants and, one source states, their work was primarily "in-office 'bookkeeping' chores collating such routine information as the whereabouts of known racketeers." While these four methodically checked plane and train schedules, Hoover's other four hundred special agents assigned to the FBI office in New York were out tracking down suspected Communists.

The Kefauver committee of 1951, investigating organized crime, had spelled out the words for Hoover in capital letters. And years before, in the 1930s, the intrepid, much-neglected director of the Federal Bureau of Narcotics, Harry Anslinger, had screamed about the existence of organized crime. In 1957, when nationwide headlines brandished the facts about the hundred most-powerful syndicate members in the nation meeting in Apalachin, New York, for a summit conference of organized crime, Hoover remained silent.

In the fall of 1958, mysteriously, and as a result of the Apalachin meeting, twenty-five copies of an FBI report which documented the existence of the Mafia were sent out to twenty-five top government law enforcement officials; each copy of the report was numbered. The following day, Hoover recalled every copy. His only remark about the report was "Baloney." No one ever saw this report again.

As late as 1962, with Attorney General Robert Kennedy pushing for an FBI investigation of the syndicate, Hoover adamantly insisted that "no single individual or coalition of racketeers dominates organized crime across the nation." He did not explain how crime across the nation could, therefore, be "organized."

But, as Kennedy had promised when he was chief counsel and investigator for the McClellan committee, he compelled Hoover to begin a crusade against organized crime.

Kennedy used to walk past the John Dillinger display in the FBI museum, an FBI aide at his side, and mutter, "What have you done for me lately?" Robert Kennedy was not a man to wait for Hoover to move. Brief months after he became attorney general, he learned of the killing of John A. Kilpatrick in Chicago. Kilpatrick was international president of the United Industrial Workers of America, and his death, on October 20, 1961, was reported as a syndicate "hit." Kennedy remembered the union leader as being a cooperative witness when he testified before the McClellan committee. Kennedy told Hoover about the killing and issued him a direct order: "Find out who's behind this killing, and get him."

Still smarting from this edict, Hoover sent fifty agents swarming through Chicago's underworld. A year later, after one of the killers confessed, two syndicate hit men were sent to the Illinois State Penitentiary to serve long sentences. It was the first major conviction of syndicate killers in Chicago since 1934.

Kennedy's crusade against organized crime proved effective in this case, but he still had to push the Director. The two were constantly at odds about Kennedy's dedication to smashing organized crime. As one observer succinctly put it, "Bobby and Edgar were both cops and both were used to being boss. But they disagreed on where to put the emphasis. Bobby wanted to zoom in on the Mafia and dismantle the [FBI's] Internal Security Division. Edgar wanted the opposite." Robert Kennedy won out.

He was the first attorney general Hoover couldn't circumvent by going to the White House, where another Kennedy was sitting in the president's chair.

Hoover reluctantly obeyed, though with constant threats of resignation on his tongue. The Director's moves against organized crime were often unexplainable. Refusing to allow his agents to arrest syndicate racketeers at all hours of the night in a raid, Hoover reportedly mused, "We'll arrest them at breakfast, not in the middle of the night, because that's the American way."

Hoover was not so gentlemanly in his handling of the Joseph Valachi case. In 1962, when inmate 82811 of the federal penitentiary in Atlanta made his rambling confession to save his own hide after brutally killing a fellow prisoner, Hoover realized he was off the hook as far as organized crime was concerned.

After denying its existence for years, Hoover jumped at the opportunity of using Joseph Valachi as the man who finally revealed the reality of a national syndicate. Today,

Valachi is dead (no one came to claim the body), but he is best remembered for disclosing the sinister words *"Cosa Nostra"* (Our Thing) to the world.

Valachi decided to tell all and ground out more than three-hundred thousand words (1,180 pages) exposing "for the first time" the evil background of the *Cosa Nostra.* Outside of the name itself, which, coming from an admitted killer like Valachi, euphonically suggests dark terror, the exposé was little more than a rambling, self-apologetic, self-excusing document that told what was then commonly known by crime experts. Valachi's information was "safe" information dealing mostly with internecine wars between Mafia factions in the early 1930s. Valachi's description of his blood-brother-type initiation into the *Cosa Nostra* (the name was indigenous to the East, not the rest of the United States) is almost identical to that of Tony Nataro's of 1918:

"So Joe Bananas [Valachi's godfather] . . . comes to me and says, 'Give me that finger you shoot with.' I hand him a finger, and he pricks the end of it with a pin and squeezes until the blood comes out. When that happens, Mr. Maranzano [the Mafia boss of bosses until his murder in 1930 at the behest of his successors Lucky Luciano and Vito Genovese] says, 'This blood means that we are now one family.' In other words, we are all tied up."

Beyond this intriguing cabalistic rite and the name *Cosa Nostra,* nothing Valachi had to say was of real importance. It was ancient gossip of the dead, dying, and imprisoned. That Valachi was employing one of the oldest tricks a convict up for murder resorts to—confessing all for immunity against a death sentence—was irrelevant to J. Edgar Hoover. Valachi was, as any "criminologist" should realize, employing the same technique Abe "Kid Twist" Reles, one of Murder, Inc.'s top hit men, used to avoid prosecution for murder. But this seemed to be unimportant to Hoover. If the Director had thought back a few years, he would have remembered that it was the testimony of Reles that sent Lepke to the chair; desperate finger pointing spared Reles that uncomfortable fate. Reles' action at least put Lepke and two of his most vicious lieutenants to death (though turning state's evidence didn't save Kid Twist, who was either pushed or fell from a window in a sixth floor hotel room where he was being guarded by a squad of policemen). Valachi, on the other hand, revealed nothing that could hurt his associates. Though he stood to face the considerable wrath of Vito Genovese, who was once his cellmate in Atlanta, Valachi put nobody on the proverbial spot.

Yet Hoover claimed him for his very own. He discourteously neglected to tell the world that Valachi's capture and conviction had been an exclusive affair of the Federal Bureau of Narcotics, an agent of which first got Valachi to talk. Hoover's agents then stepped into the affair and it became an FBI coup.

His statements in public before congressional hearings had a "read all about it" air. But that was all right because J. Edgar Hoover was suddenly selling newspapers.

Where he would not accept the possibility of a Mafia, Hoover now trumpeted warnings of Valachi's "revealed" organization: *"La Cosa Nostra* is a criminal fraternity whose membership is Italian either by birth or national origin, and it has been found to control major racket activities in many of our larger metropolitan areas, often working in concert with criminals representing other ethnic backgrounds. It operates on a nationwide basis, with international implications, and until recent years it carried on its activities with almost complete secrecy [or else J. Edgar Hoover would have known about it]. It functions as a criminal cartel, adhering to its own body of 'law' and 'justice' and, in so doing, thwarts and usurps the authority of legally constituted judicial bodies."

From Hoover's statement on, the FBI was syndicate conscious. The Director's combat record against organized crime is another matter.

On March 25, 1966, another syndicate get-together, ostensibly to honor Mafia hoodlum Fifi Buchieri, occurred at Chicago's posh Edgewater Beach Hotel. Although over one hundred members of the intelligence unit of the Chicago Police Department were positioned outside (a few got inside masquerading as busboys), the FBI was not present.

The only man to penetrate the meeting was an investigator from the Northwest Indiana Crime Commission, who noted the dozens of underworld luminaries present. None of Hoover's agents even knew of the summit meeting. The Director found out about it the next day when he opened the pages of the *Chicago Tribune* (the only newspaper placed on his desk each morning), which carried the entire story as the crime commission investigator reported it. Hoover exploded and put through a call to his Chicago office. He demanded to know why the Bureau hadn't covered this meeting and why the FBI received no publicity in connection with exposing the affair. The Bureau chief, Marlin Johnson, was nonplussed. He hadn't read the *Tribune* that morning.

Hoover wanted a full report of the syndicate summit meeting on his desk within hours—or else. Embarrassed Chicago FBI agents were compelled to go to the Chicago Police Department's intelligence unit, copy reports of the meeting, and hurry these along to Hoover.

The Director, if caught short in such circumstances, knew he could always excuse the Bureau's inactivity on the basis that FBI men are not permitted to do undercover work (again to avoid the possible corruption of agents).

In lieu of such assignments, the Bureau utilizes under-cover men of police departments and crime commissions, and sometimes, well-paid informants, often criminals themselves.

Recently, one such man was sitting in a roadhouse belting down drinks. "For three days I followed him [a man about to be killed by the syndicate]," he said undramatically. "I wanted to put dynamite in his car, but he was going with some girl. I didn't want to kill the broad. I didn't want to kill anybody but him."

"On the third day, he walked out of a restaurant. I put one in the back of his head. When he hit the sidewalk, I rolled him over and I put one in each eye."

This man is a syndicate hijacker, fence, and murderer on a professional scale, and he has been on the FBI payroll for the last fifteen years as an informer (preceding Hoover's admission of the existence of a syndicate). His payoff is not cash, but freedom.

Curiously, the FBI allows this vicious criminal to operate his syndicate cartel as long as he maintains and limits his operations to within the boundaries of his native state.

The Bureau's attitude toward this man is prosaic. The agents who deal with him, along with other highly-paid informants, are primarily motivated by expediency and by Hoover's statistics. His local criminal activities are of no concern to Hoover's men. As a matter of policy, the Bureau takes special note of only two serious offenses—not putting the FBI first and interstate crime.

To this informer, it's strictly business. He sells hot mer-chandise and, occasionally, he sells the seller. If a hot-wares peddler is unlucky enough to fall into this informant's bad graces, he will probably find himself in the unenviable posi-tion of being the next FBI statistic.

Syndicate or not, this informant contributes to Hoover's

assembly line of raw data that fills mountains of "intelligence reports" made out each year by the FBI. These reports, as we shall see, are the nucleus of FBI power. These reports can intimidate and destroy. Just as they were of great aid to Senator Joseph McCarthy in his witch hunts, they also serve as a dagger to the throat of any politician Hoover chooses to inspect; such are the reports, in the extensive dossier the FBI keeps on Mayor Richard J. Daley of Chicago, which claim Daley has a long history of connections with top executives of organized crime.

Its just another way J. Edgar Hoover combats the syndicate—now that it exists.

# 7

# Netting The 'Red Herring'

After World War II, both the syndicate and J. Edgar Hoover flourished. The syndicate went about its expansion of business in the late 1940s and throughout the 1950s virtually unhampered by the FBI, and Hoover's status rose with the new Red scare that swept the country after the Rosenberg-Fuchs-Hiss cases.

The Director continued to enjoy his affluence of power. In Washington, he took time out from his busy Red-hunting schedule to indulge in elaborate practical jokes. He was a regular patron of Harvey's, specialists in cuisine of the sea, and he liked nothing better than to plague the owner, Julius Lully. Hoover obtained a photo of Lully in his World War I uniform and, using this picture, had batches of FBI wanted posters made up. These fliers on Lully were posted everywhere about the restaurateur's country home and he was finally arrested by a local sheriff. When Lully protested and gave Hoover as a personal reference, the Director told the sheriff he had never heard of Lully.

On yet another occasion, Hoover, pretending to be Chef Oscar of the Waldorf, sent Lully a letter threatening to sue him for stealing the recipe of an exclusive salad dressing. The frantic restaurant owner hired a lawyer and instructed him to offer the Waldorf $2,500 as a settlement. When he asked Hoover's advice on the matter, the Director growled that the settlement was not enough.

In Miami, where Hoover regularly vacationed, the jokes were on him. There he attended racetracks which were owned by the syndicate and, according to one source, he would often "find himself posing with notorious hoods." This proved embarrassing, but Hoover, in lieu of giving up the ponies he held so dear, established a Miami-based special hoodlum squad, whose sole job was to identify hoodlums to the Director and keep the underworld goons out of the pictures.

But these were only minor problems for Hoover, easily surmounted. He was much more concerned with an announcement made by a young senator from Wisconsin before Republicans in Wheeling, West Virginia, on February 9, 1950. On that date, Senator Joseph R. McCarthy (R., Wis.) stated:

"While I cannot take the time to name all the men in the State Department who have been named as active members of the Communist party and members of a spy ring, I have here in my hand a list of 205—a list of names that were made known to the secretary of state as being members of the Communist party and who nevertheless are still working and shaping policy in the State Department."

This single statement, though McCarthy's "evidence" was nonexistent, touched off the most incredible witch hunt in American history, a nightmare of political oppression and smear that was to ruin the reputations of hundreds of American citizens who had even remotely touched the stringy fabric of communism, and of hundreds more who knew, however distantly, the fingered victims.

Hoover not only endorsed McCarthy's wild accusations, but aided the senator in his pursuit of the unnamed agents of the Soviet Union. McCarthy and his chief assistant, Roy Cohn, in turn, praised Hoover and the FBI for its diligence against the Red Menace.

McCarthy's entry into the war on communism heartened Hoover immeasurably. Not only was the ancient foe again enjoined, but it appeared to be an excellent opportunity for Hoover to even an old score. In a 1945 speech to the International Association of Chiefs of Police, Hoover had bragged, "Foreign powers tried to steal not only the atomic bomb but other military secrets. . . . The counterespionage program which we developed did more than encircle spies and render them harmless. It enabled us to learn of their weakness and their aims."

Before Hoover had spoken these words, Soviet spies had already stolen the atomic bomb secrets. It would not be until four years later that Hoover would learn the true extent of the atomic-bomb-plans theft involving master Soviet spy Klaus Fuchs (identified as early as 1946 by defector Igor Gouzenko), chemist Harry Gold, who had been arrested by FBI agents in 1947 on suspicion of espionage and released, David Greenglass (eventually turned in by Harry Gold), and Julius and Ethel Rosenberg (fingered by Greenglass).

None of this was known to the Director until 1949, when it was far too late to save any secrets. Though Hoover was to contend that the FBI really couldn't have acted since certain espionage laws had not been passed until 1946 and the atomic bomb secret was stolen before then, the FBI was responsible for counterespionage under laws existing since 1917, the very laws employed to convict the Rosenbergs, and sentence them to death.

Though Hoover, through expert public relations techniques, converted his failure into success by blandly stating that the FBI caught the spies, the sting of this defeat lingered. Senator Joseph McCarthy's emergence on the Red-hunt scene was salve to Hoover's open wound.

McCarthy, a ruthlessly ambitious politician who had twice tried to win a Wisconsin senatorial seat, finally edged past the dynastic incumbency of Robert M. La Follette, Jr. McCarthy worked against La Follette's conservatism, and received the support of many Democrats in his state (as a more vulnerable opponent against their November candidate) and, ironically, the support of the small but influential Communist party.

When asked about the Communists who backed him, McCarthy retorted, "Communists have the same right to vote as anyone else, don't they?"

Such turnabouts were not only fair play for McCarthy, but axiomatic for the progress of his phenomenal political rise. This was the same Joseph McCarthy who, in 1946, the year of his election to the Senate, sat in as a free agent on the hearings of the subcommittee of the Armed Services Committee dealing with Nazi atrocities. The committee was studying the cases of forty-three men who belonged to the notorious "Blowtorch Battalion" of the First SS Panzer Regiment. They had been tried as war criminals and held responsible for the Malmedy Massacre, in which hundreds of unarmed American prisoners and Belgian citizens were slaughtered.

The army hearings were to determine whether or not the death penalty for the SS men would be upheld. McCarthy, who was never a member of the subcommittee, badgered witnesses and totally dominated the sessions with statements that claimed the rumors of American atrocities against the convicted Nazis were true.

McCarthy's blusterings nearly caused riots in Germany, and the Communist press championed his remarks as proof of American brutality. Occupied Germany was about to explode and the subcommittee, in political anxiety, reduced the death sentences to long prison terms.

Eight years later, evidence was obtained that proved McCarthy a Communist dupe in the entire matter. "At a subsequent hearing of the Armed Services Subcommittee in Germany," the report stated, "a notorious Communist agent, Dr. Rudolph Aschenauer, admitted that he had worked up the whole case in defense of the SS men, that he had manufactured all the charges—and that he was the source of the data on which the senator had based his case."

McCarthy, a reckless mudslinger whose philosophy centered about the "Big Lie" theory, turned on his supporters, the Communists, in 1950, employing the same smear techniques he used to defend the SS men. This was the man J. Edgar Hoover backed in the wild and unfounded namecalling hearings that followed. It was Hoover's heyday as well as McCarthy's, but only the Director would survive the holocaust.

Hoover was to state in the McCarthy aftermath that his FBI was merely a fact-gathering agency. "Once we gather the facts," he wrote, "apprehend the violator, and provide our services to other agencies, our duty is fulfilled. We submit the results of our investigations to other officials of the government. We neither evaluate the results of our investigations nor make recommendations. We do not inject ourselves into the administrative operations of other agencies of government by saying who is loyal and who is not loyal or who is a security risk or who is suitable for service in the federal government."

Still Hoover didn't have to evaluate his "intelligence" reports for Joseph McCarthy. It was enough to get such reports on suspected Communists into the volatile senator's hands. McCarthy would do the rest. The reports channeled to McCarthy were never issued to his committee investigating Communists and communism on an official basis. These were slipped under the door. As one reliable reporter stated: "During the Red-hunting McCarthy era, the Bureau never funneled information on suspected Communists to the McCarthy committee. Instead the FBI gave its information to military intelligence, which then leaked it to the committee."

McCarthy's committee had a field day fostering, for the most part, sinister implications, dark insinuations, and unsupported accusations. McCarthy flaunted his power to intimidate and destroy. Because they were fearful of being labeled Communists or Communist sympathizers, few people in Washington, or anywhere else, were willing to stand up to McCarthy. Columnist Drew Pearson did, and McCarthy, adopting one of Hoover's favorite techniques, shouted that his critic, Pearson, was guilty of "complicity" with communism. The two met in the men's room of Washington's swanky Sulgrave Club one day and McCarthy punched Pearson. It was none other than Richard Milhous Nixon who stepped between the two before the brawl could continue.

No matter how much Hoover claimed his was only a fact-finding agency strictly of an investigative nature, the FBI during the McCarthy era became an infiltrative organization gathering "intelligence," which was more likely to compromise, embarrass, and ruin those investigated than merely supply "facts." The General Intelligence Division which Hoover headed under Palmer had been disbanded by Attorney General Stone, who insisted that the Bureau rigidly adhere to investigation alone, not "intelligence" of an evaluative nature. But that was in 1924, and almost thirty years later, Hoover was running the Bureau, not Stone.

Added to his penchant for special intelligence on would-be subversives was the support Hoover received from President Truman's 1947 loyalty programs, which had been brought about by the atomic-bomb-plans theft. Thus Hoover and McCarthy could comfortably ride the crest of the Red scare wave, their conduct sanctioned by the higher authority of the executive office.

"I think well of Senator Joe McCarthy," Hoover said in 1953. The thought was backed by action and intelligence reports with which McCarthy crucified any and all who would not bend to his condemnations. Further testimony on the political ties between the Director and McCarthy came from J. Parnell Thomas, who served on the House Un-American Activities Committee. Before he was sent to prison, convicted of graft, Thomas stated that "the closest relationship exists between Mr. Hoover and this committee."

The tie was severed when McCarthy went too far—not in his wild allegations, but in that he revealed his unsubstantiated source material.

McCarthy, pushed by the courageous Senator William Benton (D., Conn.) and a few others to identify the basis of facts behind his denouncing labels, blurted out on the Senate floor that he possessed a chart prepared by the FBI which consisted of photostats listing Communists in the State Department.

This was a glaring breach of Hoover's private protocol. He swiftly denied the existence of such material. He stated that the FBI "did not send any such chart to the State Department and, of course, made no evaluation of information as was indicated."

After this denial, President Eisenhower, who had also been a McCarthy target, rallied to Hoover's support. Eisenhower said, "It has come to my ears during this interregnum a story to the effect that J. Edgar Hoover, head of the FBI, had been out of favor in Washington. Such was my respect for him that I invited him to a meeting, my only purpose being to assure him that I wanted him in government as long as I might be there and that in the performance of his duties he would have the complete support of my office."

This was a curious statement in that, during this period, Hoover was enjoying immense support in Congress. But two could play the Hoover game and Eisenhower's "assurance" of Hoover keeping his job could well be interpreted as a directive to the FBI chief to keep his place and to steer clear of fanatics such as McCarthy.

Shortly after, Hoover wrote: "False accusations and careless insinuations can do more to destroy our way of life than to preserve it." Hoover never extended such thinking to his own Bureau, where thousands of "raw intelligence" files hold little more than—if not false, then extremely dubious—accusations directed at prominent Americans.

As a postscript to the McCarthy period, Hoover added in 1964 (responding to the McCarthy canard published that year), "Anybody who will allege that General Eisenhower was a Communist agent has something wrong with him."

On December 2, 1954, Senator Joseph McCarthy was soundly condemned in a vote of censure (67 to 22) by the Senate. He was through. He, like Attorney General Palmer before him, relied upon Hoover to supply him with ammunition with which to fight communism. Where Palmer got duds, McCarthy got firecrackers. Neither was lethal except to the user.

McCarthy's drinking increased thereafter and Hoover no longer lavished splendid fraternal remarks on him as he had in McCarthy's palmy days when he stated: "I've come to know him well, officially and personally. I view him as a friend and I believe he so views me."

The senator's rantings slowed to murmurs and stopped altogether on May 2, 1957, with his early death. Though McCarthy had been finished off prematurely in his political career, his chief aide, Roy Cohn, was to survive handsomely, thanks to J. Edgar Hoover.

Cohn, an executive of Schenley Industries, was the apple of Hoover's eye during the McCarthy witch hunts. The Director, one news source states, "showered Cohn with compliments, notes, and photographs."

In the year McCarthy died, Louis B. Nichols, for years considered "number two man" at the FBI, left the Bureau and became the executive vice-president of Schenley Industries through, as one source states, "Cohn's good offices." Nichols went to work for Lewis Rosenstiel, Schenley's chairman of the board. Cohn, whom Nichols also admired greatly, joined the firm shortly thereafter.

Nichols, who named his oldest son J. Edgar Rosenstiel and who has purchased large amounts of pro-Hoover books and distributed them to friends, became president of Schenley. In 1965, he and Rosenstiel and Cohn founded and incorporated the not-for-profit J. Edgar Hoover Foundation in the District of Columbia.

Initially, Cohn contributed $500 to the Hoover Foundation, channeling it through the American Jewish League Against Communism, of which he is the founder and president. Nichols contributed a small and undisclosed amount of Schenley stock to the Hoover Foundation. Rosenstiel's contribution, by comparison, was gigantic. In 1965, Rosenstiel contributed 1,000 shares of Schenley stock, valued at $35,000, to the Hoover Foundation. The following year, the charitable Dorothy H. and Lewis Rosenstiel Foundation of New York—which purchased 25,000 copies each of *The FBI Story* and Hoover's *Masters of Deceit* (making them best sellers)—contributed $50,000 more to the J. Edgar Hoover Foundation. This sum was topped in 1968 when the Rosenstiel Foundation, in the form of bonds of the Glen Alden Corp., which took over Schenley Industries in the fall of 1968, gave the Hoover Foundation $1 million.

Ostensibly, the Hoover Foundation was established to work closely with the Freedoms Foundation of Valley Forge, Pennsylvania, to which tiny amounts over the years have been paid by the Hoover Foundation.

Months previous to the time of Rosenstiel's $1 million gift, Roy Cohn was prosecuted by U.S. Attorney Robert M. Morganthau on conspiracy, mail fraud, extortion, bribery, and blackmail charges. Three FBI agents out of the New York Bureau were working with Morganthau on the case (it is a long-standing procedure with the FBI to provide agents to work with U.S. attorneys on their cases). Morganthau, taking no chances, had the agents file affidavits stating that they had no knowledge of an entrapment scheme in the Cohn case.

Shortly after the agents filed their affidavits, Cohn rushed his copies to Nichols. The ex-FBI man promptly marched into the Washington headquarters of the FBI and demanded that the three agents working on the Cohn case be censured. Hoover personally ordered their transfer out of New York. When Morganthau discovered this action, he confronted assistant FBI director and agent-in-charge of the New York office, John Malone. Malone, in turn, immediately reported Morganthau's visit to Hoover, and the Director told him to have the three agents out of town by midnight of the following day.

One newsman summed up the incident: "If Cohn, through Nichols, could bring about arbitrary transfer of three FBI agents, what chance had an ordinary citizen?"

Another pertinent question might have been: How coincidental was it that Rosenstiel suddenly upped his contributions to the Hoover Foundation by a staggering amount just after Cohn's New York indictments? Further, one might ask: How can Rosenstiel be J. Edgar Hoover's close friend *and* have a history of business associations and friendships with known leaders of organized crime?

A New York State committee studying organized crime recently heard federal agents testify that Rosenstiel was associated with such underworld czars as Frank Costello, Meyer Lansky, and Joe Fusco in a liquor consortium during Prohibition.

Moreover, Rosenstiel's fourth wife, Susan, testified before the Kefauver committee in 1957 that she and her husband were warmly greeted and entertained by Meyer Lansky on a pleasure trip to pre-Castro Havana.

Many of Hoover's friends who were involved in the liquor business had syndicate connections.

—Prendergast and Davies Company was founded one month before Repeal. The liquor company's boss was Al Capone's mentor, Johnnie Torrio (the architect of the national syndicate). One of the firm's founders was Herbert Heller, who was once Rosenstiel's brother-in-law.

—Rosenstiel owned the building in which the offices of Prendergast and Davies were housed.

—Alfred Hart, onetime executive of Gold Seal Liquors in Chicago, which the Kefauver crime committee identified as syndicate controlled by Charles "Cherry Nose" Gioe, is presently the president of the City National Bank of Beverly Hills, and a personal friend of J. Edgar Hoover.

—Arthur Samish, a California liquor lobbyist who was sent to the federal penitentiary in the 1950s for income tax evasion, and who was on Rosenstiel's payroll for some time, was a personal friend of Meyer Lansky and of J. Edgar Hoover.

And Lansky? He is reputed to be the kingpin of the syndicate (but not of the inner organization, the Mafia), with a personal fortune of $300 million. Somehow "Little Meyer" has managed to avoid jail and retribution for his many years as a syndicate leader. In 1952, denaturalization proceedings were started against him. Yet the Department of Justice unexplainably stalled its probe, and in May 1958 proceedings against Lansky, "for lack of evidence," were dropped.

While on the subject of Hoover's unusual friendships, it might be noted here that McCarthy and Hoover took trips together to California in their friendly years of the Red witch hunts. They were both lavishly entertained at the Hotel Del Charro in La Jolla, California. The hotel is situated near the Del Mar racetrack (the site of the Nisei internment), where Hoover likes to place his two-dollar bets—which he insists are in the best "American tradition." Both hotel and racetrack were owned by Texas oilman and billionaire, Clinton W. Murchison, Sr., who died in 1969, and fellow Texas tycoon, Sid Richardson.

Murchison gave Hoover carte blanche and the Director, almost always accompanied by the faithful Clyde Tolson, took full advantage of the facilities at the Del Charro. Sometimes the service at the luxury spa was not up to Hoover's expectations. Once, circa 1950, Hoover showed up late in the dining room and the *maitre d'* would not seat him on the grounds that he didn't want to keep the help late. Hoover exploded and ordered the Bureau in San Diego to open files on the *maitre d'* and the rest of the dining room help. All were questioned at length in the Bureau offices about their patriotism.

Hoover and Tolson stayed in $100-a-day suites and the living was high. One report had it that the pair ran up a $1,900 bill on one visit. Another source states that the final bill was $15,000! 

All the tabs were casually picked up by Clint Murchison and charged to one of his companies, such as the Delhi-Taylor Oil Company.

The Director was always grateful for such hospitality. According to one columnist, a typical Hoover to Murchison thank-you note read: "It is always hard to leave one's friends after such an enjoyable stay as Clyde and I have had these past few weeks . . . we appreciated the superb accommodations and your many contributions toward our comfort and enjoyment of this trip. Edgar."

This close association might explain why I. Irving Davidson, who represented Murchison's interests in Washington, had access to the Director's inner sanctum. Davidson was a registered agent of Haiti. Murchison owned the Haitian American Meat Packing Company there, which, incidently, was promoted at one time by Bobby Baker.

A national magazine reported in 1969 that Davidson had convinced his onetime client, Thomas Licavoli, a top Mafia boss in Cleveland, "to donate $5,000 to the J. Edgar Hoover Foundation." But, as we have seen, this contribution to the amazingly static Hoover Foundation does not stand alone as suspect. (Licavoli, by the way, was suddenly released from the Ohio State Penitentiary early in January of this year.)

In 1954, Murchison established a boy's club in San Diego and stated to high society there that, on certain days, track receipts from his Del Mar racing arena would go to the club.

Hoover gave the plan his endorsement. Retired Marine Corps General "Howling Mad" Smith, who lived in the area, also stumped for the club. But the general bowed out a little later when he was unable to find any of the promised receipts going to the boy's club.

Hoover, who was national director of the Boys' Clubs of America, gave only his verbal endorsement, and let Murchison operate from there. Hoover talked about the "wonderful people" in racing, and stated that the Murchison offer "helps directly in making the nation sturdy, for

Communist penetration is currently directed mainly at labor organizations and youth organizations."

Hoover's penetration of the Communist party at that time was far less exciting than his trips to La Jolla.

With the passing of McCarthy, Hoover publicized his Bureau's Red-hunting less and less, but the Director kept full squads of "Red-chasers," as they called themselves, on the job.

One agent reported that he spent twelve years on lookout, which usually meant watching the windows of apartments where suspected Communists lived. Several of those years were consumed staring across an air shaft in Washington, D.C. "The blinds in the room he watched," a fellow agent wrote later, "were never closed. He liked to tell of the lively sexual activities he had seen. He seemed to think that, in the absence of other evidence, they confirmed that something subversive was taking place."

Agents clocked another suspect as he left for work and then wrote reports on the suspect's wife, who signaled her lover down the block that her husband was gone by flashing the porchlight on and off. "The agent's report," the ex-FBI agent stated, "indicated the time elapsed from the moment when the porch light went on until the lover arrived panting at the door, and then the length of his stay."

In Chicago, one FBI agent's sole duty was to watch three Greek men in their seventies. They had long since retired from radical activities, but that made little difference to Hoover's policies. They were kept on constant surveillance. "I watched them for months on end," the ex-FBI man stated, "and all they did all day long was play dominoes. It was ridiculous."

Yet Hoover's vigilance against Communists became so thoroughly ingrained in the pattern of FBI procedures that he easily transferred his attacks from the working class radicals of the 1930s and 1940s to the white collar spies of the 1950s to the new student left of the 1960s without altering methods or philosophy. To Hoover they are all Communists.

Hoover's festering antipathy for the new student left is based on his personal identification of the radicals of 1919. No other reason would cause him to order almost a thousand FBI agents—a seventh of his entire work force of agents—to blanket the 1968 Democratic Convention in Chicago and combat unorganized bands of young leftists, radicals, liberals, and those generally opposed to elements of the Democratic party pursuing a pro-war policy in Vietnam. Hoover did this even though he knew that Chicago's more than twelve-thousand-man police force plus several thousand national guardsmen were more than capable of handling any disturbance.

The Director's hatred for all leftist groups no doubt prompted him to prematurely announce, on November 27, 1970, a plot by the Reverend Philip Berrigan and eleven "co-conspirators" to kidnap President Nixon's top adviser, Henry Kissinger, and to blow up the heating systems of certain government buildings in Washington.

This announcement was also made by Hoover to bolster his FBI's performance before appropriations committees from whom he sought Bureau-supporting funds.

As a result of the Director's charges, the Department of Justice writhed in political agony and then, as one Berrigan defender stated, rushed a grand jury to deliver indictments against the Berrigan group as "a product of Hoover's pique" on January 12, 1971.

But it was a planned pique for the Director. It was not mere happenstance that Hoover's charges against Philip and Daniel Berrigan, in a closed-door congressional hearing, coincided with his request for funds to hire a thousand new FBI agents. At this meeting, Hoover's assistants gave seventy-five copies of the Director's statements to the committee clerk with the aim of capturing frontpage headlines outlining his Berrigan charges.

Hoover's "premature" accusations served to point out to the appropriations committee the new threat to government from the Left and therefore the vital necessity of adding the one thousand new agents to his payroll.

Hoover's tactics are quite clear. There must always be an evil, godless menace threatening the very existence of the "American way of life" to justify his FBI's existence.

FBI agents are kept hopping to support this threat from "the enemy within." Only three Communist party members existed in Washington, D.C., by 1967 and yet an entire FBI squad was ordered to maintain constant vigilance on these people. As one ex-Bureau man stated: "The main function of the squad then was to verify the residence and employment of the persons who once had been subjects of FBI investigations and who were still considered dangerous enough to keep track of, even though they were no longer active with the Party or any other subversive group, for that matter."

In the year the FBI's "Red squad" in Washington was performing such useless tasks, the antiwar movement swelled and Hoover typically determined this to be "a part of the larger Communist conspiracy to overthrow the United States government," the same ex-FBI agent stated.

Of the nearly forty thousand people who marched on the Pentagon in October 1967, the Bureau named to the press twenty persons who had, at one time or other, been identified as affiliated with the Communist party. Hoover's propaganda was thus converted to illogical proof that all forty-thousand dissenters were suspect and the willing pawns of a Communist conspiracy.

This is the standard ploy Hoover uses to indict the whole

of the so-called New Left movement in America. He has also ordered his agents to perform some of the most deceitful acts imaginable to undermine the activities of any group or movement that appears to have beliefs contrary to the Director's idea of patriotism.

As an ex-FBI agent who worked on one of the Bureau's Red squads put it: "My experience has shown me that the FBI in its pursuit of Blacks, the antiwar movement, and college activists was not an impartial, disinterested finder of facts, but rather a relentless guardian of orthodoxy, a police force which sought to cause harm to movements that boldly questioned the policies of government. . . . Enemies of the public were created to justify the Bureau's role as defender of the 'national security' against domestic foes who sought, according to Hoover's propaganda, to subvert the country."

J. Edgar Hoover's dedication to this end is no more finely illustrated than in his classic struggle with the CIA and other federal agencies in an attempt to dominate the crusade against the Red Menace within—and outside—the boundaries of the United States.

# 8

# The International Hoover and the CIA

The man standing behind President Roosevelt's back listened to FDR dictate to a secretary, then, unseen, drew a Colt pistol with a special apparatus affixed to its muzzle and fired six times into a sandbag propped against the wall of the president's office. Roosevelt went on dictating as the faint *plups* sounded.

The man waited until Roosevelt finished his dictation before handing him the pistol and explaining how the silencer worked. Roosevelt, when he learned that the gun had just been emptied in his presence, grew visibly shaken. "His eyes opened wide as saucers. Carefully he examined the gun, and carefully he laid it on his desk."

Roosevelt studied the general standing next to him. "Bill," he said, "you're the only black Republican I'll ever allow in my office with a weapon like this."

Roosevelt was addressing the father of modern U.S. espionage, Major-General William J. "Wild Bill" Donovan, head of the Office of Strategic Services (OSS), whose legendary exploits impressed everyone except his arch-foe, J. Edgar Hoover.

Donovan, who as a colonel led the famous "Fighting Sixty-ninth" New York regiment at the battle of the Argonne during World War I, was everything Hoover was not. He hated bureaucracy. The chronic paper shuffling, memoranda, and tedious documentation that were a part of all government work bored and enraged him. Donovan preferred to give his orders verbally. He was a conversationalist. Still, his accomplishments with the OSS during World War II were nothing short of fantastic.

Within a year and a half of being ordered by Roosevelt to develop a new worldwide intelligence service, Donovan sent almost four hundred French-speaking American agents into occupied Europe, where their intelligence operations shortened the war by years.

In Burma, an OSS behind-the-lines group known as Detachment 101 (led by marksman Carl Eiffler, and never numbering more than one hundred Americans and Kachin tribesmen) was responsible for killing more than fifty-five hundred Japanese troops and wounding about ten thousand more. It transmitted by radio every pertinent enemy field movement and operation throughout the war, and rescued 215 fliers shot down over Burma at the cost of the lives of 15 OSS men.

In Africa, OSS agents so completely misled German intelligence that the Abwehr was convinced the U.S. invasion of North Africa would take place at Dakar, where the Nazis shifted their entire Atlantic fleet for four vital days while two thousand miles away American forces landed at Oran, unopposed by the German navy.

Such feats rankled rather than elated Hoover. He had unsuccessfully tried to take over America's worldwide espionage operations, but had been restricted by Roosevelt to the Americas. Donovan knew all too well the ambitions of the Director and his fanatical desire to control all American security. In the past, Donovan had been subjected to Hoover's long-winded queries about every action performed by the Director's agents for U.S. attorneys and Department of Justice officials (an essential part of an agent's job).

On April 8, 1928, when Donovan was assistant attorney general, he received a memo from the thirty-four-year-old Hoover demanding to know exactly what his FBI agents were doing when not reporting directly to him. It read, in part: "When I assumed the duties of Director . . . I found that the accountants and agents upon the case [the Wheeler case, see Notes] had been . . . detached from the Bureau . . . and had been assigned to the Special Assistant to the Attorney General Pratt. I didn't know even where the accountants or special agents were. And it was only after several months that I was able to have orders issued which would at least enable me to know where these men were . . . I did not even then assume direction of their investigative work nor see any of their reports nor know what they were doing."

By 1943, Donovan and Hoover were butting heads. Donovan had become, by then, the only American to get inside Soviet intelligence headquarters—the Lubianka Building inside the Kremlin, offices of the KGB—while on a special mission in December 1943. He had proposed to Russian intelligence leaders that Russia and the United States exchange intelligence teams. The object of such an exchange, Donovan stated, was to trade information concerning sabotage behind the Nazi lines.

U.S. Ambassador Averell Harriman supported Donovan, stating that the Russians already had hundreds of officials in America on various assignments, and some, it was known, were spying. He felt the KGB's Washington exchange group would hardly be a serious espionage threat since J. Edgar Hoover was on the job.

But J. Edgar Hoover violently opposed the Donovan proposal. The Director argued vehemently that the domestic reaction would create political chaos for the Roosevelt administration. FDR, a great political engineer, responded favorably to this line of thinking and canceled the scheme. It would be decades before the United States would even come near to penetrating top Soviet intelligence operations, and the Donovan plan, squelched by Hoover, proved to be, even in the light of postwar developments, one of the great lost opportunities of American international intelligence.

Shortly after the war, Hoover went after the OSS itself. Powerful congressmen and lobbyists, sympathetic to Hoover, began to pressure President Truman to abolish the OSS. The Director insisted that the OSS would exist in peacetime merely as a costly duplicate agency.

Hoover took no pains to point out to Truman that the entire wartime budget for the OSS had been $135 million, while the FBI's budget for the same years exceeded that by $65 million, and that the Bureau had accomplished considerably less than the OSS in the world of international espionage. Hoover also failed to explain in what way the OSS would be a "duplicate agency," since, divorced from the armed services, it was the only federally-authorized organization in existence that handled intelligence abroad.

However, Truman, whose understanding of espionage was not great, nodded approval to Hoover's suggestions. He abolished the OSS.

Hoover naturally put in a bid to assume the defunct agency's duties, but was stalled off. Meanwhile, Truman was sorely regretting his brusque decision. No sooner had he dissolved the OSS than his desk was flooded with contradictory intelligence reports from Hoover and the armed services. The reports left Truman uninformed, and, finally, in a rage. In desperation, he decided one morning that he needed "somebody, some outfit, that can make sense out of all this stuff."

A succession of military chiefs, who commanded the newly-organized Central Intelligence Group, then coordinated foreign intelligence for Truman. This short-lived agency was abolished in 1947 and the Central Intelligence Agency was created, much to Hoover's chagrin. At the head of the CIA was Allen Dulles, who had been given sweeping and autonomous rule by Congress.

Dulles had excellent credentials for the job; he had performed with distinction in espionage operations in both world wars. (It was Dulles, as an OSS representative, who met secretly in Switzerland in early 1945 with Nazi Generals Wolff and Kesselring to attempt negotiating Germany's capitulation before Hitler insisted on the Nazi *Götterdammerung.*)

Upon Dulles' appointment, the struggle between the CIA and Hoover's FBI to dominate intelligence activities took on titanic proportions.

Regardless of the fact that espionage and counterespionage activities abroad were and are the exclusive domain of the CIA, Hoover later began to systematically place FBI agents in foreign countries, assigning them to American embassies as "legal attachés." From these vantage points, the Bureau indulged in Hoover's fanciful cloak-and-dagger operations against the Communists.

The CIA, in its formative years, was also hampered by the snooping and the attacks of Hoover's friend Senator Joseph McCarthy, who charged that its ranks had been infiltrated by Communists. In a rare public statement, Dulles emphatically denied the charge. But McCarthy's attack caused enough political upheaval to create an ineffective congressional investigation into CIA affairs, which subsequently faded.

George ''Machine Gun'' Kelly's apprehension by the FBI along with his shouts of ''G-men'' were Hoover inventions designed to build the Bureau's image. (Wide World)

Roger "The Terrible" Touhy on trial for the Factor kidnapping in 1933; he was beaten senseless by FBI agents and railroaded into a 26-year prison term by the Bureau for a crime he didn't commit. (Wide World)

Indiana outlaw John Dillinger (right) proved to be Hoover's perpetual nemesis. This Public Enemy Number One was not killed at the Biograph Theater in Chicago in 1934, despite FBI claims. (Wide World)

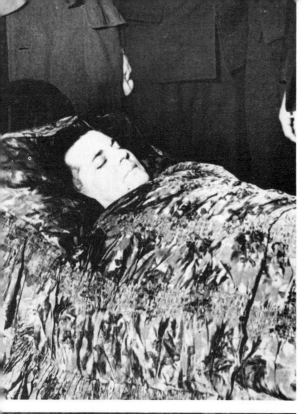

Desperado Charles Arthur "Pretty Boy" Floyd on display in October 1934 after FBI agents gunned him down for his alleged part in the Kansas City Massacre, a role he never played. (Wide World)

Counterfeiter Victor "The Count" Lustig (right) escaped from the FBI and was retaken by Treasury agents; Hoover took the credit for Lustig's recapture. (UPI)

Bruno Richard Hauptmann (right), convicted slayer of the Lindbergh baby; Hoover took the credit for his capture even though Treasury agents and a New York City policeman apprehended the kidnapper. (Wide World)

Alvin "Old Creepy" Karpis, 1930s public enemy, shown here upon his release from prison in 1968, was not captured single-handedly by Hoover, as was claimed, but was surrounded by dozens of gun-toting agents before the Chief was called out to make the arrest. (Wide World)

FBI Special Agent Melvin Purvis handled the botched-up Touhy, Dillinger and Floyd cases; competed with Hoover for publicity; and was forced out of the Bureau. Purvis' committed suicide in 1960. (Wide World)

The head of Murder, Inc., Louis "Lepke" Buchalter, was another Hoover prize catch — for publicity reasons. (UPI)

Senator Kenneth Mc-Kellar charged in 1936 that Hoover had never made an arrest, which the Director had to admit was true. (Wide World)

Hoover living up to his G-man image in 1935. (Wide World)

Militarist Hoover inspects a "weapon" of the Alumni Drill Corps of Penn Military College in 1936. (UPI)

J. Edgar Hoover placing a two-dollar bet at Bowie racetrack in Maryland, 1938. The races remain his passionate hobby. (UPI)

Hoover fingerprinting Vice-President John Nance Garner (with cigar) in 1939 while the Director's friend and publicist, Walter Winchell (center), gets the scoop. Winchell's associates were to become an embarrassment to Hoover. (UPI)

While Hoover certainly must have been delighted to see the CIA put on the spot, he grew more and more irritated with the power invested in the CIA by the National Security Act of 1947. This act placed the intelligence branch of the FBI under the jurisdiction of the CIA.

To the present, the director of the CIA serves as chairman of the board of the entire U.S. intelligence community, and all branches of the federal government working in intelligence are answerable to it, including Hoover's FBI.

Hoover, however, has never felt constrained to provide the CIA with any information other than the absolute minimum demanded of his agency. All requests for information from the CIA to Hoover must be made in writing, but at the Director's instructions the Bureau does not routinely inform the CIA of anything.

This kind of aloof uncooperativeness, critics argue, may have cost the life of President John F. Kennedy. The FBI failed to inform the president's bodyguard, the Secret Service, of Lee Harvey Oswald's long involvement in Communist activities, of which the FBI had full documentation.

The Bureau knew that Oswald had defected to Russia and returned, that he had been involved in the Fair Play for Cuba campaigns, that he had been court-martialed while in the marines for illegal possession of a gun, that he possessed weapons in civilian life, and that he loudly proclaimed himself a "Trotskyite Communist."

Yet the FBI never bothered to inform the Secret Service of Oswald's presence in Dallas, Texas, at the time of Kennedy's trip there. Hoover blandly brushed aside Oswald's background; in fact, he pretended it didn't exist.

"There was nothing up to the time of the assassination," Hoover testified before the Warren Commission, "that gave any indication that this man was a dangerous character who might do harm to the president. . . ."

The Warren Commission's attitude was wholly different. After studying and sifting mountains of evidence (the Bureau swamped the commission with 25,400 pages of reports), it concluded that "the FBI took an unduly restrictive view of its responsibilities in preventive intelligence work prior to the assassination. . . . There was much material in the hands of the FBI about Oswald: the knowledge of his defection, his arrogance and hostility to the United States, his pro-Castro tendencies, his lies when interrogated by the FBI, his trip to Mexico where he was in contact with Soviet authorities, his presence in the School Book Depository job and its location along the route of the motorcade. All this does seem to amount to enough to have induced an alert agency such as the FBI, possessed of this information, to list Oswald as a potential threat to the safety of the president. . . .

"The formal FBI instructions to its agents outlining the information to be referred to the Secret Service were too narrow at the time of the assassination. . . . The FBI's instructions did not fully reflect the Secret Service's need for information regarding potential threats. . . . Most important . . . the commission does not believe that the liaison between the FBI and the Secret Service prior to the assassination was as effective as it should have been."

Not only did the Bureau fail in this respect, which is solely attributable to a system where only one man, Hoover, is consulted on such matters before any routine decisions can be made, but it failed to preserve for proper trial the life of the man who killed the president (and who was the key to the unraveling of all the mysteries surrounding Kennedy's assassination, with which the Warren Commission was charged).

The Dallas office of the FBI received several anonymous phone calls around three in the morning on November 24,

1963, telling agents that someone was going to "kill the man that killed the president." At 11:20 A.M. that day, Oswald was fatally shot by striptease joint proprietor Jack Ruby, and died two hours later at Parkland Hospital.

A little more than a year later, J. Edgar Hoover was still claiming the Dallas assassinations were inevitable and in no way due to the negligence of the FBI. "Total security for the president of the United States is ridiculous," he said. "When he is gregarious and loves to move around you can't box him in. You can advise him to take certain precautions —but that doesn't mean he will take them." In Kennedy's case the precautions were as invisible as the security.

As late as 1970, Hoover was still preaching the same lame-duck apologia, but with a new ethnic twist. He told a national magazine: "We cooperate with the Secret Service on presidential trips abroad [odd that he should make that distinction]. You never have to bother about a president being shot by Puerto Ricans or Mexicans. They don't shoot very straight. But if they come at you with a knife, beware."

Such back-alley myths aside, Hoover has done more than "cooperate" with other federal agencies abroad. He meddled in international affairs even prior to the time he was appointed head of the FBI.

In 1923, Hoover prepared briefs for the Senate Foreign Relations Committee, which was determining whether or not to recognize Soviet Russia. These briefs, one pro-Hoover biographer stated, "traced the interlocking relationship and control of Soviet Russia over the Third International Communist leaders in the U.S. in their preparation and advocacy of the use of force and violence to obtain Communist ends."

Hoover sat at the committee's witness table while these briefs were being shown to Communist representatives, who would not comment. As a result the Senate Foreign Relations Subcommittee refused to recommend the recognition of Red Russia.

The Director won his first international victory then, resting his reputation on a simple, "half-free half-slave" world politics theory.

Hoover's rage against the Russians became a mere whimper when FDR recognized the Soviets in 1933. It was politically expedient for Hoover that he back down. The Director had been appointed and nurtured under Republican administrations, and he was walking a thin line with the Democrats and Roosevelt.

After his political roots became seemingly ambiguous, Hoover continued his activities in foreign relations.

In 1960, Hoover got verbal revenge for FDR's recognition of Red Russia. In May of that year, he stated: "The Soviet Union has maintained a large staff of officials in this country since its first recognition in 1933. These officials have been assigned to Soviet embassies, consulates, trade delegations, news media, the United Nations, and the Amtorg Trading Corporation. It is from these installations that the primary intelligence activities are directed against the United States."

By 1965 Hoover was powerful enough to affect significantly diplomatic relations between Russia and the United States. During that year the Director appeared before one of his staunchest supporters, Congressman John Rooney (D., N.Y.), head of the House Appropriations Subcommittee. He told Rooney that a proposed Soviet-U.S. consular treaty, which would allow the opening of certain consular offices in each country, was a mistake. Such a treaty, Hoover contended, would give the Russians espionage opportunities and create an unnecessary burden for the FBI.

"I did not at any time say I was in favor of or against [the treaty]," Hoover remarked later. His meaning was clear nevertheless. He didn't want the treaty passed, and he exercised enough strength on Capitol Hill to have it delayed until its ratification in 1967.

With or without consular treaties, Hoover maintains that Chinese and Russian spies are everywhere. His interpretation of Peking's intelligence apparatus is vague, at best. A good example is the case of Ch'ien Hsueh-shen, an engineer trained in the United States, who was detained by the FBI in 1950 on the suspicion he was a Communist. Ch'ien had been the director of the rocket section of America's National Defense Scientific Board during World War II. In this post, Ch'ien had access to top secret information. Years later, he became chief research analyst at Caltech's Jet Propulsion Laboratory.

After the Communists took over China in 1950, Ch'ien attempted to travel there. The Bureau was tipped off that the rocket genius was attempting to send eighteen hundred pounds of books ahead of him and they picked him up.

Ch'ien was detained in this country for five years until it was determined that his knowledge of U.S. secrets had become dated. He was released and immediately embarked for China, where he was named chief of China's program of nuclear missile development. On October 27, 1966, Ch'ien was responsible for the successful launching of China's first nuclear weapon transported by a guided missile.

This experience of losing a top nuclear scientist to the Communists may have been the reason why Hoover told Congress in 1965: "Communist China represents one of the greatest long-range security threats and the FBI is continuing to devote close attention to coverage of possible Chinese Communist agents and sympathizers in the United States. There is every likelihood that Chinese Communist intelligence activities in this country will increase in the next few years, particularly if Communist China is recognized by the United Nations and is thereby able to establish a diplomatic mission in this country."

This last statement embodied the same tactic Hoover had been successfully employing for years while interfering in foreign diplomacy. The following year he was again harping on the same subject, but now the Communist "Yellow Peril" had become a reality—in his own mind.

"The security problem presented by Red China has assumed larger proportions," Hoover emphasized in 1966. "Our work load has more than doubled during the past several months. Red China has made concerted efforts to acquire unclassified technical data shipped from this country for their libraries and government agencies. Because of their lack of basic research, it is only logical to assume that they will resort to other means, such as espionage, to obtain information they cannot get publicly."

The Chinese threat of espionage in the United States, however, was just as empty as Hoover's warnings. Up to and beyond the time of the Director's alarmist statements there had not been one arrest by the FBI of any Chinese Communist espionage agent in the United States.

The Chinese spy scare was hypoed in 1971 by Hoover, who, through the Department of Justice, announced that hundreds of Chinese seamen, recruited by a pro-Peking seamen's union, had jumped ship and were scurrying about on cloak-and-dagger activities. The Department of Justice published the information—the source was not stated—that in the past five years, 5,056 Chinese seamen jumped ship in the United States, with only 1,158 being caught. Of these, "hundreds are considered top espionage risks," stated one British newspaper.

As of this date, no FBI arrests of Chinese seamen on espionage charges have been announced. This Department of Justice release smacks very much of typical Hoover meddling in international politics, particularly now that United States-Communist China relations have softened.

Whereas the nonexistent Chinese espionage rings were "inscrutable" to the Director, Soviet spies left Hoover totally amazed, and quoting curious statistics.

During his budget sessions with Congress in 1964, Hoover, who was asking for a paltry $149.9 million to support the FBI's 20,253 people, told of the enormous monies used each year by the KGB, Russia's espionage arm. He pointed out that "a former officer of the KGB" (unnamed) estimated that the Soviets "spent about one and a half billion dollars a year" on foreign intelligence operations alone.

Where Hoover got this ball-park figure can best be determined by looking at the available records of the Soviet Twenty-first Party Congress of 1959, at which KGB Director Alexander Shelepin stated that the CIA had spent $1.5 billion a year on espionage activities aimed at Russia.

Publicly, the Soviets praised Hoover's counterespionage work. Ex-spy Kim Philby, who escaped behind the Iron Curtain, was quoted by the Soviet newspaper *Izvestia* as saying of Hoover: "He is a painfully excellent counterspy who controls an apparatus of repression amazing in size."

On the other hand, Gordon Lonsdale, who operated in the United States and in free Europe for twenty years as a successful superspy, wrote in his much-debated memoirs: "I do not propose to describe in any detail my experiences in the United States. . . . I have very good reason to know that Mr. J. Edgar Hoover is interested in me and I have no desire to satisfy his curiosity. I hope that many FBI man-hours will be wasted in search of the identity I used in the United States. They will be wasted I have little doubt because, however efficient the FBI may be in pursuing gangsters and kidnappers, they are out of their depth when trying to deal with a sophisticated intelligence network. Most of their successes in this field have been due to information being handed to them on a plate by turncoats.

"Not that I can withhold a considerable measure of admiration for Hoover. He has a genius for publicity and an unrivaled capacity for extracting money from Congress."

Lonsdale had a specific turncoat in mind, a man who was involved in the sensational FBI capture of the notorious Soviet agent, Colonel Rudolf Abel, a capture which, as facts prove, wasn't so sensational after all.

Hoover likes to tell the story of how the FBI alone diligently tracked down the Soviet's master spy, Colonel Rudolf Ivanovich Abel, alias Mark (his cover name when dealing with other Russian agents), alias Emil R. Goldfus, a Brooklyn painter and photographer.

Abel had quietly slipped over the Canadian border in 1948 and for two years crisscrossed the country, freely establishing and visiting his espionage contacts. He finally settled down to a steadily-successful ten-year operation of espionage in Brooklyn without the FBI ever detecting his identity.

The Abel saga begins in 1953 with a newsboy for the *Brooklyn Eagle* collecting for paper deliveries at 3403 Foster Avenue in Brooklyn. While making change in this building, the newsboy was given a curious nickel by one of the tenants.

Once outside, the boy examined the coin. It felt too light and had a hollow ring when dropped. The newsboy mentioned the coin, which had broken open revealing a tiny microfilm, to a New York City police detective. The detective in turn mentioned it to the FBI. Then the detective obtained the coin and the film for the FBI and they went to work on it. The film showed ten columns of typewritten numbers with five digits in each number and twenty-one numbers to each column.

Hoover's much-vaunted FBI laboratory in Washington labored over the code for years, but was unable to break the cipher. The FBI was also unable to determine exactly who had passed the coin to the newsboy.

The Abel story would have ended there if it had not been for one of the CIA's top espionage agents in Paris (cover name "John") who convinced a Soviet spy, Reino Hayhanen (cover name "Maki"), to defect.

This CIA agent spirited Hayhanen to the United States in 1957, and once there, he not only explained the meaning of the coded groups found on the film from the dummy nickel, but fingered Colonel Abel as chief Soviet agent and director of Russian espionage in the United States. Hayhanen testified at Abel's trial in 1957, and Abel was sentenced to thirty years in prison for his espionage activities. He did not complete that sentence, but was returned to the Soviet Union in a dramatic exchange for captured U-2 pilot Francis Gary Powers in 1962.

To hear Hoover tell it, the entire Abel episode was another glorious chapter in the annals of the FBI. Yet, without the CIA's Russian turncoat, Abel might be operating today. Incidental to the Abel case was the fact that Hoover told newsmen in 1970 that prisoners "should be incarcerated until they're tried, but it's absolutely wrong that they should have to wait seven or eight months before their trials."

The Director certainly couldn't have been thinking of Colonel Abel. When the FBI agents arrested him (without a criminal warrant or search warrant, mandatory even in charges of treason and espionage), they confiscated everything in his apartment, and then spirited him away to a remote town in Texas for a period of forty-seven days before allowing him to surface for proper legal action.

During these forty-seven days, Abel was held strictly incommunicado and was constantly beaten, one report states. The irony of this FBI snatch is that if Hoover had been allowed to keep his prize catch—which he attempted to do —instead of having to turn him over to immigration authorities, Abel would have been set free, as his rights had been flagrantly violated. He could have continued his nefarious activities in the United States, while Francis Gary Powers rotted in the Kremlin's Lubianka Prison.

An even stranger case involving foreign espionage, the CIA, and J. Edgar Hoover had its beginnings in Poland in 1958 during the height of the Cold War. A sophisticated and highly effective anti-Soviet network inside the Iron Curtain, known as the Heckenschuetzes and headquartered in Warsaw, picked that time to establish contact with American espionage agents through whom secrets would be channeled.

The Heckenschuetzes were certain that CIA operations in Europe at that time had been penetrated by Soviet agents, so they chose to directly contact none other than J. Edgar Hoover. Their first secret letter in April 1958 was sent to Hoover in care of Henry J. Taylor, the U.S. Ambassador to Switzerland, who was living in Berne.

That Hoover was not officially in the international spy business did not deter this highly efficient and knowledgeable underground organization. The Heckenschuetzes, led by one Michal Goleniewski—a Colonel in Soviet-dominated Polish intelligence—fed "Hoover" a constant stream of vital espionage information, all of a top-secret nature, which identified Russian espionage agents in the West, their letter-drops, radio stations, contacts, and codes.

Messages sent to the Heckenschuetzes and Goleniewski from the West were all signed "Hoover."

When Goleniewski finally defected to the West in 1961, the first man he asked to see was J. Edgar Hoover. CIA agents took him in charge and brought him to the United States, where, among many invaluable secrets, Goleniewski identified the top Russian agent in the West, Kim Philby, as a member of MI-6, the British secret intelligence service.

Throughout the CIA grilling, Goleniewski insisted that he be allowed to see Hoover. He also insisted, and had so much evidence to prove his claims that his file is permanently sealed under top-secret orders today, that he was the surviving son of Czar Nicholas II, the last of the Romanovs and heir to the Russian throne (and the Czar's millions still locked away in Western banks).

Goleniewski was never to receive total recognition as the true Czar or see J. Edgar Hoover. On September 30, 1961, in a curious interview with CIA Chief Allen Dulles (who agreed with Goleniewski that he was, indeed, the Czar's son), the defector again demanded to see Hoover.

"It was clear," Goleniewski told an interviewer later, "that Mr. Dulles was interested neither in disclosing that he knew my real identity nor in the support of my claims. He was more interested in preventing the proofs. For that reason also the CIA prevented me from visiting FBI Director Mr. J. Edgar Hoover. . . ."

But Mr. Hoover, as a matter of policy, doesn't see defectors. Goleniewski did see and talk with two of the Director's subordinates. He was then taken on a tour of the FBI museum, in which Goleniewski expressed no interest. From the end of a long corridor he caught a glimpse of a receptionist working outside of Hoover's office. That's all.

Here was a courageous spy who had risked his life hundreds of times to provide vital intelligence information to "Hoover" for a number of years, only to be rewarded with a quick tour of the FBI museum. As one writer put it:

"What would have happened, it leads one to think, if a defector from the Japanese navy, a few days before Pearl Harbor, had appeared before Mr. Hoover's receptionist with an urgent message for Hoover's ears only? Would he have been courteously bundled downstairs to see the fingerprints display?"

Although Hoover never denied that he had been in contact with and had directed the espionage operations of Goleniewski and the Heckenschuetzes (which, by government decree, would have been illegal), the FBI inexplicably took pains on numerous occasions to attack Goleniewski for his claims to the Russian throne.

On the other hand, the CIA has never explained whether or not Goleniewski was working for Hoover, or if they were merely using the Director's name in their contact with the Polish underground. The CIA certainly does know that, though unauthorized by law, Hoover operates extensively abroad on an intelligence-gathering basis. Hoover has now convinced Nixon that it is necessary to expand the FBI's foreign espionage beyond the few foreign embassies where FBI men were installed in the early 1960s as "legal attachés."

Nixon recently agreed to let Hoover secretly install FBI agents in more than twenty-five foreign capitals. This Hoover has done without congressional approval or the knowledge of the public. Even before Nixon's docile approval, Hoover had established agents in some twenty foreign countries.

Attorney General William P. Rogers and President Eisenhower first sanctioned this procedure when they assented to Hoover's monolithic takeover of certain espionage activities. Both Rogers and Eisenhower were assured by Hoover that the FBI would operate as "legal attachés" only, under the direction of U.S. ambassadors, and would never

collect foreign intelligence. They were to concentrate strictly on the apprehension of American fugitives.

As one recent report put it: "The truth is otherwise. The
'legal attachés' are *required* to send foreign intelligence reports back to Hoover through FBI channels, unseen by the
State Department or CIA. Indeed, the Director himself has
reprimanded legal attachés for failure to send him sufficient
intelligence material.

"The caliber of the intelligence picked up by the overseas
FBI agents is considered suspect by intelligence experts,
however. Barred from conducting overseas operations, the
legal attaches tend to pass along gossip picked up on Embassy Row and in the coffee houses. Whether the thousands
of tax dollars spent for this purpose is justifiable is therefore
questionable."

Tens of thousands of tax dollars are spent by the FBI on
foreign espionage in the United States alone. The Bureau
employs hundreds of its men in authenticating the patriotic
background of civilians who are entering the armed forces
and who must be authorized to handle classified material. In
many of these FBI "clearance" activities, the spending of
tax money is not merely questionable, it's clearly an outright
waste.

In one instance, the FBI cleared Dennis Channing as an
intelligence agent for the U.S. Air Force in 1950. He was
then allowed to handle classified information up to "Most
Secret." He processed this kind of material for three years.
Then, without warning or explanation, Channing's clearance was revoked. It was learned later that FBI agents
(still at work on Channing's case) uncovered something in
Channing's background that made him a bad risk. At age
twelve, the FBI discovered, Channing had "accidentally
busted a neighbor's window with an air rifle."

With such pedantic, long-range investigations using up

men and hours, it is no wonder that the Bureau hadn't enough time to concentrate upon the security of its own inner workings. Soviet spy Gordon Lonsdale insisted that the FBI had been infiltrated, not by Soviet spies, but by agents of West German General Reinhard von Gehlen, head of Bonn's secret service.

Gehlen had been a lieutenant-general and chief of Nazi Germany's military intelligence, foreign armies east section, which had concentrated its activities on the Soviets. While the Russian and American armies raced to meet at war's end, this tall, blond-haired espionage master spy packed fifty cases of indexed intelligence documents, ordered his sleeper agents behind Russian lines to remain undercover and await orders that would come sometime in the future (a future beyond the suicidal life span of Hitler and the Third Reich), and sped westward from Berlin to Bavaria, where he surrendered himself and his secrets to U.S. troops.

The CIA installed Gehlen in Munich, retrieved most of his old staff for his use, and encouraged him to continue his anti-Soviet espionage, which he did with a U.S.-paid budget of $4 million a year.

Lonsdale's associate in the United States, a Soviet agent he called Gross, told him that "von Gehlen had agents in the FBI itself."

Hoover has yet to admit that the ex-Nazi's superlative spy organization did infiltrate his agency. He could not deny, on the other hand, that the Soviets did, indeed, penetrate the Bureau more than once, operating under his very nose for years and obtaining highly classified material.

In September 1953, General Bedell Smith, acting director of the CIA, shocked the country by stating, "I believe the Communists are so adroit and adept that they have infiltrated practically every security agency of the government."

Bedell Smith's warning came almost four years too late for the FBI. Around December of 1949, through an informer, the Bureau learned that the Soviet Embassy in Washington was in possession of top-secret documents obtained from the FBI and the Department of Justice.

An informer also told Hoover that a woman who was working in the Foreign Registration Office of the Justice Department was the supplier of the top-secret documents. Only one woman in this department, Judith Coplon, corresponded to the description.

Hoover assigned a special task force to watch Judith Coplon. They chronicled her every move. She was twenty-seven years old, single, lived a quiet life, never brought men home to her Washington apartment, and had been recommended for her job by the attorney general.

On one occasion, agents trailed Judith Coplon to the Southern Hotel in Baltimore, where she stayed with a lawyer who served in the Department of Justice. The FBI agents, one historian wrote, "were able to achieve from their latest equipment for listening and looking through walls, from their post in the adjoining room . . . a practical demonstration in the art of love-making."

The following week, when Miss Coplon asked her superiors at the Department of Justice for a top-secret report on Russian agents in the United States which, she stated, she needed for her work, Hoover quickly set up fake information to be fed to her. The Director played this cat-and-mouse game with Judith Coplon for weeks. Meanwhile, his agents trailed her to New York on several occasions in January 1949, where she met with Valentine Gubitchev, a staff member of the Soviet Consulate-General in New York, to whom she apparently passed her information.

The FBI finally arrested Gubitchev and Miss Coplon months later in New York. Agents found thirty-four top-secret documents on them, all emanating from the FBI.

This proved to be extremely embarrassing to Hoover, whose big balloon of internal FBI security had been thoroughly punctured. Out of what can only be described as vengeance, he insisted Judith Coplon be tried on criminal charges rather than being dismissed. This decision proved to be one of Hoover's many mistakes.

Miss Coplon's attorneys argued that certain FBI files had to be made available in court to test the accuracy of testimony. Judge Albert L. Reeves ordered that the documents be produced.

This caused pandemonium at the Bureau, but Attorney General Tom Clark knew that if the files were not produced, the charges against Miss Coplon would have to be dropped. Such an action would certainly have inflamed the in-power Red hunters. The files were turned over and opened in court.

For the first time, it was revealed that the so-called intelligence reports of the FBI were based on rumors. As one newspaper put it, the voluminous documents were "filled with gossip, hearsay, and innuendo against innocent citizens. . . ."

These reports, based on the FBI's standard of guilt by association, were provided by informants of dubious reliability, and by wiretaps. They stated that actors Frederic March and Canada Lee, Boston University's President Daniel Marsh, and CBS's Norman Corwin were "outstanding Communist party fellow travelers." Even the most nonsensical drivel was included in these FBI files as supportive information. Helen Hayes was cited as having performed a skit in 1945 for Russian relief; Florence Eldridge had been included since her name was "mentioned" by two Communists in a conversation. Even those who had addressed a 1945 peace rally, such as Danny Kaye, Helen Keller,

Senator Charles Tobey, Jo Davidson, and Evan Carlson of the famed Carlson's Raiders, were labeled as Communists in the FBI files.

One writer stated, "If the FBI accepts and makes a record of every name that is being given by anyone, then nobody in the United States is protected against abuse. What is there to prevent a person sending the name of someone he doesn't like in to the FBI as a possible Communist?" Then, as today, the answer is nothing.

Disavowal and lack of knowledge of such reports were the standard defenses Hoover drew up when asked about the possibility of such a disaster. His memorandum at the time tersely claimed that he had urged the attorney general to seek a mistrial "rather than produce these reports with consequent devastating harm to the FBI's responsibility for internal security, as well as the disclosure of *as yet uncorroborated information in our files concerning individuals* [italics mine]."

It was another case of Hoover taking responsibility for all facets of FBI activity except when it came to error, mismanagement, and misrepresentation. The Director took no trouble to explain why "uncorroborated" items were ever included in FBI intelligence reports. But to do that, as we shall see in the cases of Mayor Richard J. Daley and others, was to admit that the very foundations of such FBI files were constructed of nothing more than wild and unfounded allegations.

Hoover's prosecution of Miss Coplon had about the same degree of effectiveness as his files; it crumbled. After months of an elaborate cloak-and-dagger game with Miss Coplon to assure her entrapment, Hoover lost his case. Miss Coplon was set free.

In arresting Judith Coplon, FBI agents had overlooked a legal detail. They had forgotten to get an arrest warrant.

# 9

# Hoover and His 'Bosses'

For as long as J. Edgar Hoover has held the directorship of the FBI, there have been only two people at any one time who were in a position to tell him what to do—the attorney general, and the president. Rarely has either been so brash as to direct the Director.

Hoover's astoundingly long tenure in office was established under Republican conservatives, Presidents Coolidge and Hoover, who took special pains to leave him to his own devices and developments, as did the attorney generals of both administrations. Those were plush years for Hoover, who flexed administrational muscles in a relatively little-known federal agency, and went about building his special brand of bureaucracy, unhampered by his superiors and by the probings of outsiders and the press.

When FDR was swept into power in 1933, Hoover curried favor from Roosevelt, who seriously considered replacing him. The Director, however, subtly ingratiated himself to the chief executive by making political appointments to the FBI, appointments which featured candidates nominated by Southern Democrats. When FDR softened relations with the Communists by recognizing the Soviets, Hoover dutifully and discreetly kept quiet. He more than once proved that he would play ball.

Yet, in the year FDR took office, some of his brain trusters had mixed feelings about Hoover. Presidential adviser Louis Howe, who was Roosevelt's closest friend (when Howe died, he lay in state in the East Room of the White House before burial), urged the president to get rid of Hoover.

FDR's response, in July of 1933, was to ask his chief brain truster, Columbia law professor Raymond Moley, to review the Bureau's performance and its ability to handle its duties.

Moley, who had always been a staunch Hooverite, wrote years later that "part of what was in Roosevelt's mind, I knew, was a doubt about the desirability of continuing J. Edgar Hoover in office. . . . When the administration had come into office in March, there were many rumors that Hoover was to be ousted in favor of a Democratic politician. I had vehemently defended the magnificent work of Hoover to the president. . . . I like to think that what I did in August 1933 gave me the opportunity to strengthen Hoover still more. . . ."

Though Moley did save Hoover's job, the brain truster was to lose his close association with FDR over this and other matters.

His position and relationship with Roosevelt tentatively secure, Hoover, as a way of making his personal role vital, frantically built up his national reputation through publicity men, who touted his mythical feats of derring-do.

Homer Cummings, then attorney general and Hoover's boss, never interfered with Hoover. Cummings, labeled a "cheap politician" by Senator Burton Wheeler (D., Mont.), authored a plan whereby the Supreme Court, which had been quashing major New Deal legislation as unconstitutional, would be legislated into accepting its role on an equal plane with Congress and, especially, with Roosevelt.

This caused consternation in the conservative Court, which the press had disdainfully labeled the Court of "nine old men," led by the venerable Charles Evans Hughes.

Chief Justice Hughes later blasted the Roosevelt-Cummings plan as being "an assault upon the independence of the Court." But at the time of the president's battle with the high judiciary, Hughes delivered his criticism of FDR *sotto voce*.

Then a curious event involving J. Edgar Hoover took place. Pathe News unearthed a 1931 newsclip of Hughes speaking about the Court in such a way that the chief justice's comments could be interpreted as an attack against Roosevelt's plan for the Court. This film clip was distributed nationwide as part of Pathe's February 13, 1937, newsreel. Nowhere was it mentioned that the Hughes clip was six years old.

Hughes went to a man who had a reputation as being a friend of conservatives, FBI Chief J. Edgar Hoover. He asked Hoover to do something about the Pathe clip. The Director said he certainly would, and he did. Within days, Hoover informed Hughes that he had "persuaded" Pathe News to yank the controversial clip from its newsreels.

"It was a pleasure to be of assistance to you in this connection," the Director said, "and if at any time this Bureau can be of any service, please do not hesitate to call upon me." One can only wonder if Hoover's reaction would have been similar if an ultraliberal Court member, say Justice Douglas, had made the same request.

Strictly speaking, Hoover's actions in the affair did not indicate unswerving allegiance to liberal Democrats Roosevelt and Cummings.

The Director took to spying overtly on FDR's cabinet members. A favorite target was Postmaster General James A. Farley, the man who had engineered Roosevelt's successful presidential campaign. A rumor reached Hoover's ever-alert ears that Farley was trying to move one of his friends from the New York City Police Department into the Director's job. This was unthinkable. Farley was tailed night and day.

"A tap was put on Farley's office phones," one journalist was later to report. "Others were put on his homes in Washington and New York. Not only that—on several occasions a rotation of different agents was assigned the job of trailing Farley. . . ."

When any of the agents performing these duties grew suspicious, Hoover explained that such assignments arose from threats on the lives of those being tailed; the agents were merely providing security.

It was about this time that the Director's paranoia increased to the point where he had agents check "against cut-ins on its [the FBI's] own wires, including [his] own private lines."

FDR's reaction to Hoover's antics was mostly indifference, and, at times, hilarity. Homer Cummings' successor, Attorney General Francis Biddle, told of the time in the early 1940s when Hoover was publicly embarrassed before FDR after one of his illegal wiretapping schemes had backfired.

According to Biddle, one of the Director's agents, while attempting to tap Communist union-organizer Harry Bridges' telephone, was flushed from cover unexpectedly by Bridges' associates, who also "captured" an FBI letterhead. Biddle insisted that Hoover tell Roosevelt all about it, and, in a foot-shuffling scene inside the White House, the Director made the admission.

"By God, Hoover," FDR said as he laughed and slapped the Director's back, "that's the first time you've been caught with your pants down!" It wasn't the first time and it surely wouldn't be the last.

Roosevelt's successor, Harry Truman, found the sledding with Hoover rough. Hoover's influence on Capitol Hill was vast by the time the Truman administration came into being. In order to retire the Director, Truman would have had to face the political fight of his life. He chose not to. Instead, he resigned himself to having Hoover around permanently. As one writer of the day stated: "Mr. Hoover has a kind of tenure that even the most carefully sheltered administrator should have reason to envy; his time-tested ability to outlast the president of the moment must always give that president pause. I cannot help wondering how often President Truman thought of relieving Mr. Hoover —and then thought a second time, sighed, and went about his business."

Truman's attorney general, J. Howard McGrath, was the first Hoover boss who tilted, albeit slightly, with the Director. McGrath enthusiastically backed legislation which banned slot machines from every state except Nevada, where they are legal. This caused him to feel Hoover's considerable anger. The Director viewed McGrath's move as a compromise of FBI duties and an unnecessary police burden.

One pro-Hoover scribe wrote, "Attorney General McGrath and the New Deal liberals who plugged for the measure . . . hoped it would put the FBI on the spot. Its enforcement being impossible, Hoover and his G-men would take the blame—either that or the FBI would have to hire thousands of fly-cops and become a new, super-prohibition unit, exposed to wholesale graft and bribery, which would please the Reds and the crooks."

This, indeed, was a perplexing pronouncement. If Hoover and the Bureau were thus blamed, so too would McGrath be blamed. It can only be interpreted that this was another item planted by Hoover to put his boss on warning. To back legislation which might prove embarrassing to Hoover was to risk public rebuff and ridicule through Hoover's considerable friends in the Fourth Estate.

Though others may have had to look long and hard to explain such a frontal attack on the attorney general, McGrath certainly knew the real reason for Hoover's wrath. In 1939, when he was a U.S. attorney, McGrath had pushed through an FBI investigation of illegal wiretapping by political foes of the mayor of Pawtucket, Rhode Island. The Department of Justice, after hearing from Hoover that there had been wiretapping, declined prosecution. The reasons were all too clear. Those being investigated would have created a hotbed of controversy, which would have trailed back to the FBI's own use of wiretapping; McGrath had bumped the Hoover hornets' nest. The feedback of this rash action would come ten years later when he became the attorney general.

President Eisenhower steered clear of Hoover quite successfully until the time came when he felt compelled to "assure" Hoover that he would keep his job after the McCarthy fiasco. These were Republican years, and strong Hoover supporters like Vice-President Richard Nixon were in office.

For the most part, Eisenhower's first attorney general, Herbert Brownell, Jr., backed the Director's every move, and yet he contributed much to one of Hoover's more disconcerting moments in connection with Soviet agents, who were known to the FBI and were allowed to operate without interference.

While addressing the Executives' Club of Chicago,

Brownell, in an attempt to tar his Democratic predecessors, announced that Harry Truman had appointed Communist Harry Dexter White to the International Monetary Fund despite two FBI reports which detailed White's "spying activities." The upshot of this speech was political pandemonium and a hearing by the Senate's Internal Security Subcommittee, which immediately demanded that Hoover confirm or deny Brownell's charges.

Newspapers began to print stories to the effect that Hoover had allowed White to continue his espionage activities, and the *New York Times,* which, next to the *Washington Post,* heads Hoover's "drop dead list," reported that "J. Edgar Hoover suggested or at least agreed to the procedure recommended to and followed by President Truman" regarding the retention of White.

Hoover, who had refused twice to testify before the Senate subcommittee, finally answered a third summons, to avoid a subpoena, and stated, "I did not enter into any agreement to shift White from his position in the Treasury Department to the International Monetary Fund. This was not within my purview. . . . At no time was the FBI a party to an agreement to promote Harry Dexter White and at no time did the FBI give its approval to such an agreement. . . . The decision to retain White was made by a higher government authority."

With such testimony, Hoover turned a nearly disastrous incident into a deft political statement directed at Democrat Truman and his administration. Yet, the Director did not elaborate on the fact that he did have knowledge of White's spying and did nothing with it other than to store it as future grist for his political mill. Then, as now, Hoover's tactic when dealing with such touchy areas involving his superiors is to dictate a memo into the permanent FBI archives exonerating himself from any initiative action, as he did in the White case when he placed responsibility squarely on the shoulders of his bosses.

Eisenhower's second-term attorney general, William Rogers, was very chummy with Hoover and never got in his way. The only significant breakthrough Rogers ever achieved with Hoover was getting him to come to his home, where the Director sang songs with a group gathered around the piano. "He has even smiled at the Rogerses," one weekly magazine commented.

During President Eisenhower's second administration, Hoover's power grew. He became the very essence of the ivory-towered, unreachable bureaucrat. Later, the *New York Times* would say: "Mr. Hoover's very independence has been seen as dangerous. Successive attorney generals have found that they have little or no control over him; he often refuses, as a minor example, to conform his speeches to official government policy."

But Hoover's most unsettling moments were before him. With the coming of the brothers Kennedy and the return of the Democrats, the possible loss of his autocratic rule and even his job became alarmingly real to the Director.

Almost moments after his victory, President-Elect John Kennedy asked for and received Hoover's reappointment to the FBI directorship. At that time it was understandably expedient to do so. But later, after having been inundated with Hoover's gossipy memos outlining "sexual 'goings-on' " concerning Kennedy politicians—a puritanical fixation with Hoover—the president had had enough. Hoover was within a hair's breadth (or the firing of a bullet in Dallas) of being terminated as the Director. Aides told Kennedy that a special presidential proclamation would have to be made to justify Hoover's continuance as FBI chief in view of his exceeding the mandatory retirement age.

Kennedy's terse reply summed up his sentiments for

Hoover: "We are not going to have such a proclamation!" Before the president could oust the Director, Oswald's bullet claimed Kennedy.

The dissipation of Kennedy's naive admiration for Hoover was based on the frustrating experiences his brother Bobby endured while he was the attorney general. One report had it that Bobby Kennedy sought Hoover's advice on taking the job, and the Director urged him to do so, comfortable in the knowledge that here was the son of an old friend, Joseph Kennedy. To Hoover's mind, Bob's youthful bumbling posed no threat.

Hoover's illusions ended when Kennedy tried to exercise immediate control over the Director and the Bureau, which was his prerogative by law. Stung by Kennedy's rapid-fire orders, Hoover reacted in a grandfather-to-whelp manner. His agent who led tourists through the FBI museum was directed to add something new to his spiel: "Mr. Hoover became Director of the Bureau in 1924," the tour guide would boom, "the year before the attorney general was born." When Kennedy discovered this bit of brazenness, he ordered the demeaning line cut.

Kennedy's hard-line policies on pursuing the national crime syndicate and uncovering civil rights abuses unnerved Hoover, but he reluctantly expanded the Bureau's activities into those formidable areas. "At first it was like pulling teeth to get the Bureau to enter these areas," one of Kennedy's aides recalled, "but by 1963 all that had changed."

Hoover balked every step of the way with his new boss. He was particularly reticent in agreeing to aid in the development of a national crime commission, which he viewed as a deep inroad into his authority, influence, and reputation as America's top cop.

An observer, who was visiting Hoover during the time Kennedy was the attorney general, was shocked at the liberties the young man took without comment or apology: "He [Kennedy] hadn't called or made an appointment. He had just barged in. You don't do that with Mr. Hoover." When the visitor's turn to see Hoover came, he found the Director bursting with rage, a stream of unprintables rolling off his tongue. Kennedy had proposed a new investigative team to assume work the FBI had been doing. The observer surmised that Hoover told Kennedy, "If you're going to do that, I can retire tomorrow. My pension is waiting."

Of course, this was the last thing Hoover intended to do, but the threat of quitting the fledgling attorney general was enough to suggest political repercussions, and it was Hoover's first line of defense and usually the first words out of his mouth when skirting Kennedy's orders.

Kennedy was forever buzzing the Director's office, delightedly chipping away at Hoover's crusty protocol. Once, Kennedy buzzed Hoover's intercom and asked, "Edgar, how many agents do we have in Birmingham?"

"We have enough," the Director responded. "We have enough."

Kennedy violated every Hoover-enforced regulation concerning the lines of communication between the attorney general's office and the FBI. Kennedy would contact specific agents or Bureau chiefs if he wished, without first getting Hoover's permission. The result was internal chaos, with each agent worried that he would be discovered talking directly to Kennedy without the Director's sanction.

Hoover refused to attend Kennedy's staff luncheons throughout his term. It got close to the point where Robert Kennedy was about to ask Hoover for that much-promised resignation. But never more than close.

Hoover's phone call to Robert Kennedy on November 22, 1963, changed all that. "I have news for you," Hoover unfeelingly blurted out, "The president has been shot." Then he hung up. Later, the Director was on the line again. His terse words were, "The president is dead." He hung up, and, from that time on, rarely spoke to the attorney general while he was in office.

Kennedy later described these phone calls to aides, stating that Hoover "was not quite as excited as if he were reporting the fact that he had found a Communist on the faculty of Howard University."

Hoover's vengeance on Bobby Kennedy was swift. After the president had been killed, the Bureau no longer sent a car around to pick up the attorney general, which had been its standard policy. Hoover went directly to the White House and President Johnson with his reports. One Kennedy aide was quoted as saying, "Starting at 1:10 on November 22, they [the FBI] began pissing on the attorney general."

Though Hoover later maintained that he did not speak to Bob Kennedy during the last six months of his administration, the brawls between the two continued. After Kennedy had compelled Hoover to actively combat organized crime, he pushed the Director to assume his proper responsibilities in civil rights investigations. He succeeded on both counts, but was bloodied for it.

In 1970, Hoover was quoted as saying, "My differences with Bobby were very unfortunate. His father was one of my closest friends. He [Bobby] wanted me to lower our qualifications and hire more Negro agents. . . . I said 'Bobby, that's not going to be done as long as I'm director of this Bureau.' He said, 'I don't think you're being very cooperative.' And I said, 'Why don't you get a new director?' I went over to see President Johnson [here admitting a direct breach of conduct by dodging his superior] and he told me to 'stick to your guns.' But there was no disagreement about organized crime."

Certainly there was no debate on organized crime since Hoover refused to admit to its existence until Kennedy insisted upon its reality. As far as Black agents were concerned, the Director couldn't lower his standards since he had few Black agents in his ranks.

Among these Black agents was one who, for thirty-two years, Hoover had pointed to with pride as an example of the Bureau's early integration. In 1901, President Theodore Roosevelt, who first established the Bureau, asked a Black policeman guarding him: "Have you got a boy you would like to go to work?"

"I've got one I can't control," Policeman Joseph Amos replied. His son Jim became the president's bodyguard, and was with him the night he died in 1919. Jim Amos was appointed an agent for the Bureau in 1921, and Hoover kept him on the rolls until he died at seventy-four in 1953, twelve years beyond his retirement age.

Two aging Black agents serve Hoover's needs in Washington today. One, his chauffeur, drives the Director to work each morning. The other is Sam Noisette, who has been Hoover's receptionist for more than thirty years. Neither man was trained for anything other than these domestic duties.

Shortly after Kennedy demanded more Black agents be included in the FBI ranks, a reliable source stated that the Chicago Bureau received a hurried call from Washington. The Bureau chief was ordered to add a Black agent, and fast. This was followed by another call within hours, the caller demanding to know if a Black agent had been added to the Chicago Bureau's work force. He was promised prompt action.

A Black man who had been working primarily in a janitorial capacity in the Chicago Bureau was ushered in front of the Chicago chief.

"Would you like to be a special agent of the FBI?" he was asked bluntly.

The man was dumbfounded. When informed that his beginning salary would be more than eleven thousand dollars a year, the janitor quickly nodded yes. He was handed a badge, credentials, and told to buy a new, conservative suit. The following day he became the chauffeur for the Bureau chief in Chicago.

Aubrey C. Lewis, a Black All-American football star, who played for Notre Dame and the Chicago Bears, was admitted into the FBI training school at Quantico, Virginia, in 1962, becoming the first official Black agent in the Bureau. Following Kennedy's edict, Hoover used Lewis as a showpiece to prove he wasn't the racist so many had thought him to be (even though he has been quoted as saying that interracial sex is "moral degeneracy").

A photograph of Lewis appeared in a feature story published by a Black magazine, and in the story Hoover was quoted as saying, "We've paid no attention to race, creed, or color. This has been my strict FBI policy." Other Black "agents" surrounded Lewis in the photos. When Hoover was pressed by a reporter who asked where other Black agents were stationed, the Director coyly responded: "On cases in every part of the country." He regretted to state that he could not divulge the number of Black agents in the Bureau because, you see, that would be revealing "the tricks of the trade."

One of these neat little tricks was the fact that out of 6,014 special agents of the FBI in 1964, 28 Blacks were alleged to be in their number. Of the more than 8,000 special agents today, 108 are reportedly Black. Where these agents may be found is still a trade secret with J. Edgar Hoover.

A delayed reaction of the Kennedy administration was

the civil rights explosion of 1966 upon the discovery that Martin Luther King's phone had been tapped. Hoover blamed Kennedy for the unauthorized wiretap, and Kennedy charged the whole episode to the Director. Both produced letters "proving" the other was responsible.

But it was Hoover, with a long record of questionable racial attitudes, who appears to be responsible. He dragged his feet in opening and expanding Bureau offices in the Deep South during the height of civil rights activities there. It was all Kennedy and subsequently Lyndon Johnson could do to prod the Director to open and staff these offices.

As long ago as 1943, national publications were attacking Hoover for his "long record of hostility to Negroes." Though Hoover strongly denied such charges, he admitted that his one favorite radio program was *Amos 'n' Andy,* in whose stereotyped malapropisms he delighted. Hoover's attitude toward Blacks (and Orientals too, for that matter) appeared to be to mark them "all right" in their places, which is where Hoover kept a representative showing of "house niggers," as one ex-FBI agent termed the Black agents.

Martin Luther King changed all that. King's popularity seemed to serve as a goad to Hoover. Dr. King's sexual life was thoroughly gone over by the Bureau, and the most scandalous reports were delivered to President Johnson, who reserved these, and other reports on Black civil rights leaders, for his bedtime reading enjoyment. One of these Hoover-to-Johnson memos reported on the illicit love affair a prominent civil rights leader was having with a Los Angeles woman. According to Hoover, the man "calls this woman every Wednesday and meets her in various cities throughout the country. The source [Hoover did not state whether it was a bug or an informant, probably the former] related an incident which occurred some time ago in a New

York hotel, where [the man] was intoxicated at a small gathering. [He] threatened to leap from the thirteenth-floor window of the hotel if this woman would not say she loved him."

No reports have clearly stated that this particular Hoover memo referred to Dr. King, but it appears logical that he was the memo's subject, since the Director concentrated upon him more than any other civil rights leader. One source stated, "As King gained more and more renown and respect, the FBI increased its flow of anti-King memoranda."

Hoover's sniping at King broke out into open, bloody battle when the great civil rights leader had occasion to confer with the Director in a historic meeting on December 1, 1964.

According to Hoover, King had asked for the audience, and the Director, discarding his usual procedure of remaining aloof, agreed to see him. King, by that time, had reportedly advised civil rights workers not to register complaints with FBI men, because they were Southerners. He had also stated that Hoover had "faltered" in his application to civil rights duties under the stress of his job.

Hoover relished the meeting in a later interview in which he stated: "I got a wire from the Reverend Doctor King in New York. He was getting ready to get the Nobel Prize— he was the last one in the world who should ever have received it. He wired asking to see me. I held him in complete contempt because of the things he said and because of his conduct.

"First I felt I shouldn't see him, but then I thought he might become a martyr if I didn't. King was very suave and smooth. . . . [He] said he never criticized the FBI. I said, 'Mr. King'—I never called him reverend—'Stop right there. You're lying.' He then pulled out a press release that he said he intended to give it to the press. I said, 'Don't show it to me or read it to me.' I couldn't understand how he could have prepared a press release even before we met. Then he asked if I'd go out to have a photograph taken with him. I said I certainly would mind. And I said, 'If you ever say anything that's a lie again, I'll brand you a liar again.' Strange to say he never attacked the Bureau again for as long as he lived."

With the coming of Lyndon Baines Johnson to the White House, Hoover's position was once again secure. Johnson had been close to the Director; the ambitious Texan lived across the street from Hoover in Washington for nineteen years. Hoover had helped the Johnson children find their pet beagle when he was lost, and once, when one of the beagles died, the Director presented the president with another one.

One quaint story had Johnson frolicking on the White House lawn with his dog, while the Director stood nearby. "Edgar, come here," Johnson suddenly shouted. Hoover, stunned at being addressed in such a fashion, stated, "I am here, Mr. President."

"I'm not calling you, I'm calling the dog," Johnson said. He had named the pet after Hoover.

No other president before or since has enjoyed the super privileges Hoover heaped upon Johnson. But Johnson, unlike most others, had long been privy to the nation's top secrets. While he was vice-president, Johnson was also a member of the National Security Council, and in this capacity, was given "more government secrets than any of his predecessors."

This tradition was upheld by Hoover, who, upon Johnson's request when he first moved into the White House, turned over to the president twelve hundred files concerning the activities of Johnson's political foes. In these confidential files were the extensive reports dealing with Bobby Baker. Johnson then gratefully waived the mandatory retirement age regulation for Hoover in May of 1964 (which was Hoover's seventieth birthday, and his fortieth anniversary as the Director of the FBI).

On that occasion, Johnson's accolades for his faithful FBI Chief were boundless: "He is a hero to millions of decent citizens and anathema to evil men. No other American now or in our past has ever served the cause of justice more faithfully or so well. No other American has fought so long or so hard for a safer and better national life."

Johnson could have added that no other American had provided him with so much political ammunition as had Hoover.

The only real threat to his position during the Johnson years came after Hoover's public attack on Martin Luther King. Hoover, a week after the King conference and his rabid denouncements of the civil rights leader, further inflamed the situation by attacking "zealots or pressure groups, spearheaded by Communists and moral degenerates, who have no compunction in carping, lying, and exaggerating." The White House felt constrained to issue one of those "unofficial" leaks which reported that the president "must find a new chief of the FBI," an endeavor which was quickly discarded after the public furor over Hoover's agitating remarks faded.

Nicholas Katzenbach, who succeeded Kennedy, at first sidestepped the Director, who was busy setting up squads to handle "racial matters." These highly-trained FBI agents wasted their time investigating high school students who were complaining that their school's cafeteria fare wasn't fit "for human consumption"; a newly-opened bookstore on Fourteenth Street in Washington run by SNCC (Student Nonviolent Coordinating Committee); steelworkers who protested job discrimination at the Bethlehem Steel plant near Baltimore; and those who participated in the Poor People's March on Washington.

The Bureau paid informants to attend the opening, in Washington's Black ghetto, of the Smithsonian's new annex, which featured a Black History Week program detailing the life and work of Frederick Douglass.

Fifty agents were assigned to watch Stokely Carmichael after Dr. King's assassination. The FBI fruitlessly attempted to build a case against him for "inciting to riot."

One of the agents who worked in the fifty-man Carmichael detachment later recalled, "Had Carmichael not decided to leave this country and go to Africa, the FBI, I am confident, would eventually have found something with which to bring an indictment against him."

Attorney General Katzenbach, about this time, chose to make a nuisance of himself by announcing that the Bureau was rent with "organizational jealousy." Hoover immediately retorted, through a spokesman, that no such discontent existed in his FBI.

Katzenbach then ordered Solicitor General Thurgood Marshall to tell the Supreme Court exactly how FBI wiretaps had been employed in obtaining evidence. Hoover exploded. There was to be no peace with this man either. Curiously, the Director's problems with Katzenbach ceased abruptly. The attorney general was suddenly made undersecretary of state by Johnson, a definite demotion.

His replacement, Ramsey Clark, wasn't any more tolerant of Hoover and his methods than was his predecessor. Clark obstinately refused to condone the use of electronic bugging to obtain information. He intimated that Hoover's successor should come from outside FBI ranks (this was tantamount to sedition). In 1967, Clark created special local "strike forces" to be used to attack organized crime (the "strike forces" consisted of Department of Justice lawyers, U.S. attorneys, IRS, Secret Service, and Department of Justice immigration agents). Hoover refused to commit any of his agents to these groups.

Hoover, Clark was later to point out, had his own exclusive way of dealing with organized crime. Clark reported that, in one instance, the FBI illegally bugged the Milwaukee, Wisconsin, offices of alleged hoodlum Frank Peter Balistrieri. He said that agents removed documents from a file, photostated them, and then returned the originals to the files without advising the owner. "This was a clear violation of law," Clark insisted.

Clark and Hoover then came into violent conflict over the Democratic Convention riots of 1968 in Chicago. Speaking of the Chicago fiasco, Clark argued that "experience to date shows crowds can be controlled without denying rights of speech and assembly. . . . Of all violence, police violence in excess of authority is the most dangerous. For who will protect the public when the police violate the law? . . . It is the duty of leadership and law enforcement to control violence, not cause it. To seek ways of relieving tension, not to look for a fight."

Hoover ignored his superior's oblique criticism of how Chicago handled protest crowds, and endorsed the hotly-debated police actions there. Hoover stated before the National Commission on the Causes and Prevention of Violence (Clark spoke at the same meeting) that "months before the Democratic National Convention was held, authorities were fully aware that it was the target of disruption and violence on the part of dissident groups and individuals from all over the country. . . . [Hoover had dispatched close to one thousand agents, a seventh of his entire work force, to the convention.]

"If it is true that some innocent people were the victims

of unnecessary roughness on the part of the police, it is also true that the Chicago police and the National Guard were faced with vicious attacking mobs, who gave them no alternative but to use force to prevent these mobs from accomplishing their destructive purposes."

Clark's dislike for the Director's techniques again erupted into headlines in 1969 when he stated that "Mr. Hoover repeatedly requested me to authorize FBI wiretaps on Dr. King while I was attorney general. The last of these requests, none of which were granted, came two days before the murder of Dr. King [April 4, 1968]."

In a CBS interview, Clark went on to add that Hoover should quit. "I think perhaps the time has come when he should retire. . . ."

But Clark's suggestion was belated. President Nixon was in office. He was and is one of Hoover's closest supporters, and the man who had belittled Clark's anticrime measures when he was in power. Nixon's response to Clark's attack on Hoover was negative. The president supported the Director, reporting that he had checked and found that the attorney general (Clark) had approved the wiretap of Dr. King's phone.

Clark might have figured this would be Nixon's position since one of Clark's last acts as attorney general was to challenge the sources of Nixon's campaign funds. Clark wanted to know why twenty Republican organizations that backed Nixon were tardy in stating where they received the money to finance his campaign, and implied that the rarely-used Federal Corrupt Practices Act might be enforced. Clark was told that the Bureau could never complete such an investigation before Nixon took office, and Clark's attack evaporated.

Clark made one more stab at Hoover in a recently published book in which he described the FBI Chief's "self-centered concern for his reputation" as being a detriment to good law enforcement. "The FBI so covets personal credit that it will sacrifice even effective crime control before it will share the glory of its exploits."

Hoover knew this to be a parting shot and casually remarked that Clark was a "softie" and a "jellyfish." Clark, Hoover explained, was the worst attorney general he had ever encountered.

More to his liking, politically and professionally, were his new bosses, Attorney General John Mitchell and President Nixon.

Hoover's friendship with Richard Nixon, as previously outlined, more than assured the Director that his position was secure. Hoover paternalistically calls Nixon "one of my boys," even though he turned Nixon down for a job with the FBI in 1937.

Hoover prepared well for Nixon. He ingratiated himself to the president by assigning FBI agents to protect him when he was running for the presidency in 1968, and by augmenting security forces at the Republican National Convention. (Missing no bets, Hoover did the same for candidate Hubert Humphrey.) FBI agents also tailed newsmen who might have proved annoying to Nixon.

Nixon calls the Director on his birthday each year. Though wary of Hoover and seriously contemplating his proverbial retirement, Nixon realizes his great indebtedness to the Director.

When Nixon's sun went into eclipse in 1960, another one of Hoover's "boys," ex-FBI heavyweight, Lou Nichols, who had retired from the Bureau but who still functioned as the Director's "outside man," bolstered Nixon's ego considerably. He displayed his loyalty to Nixon whenever possible. "For years after 1960," one report has it, "it was Lou Nichols who met Nixon at the airport with a chauffeured limousine every time he came back from any place —and that was when everyone else was treating him like a has-been."

It was also Lou Nichols who organized Operation Eagle Eye for Nixon in the 1968 election. Nichols organized a nationwide group of ex-FBI men and lawyers who watched polls and checked for fraud.

If Nixon is close to Hoover in almost everything, Attorney General Mitchell was closer. He was hard-headed and unswerving when it came to meting out justice to offenders. In 1971, Mitchell complained that the system of justice in the United States was stricken with "a preoccupation with fairness for the accused."

This is Hoover's kind of talk, and Mitchell is his kind of man. Mitchell's unstinting support for Hoover has been proved time and again. When Boggs' anti-Hoover charges on wiretapping erupted, Mitchell demanded that Boggs "recant at once and apologize to a great and dedicated American."

Mitchell consistently assumed hard-line and hard-headed stands on law and order. He assumed the right to keep records on protestors without being subjected to Constitutional regulations, laboring under the idea that such record keeping was involved with providing protection for "the internal security of the nation."

He sponsored wholesale police bills which called for any suspect to be booked without formal arrest.

He truculently condemned liberals in education by calling such students and professors "stupid bastards who are ruining our educational institutions." He also predicted that "this country is going so far right you are not even going to recognize it." His wife, Martha, has more than once created headlines in her fanatical partisan support of her husband's interests.

One news account has it that she called the *Arkansas Gazette* in Little Rock to demand that the paper attack the state's outspoken critic of the administration, J. W. Fulbright, who helped to defeat the confirmation of Judge G. Harrold Carswell to the U.S. Supreme Court in 1970.

At 2:00 A.M., only hours after the Senate voted down the nomination, Martha Mitchell called the *Gazette* and was quoted as stating, "It makes me so damned mad I can't stand it. I want you to crucify Fulbright and that's it."

Fulbright shrugged off the attack as "flamboyant," and typical of Mrs. Mitchell.

Eleven days later, Mitchell was accused of not having bothered to order the FBI to check Carswell's background, as well as that of another rejected Nixon nominee, Judge Clement F. Haynsworth.

*Life* got into this act by stating that Mitchell had given Nixon "bad advice" and "should leave."

But Attorney General Mitchell, like J. Edgar Hoover, would leave in his own good time. This year, the right-wing former lawyer, whose practice once brought him an average income of two hundred thousand dollars, did leave to become Nixon's campaign manager for the coming election.

The attorney general designate, Richard G. Kleindienst, is essentially a carbon copy of his predecessor; his views are largely conservative and pro-Hoover. It was Kleindienst who, while he was deputy attorney general in 1971, had rabidly defended Hoover against Congressman Boggs' wiretapping charges.

Kleindienst stated in an interview that Boggs must have been "either sick or not in possession of his faculties" when he charged Hoover with wiretapping his phone. Kliendienst also went on to add that the Director, although seventy-six in 1971, was "able, agile, alert, hard working," and "conscientious."

It is not difficult to imagine Hoover performing gleeful pirouettes at the appointment and confirmation of Richard G. Kleindienst as attorney general this year.

With such supporters as Nixon, Mitchell, and Kleindienst, Hoover can now fearlessly indulge himself as he did in 1969 when he wrote: "I have been fortunate to serve under eight presidents and sixteen attorneys general who have shared my conviction that the FBI must be completely divorced from politics, and that it must be a career service dedicated to honest, prompt, and impartial enforcement of the law. Had other conditions been imposed at any time, I would have resigned immediately."

# 10

# Hoover's 'Boys'

The successful candidates stood in a long, even line and at attention. These men had just finished the rigorous training program at the FBI school in Quantico, Virginia, and they had been preparing for hours to meet their boss. One of the things they had been told was to make sure they had a handkerchief near at hand. The Director had more than once fired a man who was careless enough to shake his hand with a sweaty palm.

Suddenly J. Edgar Hoover appeared and walked stiffly down the line, shaking briefly the hand of each graduate. One man in the line received more than the casual glance. His complexion was sallow and that disturbed the FBI Chief. The reason for this condition, it was explained, was that the man, a war hero, had been wounded in combat, and the subsequent plastic surgery on his face left him with a yellow pallor.

Hoover was unconcerned with the man's personal history. He kept glancing back at the war hero, who had achieved consistently high marks at the FBI school. *He didn't look like an FBI man*. The Director stopped and whispered to an assistant. Only a few hours later the war hero was told that he was being dropped from the ranks; it seemed he had flunked the final exam after all.

One report on the incident stated: "FBI agents must not only act as Hoover wishes, but also look like the Hoover image."

Just as glossy statistics and the "G-man" of the 1930s served to create the image Hoover sought for the Bureau, he is now fully convinced that today's FBI man must be a carbon copy of television FBI hero Efrem Zimbalist, Jr. "I want our special agents to live up to that image," he told Congress in 1966.

The suave, cool-headed FBI inspector who always gets his man, portrayed by Zimbalist, is, from head to toe, Hoover's alter ego of the 1930s. The only thing missing is the Director's snap-brim hat. FBI special agents must wear dark, conservative suits. Their ties and socks must be color-coordinated. Hair, a Hoover fetish, must always be freshly trimmed.

"They all have to be above average in personal appearance," Hoover once told interviewers. "You won't find long hair or sideburns a la Namath here. There are no hippies. The public has an image of what an FBI agent should look like." On another occasion he stated, "I certainly would not want to have any of the beatniks with long sideburns and beards as employees in the Bureau."

Zimbalist takes his role as the heroic Inspector Erskine seriously. He was initially involved in the "Friends of the FBI" group comprised of ex-FBI agents, lawyers, and right-wing people from a wide variety of professions. Essentially, these Hoover-backers are pamphleteers, whose sole activity appears to be the squelching of criticism, particularly in the press and on Capitol Hill, of J. Edgar Hoover.

Quinn Martin's weekly FBI show does more **than reflect**

Hoover's idea of what a special agent should look like. According to the Bureau's assistant director, Thomas E. Bishop, the FBI Recreation Association (a Bureau employee's group) receives "a contribution of $500 for each new episode" of the show.

Much as he loves "The FBI" program, Hoover will not allow Quinn Martin's producers and writers to delve into Bureau files for case history material. Two Bureau employees, working under the Director's guidance, perform research jobs for the show while on the Bureau's payroll. Their chores include furnishing technical aid, offering story ideas, reviewing scripts (to check for any discrepancies in the image), and suggesting the "proper" changes, which are invariably made by Quinn Martin.

The producer is rewarded for his loyalty to the FBI with the friendship of Hoover and of his sidekick, Associate FBI Director Clyde Tolson, who has been with the Director since 1928. Each Christmas, Martin and the two G-men exchange gifts.

"The FBI" program is probably the greatest sales promotion job ever performed for any federal agency. According to Hoover, selling the public on the FBI is the most important aspect of the Bureau's daily functions. "They [agents] have to sell themselves [to the public] to get their confidence to obtain the information they need," he once commented.

It is mandatory therefore in Hoover's publicity schemes that all FBI men be hero-oriented, larger-than-life warriors battling injustice. "Youth must have its hero," he insisted in 1960. "They should have a decent hero . . . instead of having some hoodlum like a Jesse James or someone of that type." And that hero is the clean-cut, badge-flashing special agent of the FBI.

Hoover's agents are run through a fourteen-week course at Quantico, Virginia, where they are taught a host of FBI procedures (the most important of which is how to maintain silence), as well as capture and arrest techniques. Future agents must qualify with hand and machine guns. The pictures on the target dummies are those of John Dillinger and Lester Gillis ("Baby Face" Nelson) who represent ancient but successful FBI cases.

Candidates for the FBI usually come from conservative schools. Hoover prefers to enlist men who have served as line officers in Vietnam (about one thousand new agents have been recruited from this category in the last two years). "You get a man who has been in command of men and he has to use good judgment," the Director said of his Vietnam veterans in 1970.

But even these must have the proper backgrounds as specified by the Director: "[Agents] must be graduates of an accredited law school . . . or must have graduated from an accredited four-year college with a major in accounting and have had three years' personal experience in that field."

New agents begin at the Bureau at an annual salary of $11,500, which is approximately $4,500 more than that paid initiates of the Secret Service and the IRS, and $3,500 more than that received by beginners in the CIA. Hoover prides himself on the handsome FBI pay scale. His reason for demanding such a salary level is simple; this kind of wage, he argues, eliminates the temptation of bribes and kickbacks.

When advertising for new agents, Hoover points out that an agent can retire at age fifty after serving the Bureau for twenty years, and receive approximately forty percent of an average wage based on the agent's highest annual wage. After forty years, an agent can retire with eighty per cent of his highest-earned annual wage. For those who can somehow manage to avoid the political pitfalls of the Bureau, the retirement program is lavish.

According to one source, Courtney Evans, the Director's liaison to Attorney General Kennedy, retired (he was eased out after being too friendly with Kennedy) with a pension that had "an actuarial value of over a quarter of a million dollars."

For most agents, the hazards of keeping the Director happy preclude reaching retirement status. Any agent whose actions run contrary to Hoover's views risks dismissal. James Sturges, a special agent, was once told to stop reading *Playboy*. It was explained to Sturges that Hoover considered readers of that magazine "moral degenerates," and he could be fired for reading it.

Any violation of the Director's strict code of attire can be an immediate ground for dismissal. One agent ushered into Hoover's presence was sporting a tie with loud colors. He was fired the next day.

Those exceeding the gambling and drinking habits of the FBI chief face the same fate. Hoover takes one drink in the evening and occasionally places a two-dollar bet at Maryland, Florida, and California race tracks.

Sex and marriage are also decisive factors in the jobs of all agents. When Hoover, for example, learned that one of his agents had married a woman of Arabian extraction, he summarily fired the man. Such autocratic action on Hoover's part is possible because he has successfully kept the Bureau outside of the Civil Service umbrella, stating that only in this way can he maintain the proper discipline and chain of authority in his agency.

In 1968, Hoover fired Thomas H. Carter, a clerk in the Washington offices, for "unbecoming conduct." Hoover had received a note from an informer stating that Carter had been "sleeping with young girls and carrying on." The clerk admitted to agents that he "had twice gone to bed with a young lady, but insisted he hadn't undressed."

Carter sued Hoover, and even though a federal appellate court in July of 1968 determined that Carter had merely been "necking," his case was hopeless. Hoover does not make mistakes in determining the morality of his employees.

The Director wields this enormous power over his eight thousand agents and an equal number of clerks in fifty-eight field offices, located in the larger cities, and another fifty resident agency offices in smaller towns, firing at will anyone who breaks his codes of conduct.

Each agent usually handles approximately twenty-five separate cases at the same time. These include car thefts, bank robberies, antitrust and Selective Service cases. He must report on all of these in elaborately detailed memos within a fixed deadline for each case, say every two days on a bank robbery and every fifteen days on a car theft, until all of his cases have been solved.

The agent-in-charge receives the reports of each of the agents under his command, and these reports are speedily dispatched directly to Hoover, whose office hours are chiefly consumed with reading these reports. One ex-FBI agent stated that "the only thing Hoover gets in his daily reports is what he wants to read."

It is quite true that progress concerning every case being handled by the Bureau is what the Director wants to hear. To illustrate this progress the agent's job becomes nerve-wracking drudgery where inventiveness and cleverly-worded synopses of cases become the focal point of his job, rather than investigation and apprehension of criminals (which is generally left to police, who are seldom credited with the results of their efforts by FBI men making the reports). These reports take up almost all of an agent's work hours. He is also obligated by Hoover's procedures to put in daily overtime, one hour and forty-nine minutes minimum, but each agent is expected to contribute more hours than this.

The same kind of regimen applies to Hoover's clerical workers. Typists working in Bureau offices throughout the country are required to record the number of pages they type each hour.

An agent's life belongs wholly to the Director. He signs in and out of his office each day, and whenever he is out of the office, he must inform his superior, the agent-in-charge, of his exact whereabouts.

Life for FBI clerks is no less rigid. Each new clerk is given Hoover's handbook of conduct, to which he must adhere at all times. The booklet describes suitable attire for clerks and forbids their attendance at any public meetings that could even remotely be construed as political.

In April of 1971, two Bureau clerks, Linda Janca and Christine Hoomes, were fired for working after hours in the offices of the National Peace Coalition, which was preparing antiwar marches on Washington and San Francisco.

Their supervisor in the identification division, J. Allison Conely, grilled Linda Janca on her work for the antiwar group and what she thought of the war in Vietnam.

"I just told him 'I think the war is wrong,' " Miss Janca later reported.

Within two days, Conely told Linda Janca to "either quit NPAC or give up your job at the FBI."

The two women were finally compelled to resign. They filed suit against the Director through the American Civil Liberties Union, which also sought to prohibit Hoover from interfering with the off-hour activities of FBI personnel, but the case, as is always the situation with complaints against Hoover, came to nothing.

Hoover's booklet also instructs his clerks that excessive use of alcohol and credit are also grounds for their dismissal. Anything that "might result in embarrassment to the Bureau," such as auto accidents and "divorce or separation from your spouse," must be reported to FBI officials.

FBI personnel must also seek permission "to serve as an officer of a civic or other type of organization." The booklet warns that "employees will not be considered for promotions while on record as seeking other full-time employment."

Those wishing to hire FBI agents cannot approach them while they are still with the Bureau, but must wait for them to leave before making any offers. This, one ex-FBI agent reports, has led to massive numbers of clandestine meetings, where agents scurry about apprehensively in dark bistros, conferring in a conspiratorial manner with future employers.

The enforcement arm of FBI discipline is the Inspection Division, whose specially-trained agents swoop down unannounced on various field offices to check on the performance of agents. These inspection teams grill agents for hours, demanding to know why cases haven't been solved. "The logical but unspoken answer to such ridiculous questions," an ex-Bureau man reported, "is that the agent is too damned busy writing those book-length memos to solve anything."

Each agent's conduct is also thoroughly examined by the Inspection Division agents. At these times, agents are reminded that they must report any questionable actions or words of their fellow employees.

This directive from Hoover has created an anxiety-producing spy system within his own Bureau whereby one agent is compelled to report the slightest infraction of Bureau rules, whether real or imagined, by a fellow agent.

A recent example is the story of two agents who were close friends and who worked in the Chicago Bureau. The two men took their wives to dinner one night; one of them went directly from the office, carrying his briefcase. When he and his wife were driven home by the other agent, the briefcase was forgotten and left in the car. The agent driving the car was in a quandary. He did not know if his friend had really forgotten the briefcase or if he had used it as a plant to see whether he would be "properly" reported. If the report was not made, then the agent driving the car could be reported. He took no chances and reported the incident. Unfortunately the briefcase had not been a plant. The agent who forgot it was fired immediately by Hoover for negligence.

The threat of transfer to the Bureau's distant outposts, such as the Butte (Montana) office, is constantly hovering over agents. One agent complained to a national newspaper that he had "been transferred six times because he didn't meet the weight-loss strictures ordered by the Director, who also diets."

The Director's rigid rules extend to the minutest actions of FBI personnel. Men, but not women, may smoke on the job. No one, man or woman, is allowed to bring coffee to his or her desk.

One newsman recalled the time when an agent spilled coffee on Hoover's exquisite office carpet while the Director was vacationing in La Jolla, California. The entire staff of the FBI crime laboratory went to work, but, though they were experts in analyzing blood, paint, and hair, they failed to remove the coffee stain. The agents pooled their money and, because the carpet was an especially rare one, had the original carpet's manufacturer weave a perfect duplicate which was installed in Hoover's office before his return. The switch was never detected by the FBI Chief.

In addition to the no-coffee rule, agents are subjected to censure by the Director if any unfavorable reports reach him, about such things as playing a stereo too loudly at home. Demerits are handed out regularly for the most trivial infractions.

One agent-in-charge who was visited by Inspection Division snoopers was given a demerit for dirty windows. FBI critic and ex-agent William Turner was scolded by his superior for leaving the windows down in a Bureau car in ninety-degree heat. An assistant director was criticized for misspelling a word in one of the Bureau's reports (and the written reprimand he received contained a misspelling).

The slightest indiscretion on the part of any agent can result in disaster. Agent Jack Shaw, who had been with the Bureau for seven years, wrote a letter to a professor at John Jay College of Criminal Justice, where he had been taking Bureau-approved courses. Shaw's mistake was two-fold: first, he stated in the letter a few mild criticisms of the Bureau in his overall defense of the FBI. The most offending line involved the personality cult in the FBI, exemplified "by a haunting phrase that echoes through the Bureau: 'Do not embarrass the Director.' "

Shaw's second mistake was having his innocuous letter typed in the Bureau's Washington office. Suspicious agents watched the typist prepare the letter for Shaw, and retrieved eight bad copies of the letter from wastecans. A senior agent took Shaw aside and began grilling him, writing down everything Shaw said.

"I told him to stop writing," Shaw said later, "that we were talking about a life and a career."

The following day, Shaw was grilled by three more agents. "They hit me with everything but their fists," Shaw stated. "There was no gentlemanliness. It was a series of broadsides. There was no question of fair play. It really got them that an agent whose loyalty had never been questioned, whose Bureau record was impeccable, should say these things."

It also got Hoover. The Director sent Shaw a telegram stating that he had "atrocious judgment" and ordering him to the Bureau's Siberia, the field office of Butte, Montana. Shaw refused on the grounds that his wife was seriously ill (she died a month later) and resigned. Employing one of his favorite tactics, Hoover accepted Shaw's resignation "with prejudice." This stamped Shaw an undesirable and made getting another job difficult (and, in the field of law enforcement, almost impossible).

Though Senator George McGovern took up Shaw's case, his suit against Hoover for the vicious blackballing was ineffectual. Shaw is now just another Bureau exile looking for work.

The Shaw case is not an isolated occurrence at the Bureau. Hoover has been arbitrarily firing agents for years. Sometimes the innocent as well as the guilty are punished (the guilt always being determined by the Director).

A few years ago, a special agent in the Kansas City office was maintaining contact with a specially-developed informant (the FBI's most valuable source of information), who was serving a prison sentence. The informant, who had served this agent and the Bureau well over many years, asked one favor. The convict wanted to arrange a pass to attend his father's funeral. The agent weighed the man's request against the firm Hoover rule that no FBI agent can ever effect the premature release of a convict, irrespective of reasons.

The agent decided that the inmate's information greatly benefited the FBI and agreed to honor his request.

Following the funeral, the agent safely returned the convict to prison. He then wrote and promptly delivered a report to the agent-in-charge of the Kansas City office and to the Director outlining what he had done.

Hoover read the honest confession describing the breach

of conduct. The Director immediately fired the agent and his boss, who had no prior knowledge of the action.

The agent flew to Washington and spent three days in Hoover's outer office, staring at the death mask of the man Hoover insists was John Dillinger. The agent wanted to beg, not for his own job, but for his boss' position. Hoover ignored them both and they remained fired.

Hoover's perplexing wrath extends to both lowly agents and to those laboring in the FBI's hierarchy. For years, the man most likely to succeed Hoover in his position as director was William C. Sullivan, a scholarly and thoughtful assistant director whose work performance was excellent.

Sullivan created a stir in the fall of 1970 by announcing plots by the Weatherman group to kidnap certain federal officials, but, according to one national magazine, Sullivan's speech also debunked "the menace of the Communist party."

This was sacrilege to J. Edgar Hoover. Here was a high-ranking FBI official who not only stole some of the Director's publicity, but also made light of Hoover's gigantic phobia, the Communists.

Within a few months following this statement, Sullivan took a sick leave (he had been disagreeing with Hoover on a number of FBI policies). While Sullivan was absent, Hoover chose a unique way of informing him that he was no longer associated with the Bureau. The assistant director learned that he had been dismissed by reading the *Washington Post,* which reported that his name had been removed from his office door and the locks changed, information which had been leaked to the *Post* by the Director.

The FBI then issued a formal statement announcing Sullivan's retirement and the appointment of Alex Rosen as head of the FBI's general investigative division.

The newspaper reported that Sullivan had been resisting

Hoover's repeated demands for his resignation "as late as 10:00 P.M." on October 2, 1971. Since this was a Saturday it is fair to assume that Hoover had been badgering Sullivan at home. The paper also stated that a refusal to resign on Sullivan's part would be to "challenge openly his one-time benefactor [Hoover] at the risk of his government pension."

Another reason given for Sullivan's dismissal was that he enjoyed a strong relationship with Attorney General Mitchell and other top Department of Justice officials, "apparently casting doubt on his loyalty to the Director."

Sullivan disappeared without comment into ex-FBI-man limbo, emerging on January 11, 1972, as the assistant director of the Insurance Crime Prevention Institute, a national organization recently founded to combat insurance fraud.

Sullivan's remarks at the time of his appointment were thinly-veiled blasts against Hoover, Inc. He stated that he joined the institute because it "does not suffer from fossilized bureaucratic traditions and obsolete policies.

"It is stimulating to realize that at the institute the stress is on original thinking, experimentation, and progressive procedures, with the measure of success a practical one—results. The institute's newness guarantees willingness to think in terms of change and flexibility as a means of achieving superior results."

When asked to speak directly about his FBI years, Sullivan stated, "I came to realize how infinitely complex human relations really are."

No doubt Sullivan was describing his former relationship with the Director, the kind of relationship that ends only one way after you disagree with him on anything—you go, he stays.

It has been that way since the beginning. Melvin Purvis, the super special agent of the 1930s who stole too much of

Hoover's publicity (and who has been eliminated from all official FBI history by the Director), discovered the cruel facts in 1935. By then, Purvis had built up his own image as an impressive gangbuster through the Dillinger, Nelson, and Floyd cases.

The press lionized him. And he played the part, scooting about the streets of Chicago in his expensive roadster (he was agent-in-charge of the Chicago Bureau), and giving flamboyant interviews to eager reporters. Hoover had always wanted his FBI men to appear as heroes to the public, but Purvis was too much of a hero and the publicity he received too aggrandizing to suit the Director.

Hoover fixed that by assigning his anointed super agent to tedious recruiting chores, according to ex-FBI man Virgil Peterson, who was one of Purvis' best friends and who worked under his command in Chicago in the early 1930s.

In 1935, Purvis was fed up with the Director's humiliating assignments, so he quit. To Purvis, the resignation was a relief. As reporters faced him when he left the Bureau offices in Chicago for the last time, he breathed a sigh of relief, and commented as he brushed past them, "I'm glad to be out of here."

But there were, in the next four decades, thousands of agents glad to remain in the anonymous employ of J. Edgar Hoover, ready to serve him in any capacity, no matter how ridiculous the assignments might be. Many agents would find their careers highly stimulating, though perhaps not always sane.

# 11

# Your FBI in Action

Techniques practiced by the Bureau haven't drastically changed since Purvis' day. Although many FBI agents have a strong sense of proper conduct, others, in the name of justice, arbitrarily employ strong-arm methods that would make Giles de Raiz wince.

In 1969, Hoover cautioned his agents and other law enforcement officers against using third degree and other illegal practices to obtain evidence. "The test tube is mightier than the rubber hose," he loftily concluded.

Yet many in the FBI have consistently, through the years, used rough measures in their zeal to get results for the Director. And Hoover has never been unaware of the third degree methods his agents have employed.

Agent Melvin Purvis' offices in Chicago during the 1930s became a regular torture chamber. Doris Lockerman, Purvis' private secretary, wrote in 1935, "I sometimes saw the bruised knuckles of agents who had used more primitive arguments with refractory prisoners."

Agents of that day were also in the habit of attending Hollywood's latest G-man films to get the hang of administering persuasive arguments to prisoners. Purvis himself admitted that strong-arm methods were standard for the day: "The escaped prisoner was 'invited' to accompany the special agent to the federal building or the nearest police station, and sometimes these invitations were engraved on the minds of the escape[e] in a very definite fashion and they were accepted."

Another method of grilling suspects, according to prisoners' statements, was dangling them by the arms outside a nineteenth-floor window of the FBI offices in Chicago. John J. "Boss" McLaughlin complained of this method in 1935. James Probasco, a minor suspect in the Dillinger case, did not. Probasco fell nineteen floors to his death from Purvis' offices after being brought there for questioning. Agents stated that Probasco had appeared "despondent" while being interviewed. His death was ruled a "suicide."

As late as 1965, similar charges against the Bureau were being made. On October 4 of that year, according to a Brooklyn motel owner, Anthony Polisi, four agents questioned him about two suspected bank robbers who had stayed at his place. Though Polisi had no criminal record, the agents, he said, worked him over thoroughly.

They choked him with his own tie, punched him repeatedly in the area of the heart (after he informed them that he had a heart condition), punched him several times in the face, kicked him, and dragged him by the hair. As they were pulling him, one agent, Polisi insists, said: "Give us the information or we'll kill you."

Polisi had no information to give, but he went to the hospital anyway.

The *Baltimore Sun* revealed that between July 1968 and August 1969, David O. Hale, an agent in the FBI's Tucson, Arizona, office, set and exploded eighteen bombs at houses, businesses, and in cars "on the theory that some selective bombing would get the Mafia fighting internally and drive it out of Tucson."

Hale had reportedly been assigned "to investigate organized crime." Adding to the mystery, an Arizona judge, William C. Frey, stated that Hale had "misled" two men who helped him in the bombings by telling them they "were acting for him in an official capacity." Frey condemned the agent's actions and termed them "a frolic of his own." He considered Hale's conduct "a dereliction, gross dereliction of duty."

The Department of Justice refused to discuss the Hale case, but fired the agent when the bombing exploits were revealed. Assistant Attorney General William Wilson wrote to Congressman Morris Udall (D., Ariz.) on April 2, 1971, that the Justice Department would not institute any federal case against Hale and that it considered the matter closed.

Hale hired a lawyer, Lawrence P. D'Antonio, to argue his case. The attorney insisted that evidence which attributed the bombings to Hale was based on rumors, that the charges were designed to "frame" his client, and that the entire affair was "a plot to discredit the FBI." Hale remained fired.

That Hoover's agents have resorted to violence to achieve results for the Chief is clear. Such conduct may put them in an untenable position, but they invariably perform these violent acts confident that the Department of Justice will ignore embarrassing accusations by closing its books and remaining silent.

Surveillance and arrests by Hoover's agents have been equally questionable down through the years. Sometimes the pose an agent has affected while on the job has been not only conspicuous in the best Hollywood manner, but so absurd that *he* became the observed.

Following the theft of FBI files from offices in Media,

Pennsylvania, on March 8, 1971, a horde of FBI agents descended upon the politically liberal community of nearby Powelton Village (located just outside of Philadelphia). The entire town, which had developed a freewheeling life style, was suspected by the Bureau of being involved in the Media theft.

Agents appeared on the streets of Powelton in March of 1971, unshaven and wearing rumpled suits, attempting to appear as "hippies." But their efforts at disguise were feeble if not futile. Residents came from their homes and pointed at them. Everything about them was obvious. According to one report, "The FBI cars were all late-model sedans of the Belair or Impala type, with rear radio antennas, two-way radios under the dashboard, and license plates beginning '92' or '93.' They moved slowly when they moved. The drivers all had short hair and wore white shirts with dull suits. They appeared aimless or humorless or fatigued."

Powelton residents were amused by the sudden attention the Bureau was giving them. They created such nicknames as "Captain New Beard," "Hippie Fake-Hair," "Bell-Bottom Conservative," "Off-Duty Construction Worker," and "Aging Fraternity Boy" for agents affecting particular disguises.

Powelton's residents were approached by agents who revealed that they had knowledge of the residents' backgrounds. Then the agents attempted to interview these residents, but were told to go away.

A group of people assembled next to a car in which two agents were sitting. They tried to converse with the agents. One resident ambitiously offered to clean the windshield with a bottle of Windex. With that, "the agents jumped out, grabbed him, locked his arms, cuffed his hands, and sped away. He was taken to the central office [of the FBI] for the rest of the day. One interrogator told him, 'If you people in

Powelton don't stop this circus, this is what you'll get.' "
Obviously, the agent meant arrest (with or without a
warrant), but the man was not hurt and was released later
that day.

One Powelton resident, a woman, did "get" more. In her
possession were "third generation (twice-Xeroxed) copies
of some Media files," which she planned to publish as part
of an analysis of relations between the FBI and local police.
FBI agents, who had learned of this, knocked down her
front door with a sledgehammer, and ransacked her home
while over one hundred persons watched from the sidewalk,
including a lawyer who was not permitted to view the FBI
search inside. The agents confiscated her typewriter and
stapler. Neither was returned to her (and a $95.97 bill for
damages remains unpaid by the FBI).

With this minor, noisy victory, the FBI men withdrew
from Powelton's quiet streets and the residents went back
to their normal life. As one observer put it, the FBI "is
probably still doing most of the things it's always done, but
it's now doing them much less brazenly in Powelton."

A courtroom episode in San Francisco the year before
was equally ludicrous. On February 12, 1970, three FBI
agents jumped an alleged draft dodger in the federal court
of Judge William T. Sweigert. The man, Robert Kimball,
an archdeacon, was sitting quietly in the spectator section of
Sweigert's court watching his superior, Bishop Robert N.
Skillman, testify in a case.

Three agents of the San Francisco office, F. Wiley Davey,
Duane Franklin, and Joseph Dushek, watched Kimball in-
tently. Suddenly, the three pounced on Kimball. The archdeacon went limp, and the agents began dragging him down
the courtroom aisle. Bishop Skillman shouted, "Your honor,
that's my archdeacon! Tell them to stop!"

Judge Sweigert, who had been absorbed in the court file

and had not observed the initial fracas, looked up in time to see the agents bang out the door, carrying Kimball. "I don't know what's going on here," Sweigert cried out.

James Comerford, a deputy marshall for the court, told the judge that "FBI agents arrested a man on a selective service charge."

"In the courtroom?" Sweigert asked. "Tell them to come back here."

Comerford brought back the struggling group. The FBI agents identified themselves and explained their mission.

"Was it necessary to arrest him [Kimball] in this court?" Sweigert demanded.

"We thought so," agent Davey said. "We made an arrangement with the marshal."

"I thought they were going to bring him to our lockup," Comerford shot back rapidly, defending himself.

"As far as I'm concerned," Sweigert said angrily, "he is released from custody. Hereafter there will be no arrests in this court without prior consultations with the court. Or someone will be in trouble."

When Kimball left the court, he was promptly rearrested by the three agents, who were later called before Sweigert. The judge told them, "You violated the sanctuary of the courtroom where no violence should ever occur, nor any intimation of violence." He held them in contempt of court, but imposed no punishment on the three.

Kimball, who had not reported to his draft board, was later released on his own recognizance.

Assuming the image of circus performers to effect the arrest of a draft-dodging suspect does not daunt Hoover's agents, as long as it helps to complete their deadly daily reports.

Sometimes a criminal offense may not exist to prompt the FBI to action. A Washington businessman at a cocktail lounge once overheard someone making a critical remark about the Director. To the man's astonishment, two agents were on his doorstep the next day to quiz him about the statement.

Bob Freed, the announcer of wrestling matches in Washington's sleazy sports arena, stepped before TV cameras on the Director's seventieth birthday and extended greetings "to our favorite viewer, J. Edgar Hoover." No sooner was Freed out of the ring and the first match begun than he was called to a phone. An angry FBI man was on the line, and he informed Freed that Hoover did not watch wrestling matches, a sport apparently beneath the Director.

But when it comes to investigations, nothing seems to be beneath the FBI. According to one writer, "The FBI . . . pays a fair price to building superintendents who are willing to turn over the garbage of suspected security risks and other subversives."

The garbage is then inspected carefully and anything found that could be interpreted as incriminating is copiously detailed in the daily reports.

In 1963 the FBI couldn't get enough information on syndicate chieftain Sam "Momo" Giancana, so agents parked night and day in front of his home and dogged his footsteps on the golf links. Giancana filed a suit charging the Bureau with harassment. The case was tried in the court of Chicago's Judge Richard B. Austin (who was also a golfer).

After hearing the evidence, Austin granted an injunction which limited the FBI's surveillance of Giancana to a single car. The Bureau car, the judge specified, must be parked at least a block away when near Giancana's home and must stay a block behind when following Giancana's car. Austin also ordered that an impartial foursome play between Giancana and his FBI tailer when on the golf course.

When the chief of the Chicago Bureau refused to testify in the Giancana case about FBI surveillance techniques, he was fined $500 by Judge Austin, who commented, "I know there are some not interested in civil rights and not concerned with privacy who will in the future approve of this type of harassment. I cannot give my sanction."

Though the fine was never paid by the FBI, Giancana, who subsequently disappeared in Latin America, had beaten Hoover's men. There is no denying that Giancana, as a leader of the Mafia, certainly deserved FBI investigation. But, again, the Bureau was too obvious in its assault against a member of the crime organization, a trait indigenous, it appears, to FBI agents. As a result, the FBI failed to nail this top mobster.

The FBI's indiscriminate interviews of suspects or of those who may have information about cases also display a talent for bungling and meddling. In one instance, a call girl (who also belonged to the United Daughters of the Confederacy and the Daughters of the American Revolution while practicing her trade) complained of FBI harassment.

"If there is any reason why I'm in antisocial activity at this time," she stated, "I think it is the FBI, who in one year questioned me 173 times [meaning 173 precious reports] looking for missing people and other characters that my husband was supposed to know. I felt when they had come to question me that I disgraced my grandfather's name, who was, after all, a federal judge. Even to this day they'll question me about missing people, robberies, and things of that kind. And when I had legitimate jobs, they lost two or three of them for me by coming around to the offices where I worked."

Information is also obtained by the Bureau from other allegedly confidential sources, such as banks, stock brokerage firms, and insurance companies.

The Bureau, according to a well-documented investigation, taps these sources whenever information is needed on potential jurors involved in cases where the United States is a litigant. No firm or bank refuses this information to the FBI. As one writer aptly summed it up: "The guess may be ventured that in the overwhelming number of cases mere display of FBI credentials is a guarantee of rather full disclosure of all information sought."

One expert in this field estimates that the Bureau receives an average of twenty-five thousand credit reports each year; they are handed over by credit agencies who have vowed privacy of information to their clients. Executives in any credit bureau know that to do otherwise is futile. Almost any credit file can be subpoenaed. It is better, they feel, to curry favor with the Bureau in the hope of getting reciprocal deals (which they never do).

In stubborn cases, the Bureau will skirt executives of credit firms and establish liaison with one of the firm's investigators, who provides any dossier the FBI wants—for a price. Unlike the previously-mentioned syndicate killer who is on the Bureau's payroll as an informant, and sells his information for his freedom, is another informant who is a financial investigator for one of the world's largest credit reporting firms. This man sells and *trades* secrets. That is, he is allowed to get information, for his own use, from FBI files. He has been on the FBI payroll for the last twenty years.

The files of the credit agency for which this investigator works contain significant personal and business data on almost every prominent American businessman. Through this man, these files are instantly available to Hoover's FBI, for money. This information changer, like all other secret sellers of information to the FBI, must feed more than his bank account. He nurtures a cloak-and-dagger ego, and is

Hoover at the height of his fame as a spycatcher in 1942, flanked by his loyal associate FBI director, Clyde Tolson. (Wide World)

Hoover receives 500 sets of fingerprints for his files from two members of the Junior Chamber of Commerce of San Francisco in 1940, as a result of an FBI drive to get all civilians fingerprinted. (Wide World)

Ex-Yeoman Harry Thompson spied for the Japanese in the 1930s. Naval authorities, not the FBI, effected his capture. (UPI)

The FBI knew that ex-Lieutenant Commander John S. Farnsworth was handing secrets over to the Japanese, but failed to arrest him until a newsman suggested the Bureau do so. (Wide World)

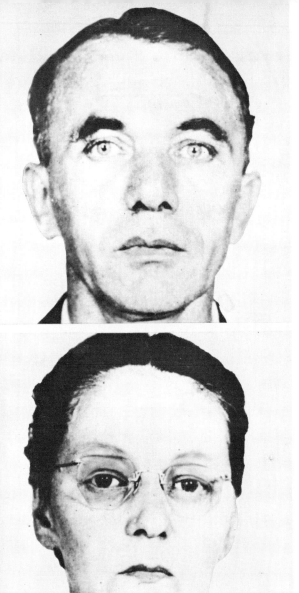

Master Axis spy Dr. Bernard Julius Otto Kuehn and his wife, Friedel, gave the Japanese the exact positions of American warships in Pearl Harbor up to the moment of and throughout the attack—even though the FBI knew the Kuehns had been spying in Honolulu since 1937. (Wide World)

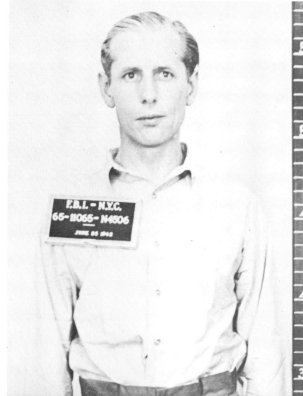

Nazi spy Hermann Lang stole the plans of the Norden bombsight before World War II. Hoover had boasted that the Bureau had controlled all espionage. (UPI)

Abwehr spy George John Dasch told Hoover that eight Nazi saboteurs had landed in Florida and got thirty years in prison for his cooperation. (UPI)

A particular object of Hoover's wrath was Benjamin "Bugsy" Siegel (left), shown with movie actor George Raft in 1944. (Wide World)

Sportsman and millionaire Del Webb built the Flamingo Hotel for Bugsy Siegel. Hoover, a personal friend of Webb, had every Las Vegas casino bugged except the Flamingo. (Wide World)

J. Edgar Hoover taking Clyde Tolson's picture
while vacationing. (Wide World)

a self-styled arbiter of national security. He is firmly convinced that neither organization—the credit agency or the FBI—could exist without his paid assistance. (This informant is also one of the few persons in the world who works directly for Howard Hughes.)

After being an FBI informant for over twenty years, and earning more than fifty thousand dollars (tax free) for his secrets, this informant described the detecting abilities of FBI men thusly: "They couldn't find their asses with both hands. If you took away that badge and their powers of subpoena, they'd be lost.

"One night, I received a telephone call at my home. It was an emergency. The FBI needed to find somebody quick. A federal arrest warrant had been issued. I told them I could help to locate this individual for $150. That was fine with them.

"After I hung up, I checked the telephone book. The man they were looking for was listed and I drove out to his house to make sure it was him. I waited a couple of hours before calling the FBI back. I wanted them to think that I was really working. They were happy to get the information and I was happy to get the money."

Among this informant's cherished souvenirs is a letter from Hoover, signed in the Director's own hand, thanking him for his services on a particularly difficult investigative job which Hoover said saved the Bureau years of spadework.

Apparently unknown to Hoover is the fact that this informer has been selling the FBI *and* another federal agency the same information for years.

In addition to supplying credit company information, this informer is an occasional wiretapper for the FBI. The reason this informant gives for the Bureau using a non-FBI wiretapper is to protect the image of J. Edgar Hoover.

This reasoning appears logical in that Hoover subjects himself to open criticism by using agents such as William Turner (who admitted he illegally entered private homes to hide electronic listening devices). Turner, like other agents, can always exercise the right to quit the Bureau and make public his nefarious activities on the FBI's behalf, whereas the informer is chained, by virtue of his position, to anonymity as well as to guaranteed swift denials from the Bureau regarding its connection to him should someone attempt to make the facts public.

Because of his long service to the Bureau, the credit investigator-FBI informer has access to the most sensitive intelligence reports in FBI files. He is permitted to read these secret reports into a tape recorder. If a photocopy of any report is required by this man, it is provided, but any letterheads or logos identifying the FBI as the source of this information are removed first. This secret intelligence information in the Bureau's files is sometimes needed by the informant's credit firm to prevent civil suits for libel. The firm is unaware that its own files are outgoing to the Bureau, and believes that the investigator is performing his job in obtaining FBI leaks only through strong friendships.

In short, this informer is able to save his own firm considerable legal research fees by manipulating the tax-supported FBI as one would a pool of law accountants and clerks.

Though it is probable that any ethical man would find the practice of having informers on the FBI payroll intolerable, the truth is that these dark-alley denizens are the mainstay of the Bureau's "fact-finding" force. Almost every criminal case that Hoover has claimed his agents solved was actually resolved through the disclosures of informants.

Not all FBI informers are of the pay-me-now variety; some are conscientious citizens attempting to perform what they think to be civic responsibility. Many of Hoover's most famous cases have been solved by just such people. An incidental but interesting track-down investigation of 1923 illustrates the Bureau's tremendous dependence upon citizen informers. On October 23 of that year, the Southern Pacific's Train No. 13 was stopped by train robbers outside of Siskiyou, Oregon, and four trainmen were shot.

This federal case moldered until March of 1927. The FBI examined all trails left by the gunmen and came up with nothing. Then, an independent criminologist, Edward Oscar Heinrich, determined the identity of one of the killers after railroad detectives gave him a pair of overalls found at the robbery scene. Heinrich determined that the overalls "were worn by a left-handed lumberjack who has worked around fir trees somewhere in the Pacific Northwest. He's a white man, between twenty-one and twenty-five, not over five feet ten inches. He has medium light brown hair and he weighs about 125 pounds . . . he's very fastidious in his habits."

Heinrich had learned, where the FBI had not, that a stain found on the overalls was fir pitch; Heinrich's powerful microscopes also revealed that tiny pieces of fir needles found in the pockets of the overalls came from Douglas fir trees of a kind unique to the Northwest. He determined the man's height and weight by the garment's measurements.

Discovering the man's race, age, and hair color was easy. Heinrich analyzed a hair caught on one of the buttons of the overalls. The gunman's meticulousness was indicated by extremely even fingernail cuttings found in a pocket seam. That the man was left-handed was indicated when Heinrich found bits of tree chips in the right-hand pocket of the overalls. "A left-handed lumberjack, you know," Heinrich explained, "stands with his right side to the tree he's cutting and the chips fly to the right, not to the left."

In addition, Heinrich found a receipt for registered mail jammed down inside of the pencil pocket on the bib of the overalls. This receipt was traced by authorities to one Roy D'Autremont, a left-handed lumberjack with light brown hair, who, with his brothers Hugh and Ray, had disappeared from Eugene, Oregon, shortly before the train robbery.

The Bureau searched for the D'Autremont brothers for close to four years, but they had vanished. In March of 1927, Albert Cullingworth was reading the Sunday paper in Steubenville, Ohio, when he noticed a story concerning the Oregon train robbery (planted by postal authorities) and recognized the photos of the robbers as "the Goodwin twins" who "worked out at the mill."

Cullingworth phoned a woman acquaintance, a Mrs. Maynard, and told her of his suspicions. Mrs. Maynard promptly called the FBI who arrested the D'Autremonts. The FBI had finally caught their men. That the amazing Heinrich had established the identity of one of the killers for them and that informers had provided the information on their whereabouts were, as always, incidental.

Another much heralded FBI coup, the solving of the $3 million Brinks robbery in 1956, was also accomplished through information funneled to agents from an informer.

Mass slayer Melvin Davis Rees, who had slaughtered whole families in Virginia in 1959, might have escaped detection to this day were it not for the fact that his best friend turned him in to the FBI. The friend not only turned Rees in but had to do the spadework that should have been done by the Bureau to discover where Rees had taken cover; then he virtually led the FBI agents by the hand to Rees' place of employment so Rees could be arrested.

The paid informer, as opposed to the duty-bound citizen, concentrates on making money. The subjects of his observations vary from suspected political subversives to politicians on the take. This kind of informer is in it for only one thing—the money. Several reports have it that if informers have to break the law while serving the Bureau, they do so.

When an FBI spokesman was asked if informers are ordered to break the law in the line of duty, he responded with: "Absolutely not, under no circumstances. The reverse is true. We make it quite clear that they are not to violate the law. That is unequivocal."

Yet admitted FBI informer David Sannes, who worked out of the Bureau's field office in Seattle, Washington, stated on June 1, 1971, that "a member of the FBI" instructed him to involve himself in acts "of a criminal nature," which included bombings. The Bureau denied Sannes' charges.

Sannes also stated that as an FBI informer he had been assigned to infiltrate a group subsequently charged with conspiring to bomb federal buildings in Seattle. He said that "on many occasions I was encouraged and instructed to take part in acts of a criminal nature that would further give me credibility within the revolutionary movement."

Sannes added that "a member of the FBI" explained that "the proper procedure was to allow . . . the bombing to happen and insure that the man who set the bomb died in a booby trap explosion."

Herbert Itkin was also identified as an FBI informer in New York City by the U. S. Court of Appeals in the fall of 1970. Itkin, the court stated, was involved in a plot to bribe a New York City official while "the FBI sat by." The court, ruling on the legal boundaries informers might exceed, stated that, even though Itkin actually helped carry out a crime of extortion while working in liaison with FBI agents, curbs on his conduct "had best be left to the executive branch, which is accountable for its conduct to Congress."

A West Coast newspaper identified another FBI informer as Alfred R. Burnett, who also worked with local police, and whose actions on May 15, 1970, reportedly involved an attempted bombing which resulted in the killing of a much decorated Vietnam veteran. Police statements verified that the exsoldier had been recruited by Burnett to bomb a business office. Burnett was quoted as telling a penal officer of Washington State that "the police wanted a bomber and I got one for them. I didn't know Larry Ward [who was shot to death at the scene of the bombing] would be killed."

As the tempo of the civil rights movement increased in 1968, Hoover issued memos to all headquarters agents throughout the United States, ordering them to develop a network of paid Black informers in various ghettos. Likely prospects, FBI memoranda pointed out, would be tavern operators, liquor store owners, barbers, salesmen, cab drivers, bill collectors, and newspaper, food, and beverage distributors. Such recruitment poses little problem to the Bureau since many large cities, such as Los Angeles, issue business permits to the owners of almost all of these businesses. Before this permit is issued, the FBI is consulted. Ostensibly, the Bureau is contacted by local police to check previous criminal records. It is safe to say, however, that any businessman whose permit must be okayed by the FBI is a likely prospect for the Bureau's informant list.

In Hoover's 1968 instructions every agent contacted was ordered to produce at least one racial informer. Information gathered by these informers was to be detailed in memos to the Director, "with copies for the files on any individuals or organizations mentioned."

The fact that the FBI was aligning itself with veterans' organizations to create a huge system of informers was clearly spelled out in one directive: "We are exploring other sources which may produce large numbers of prospects, such as men honorably discharged from the armed services, members of veterans organizations, and the like."

These extensive spy systems are established to supply information for the FBI agents' voluminous reports, which are fed into the burgeoning files in the Bureau's Washington office. This office alone—field offices also have great amounts of duplicate files—contains more than five million individual files according to one estimate, more according to others. Of these, half a million have been started and fattened with information on individuals branded by the FBI as internal security risks (chiefly those involved in political activity Hoover considers threatening).

An analysis of FBI files stolen from the Bureau offices in Media, Pennsylvania, on March 8, 1971, by parties unknown, indicates that forty per cent of the contents applies to surveillance of political groups, thirty per cent involves procedural matters, seven per cent is concerned with military AWOL's and deserters, seven per cent with draft resistance, fifteen per cent applies to "ordinary crime," and a miserable one per cent is concerned with organized crime.

At times when the Bureau is not concentrating on Hoover's pet targets—political activists—agents gather information that can be interpreted as nothing more than potential blackmail material. One such batch of information involved the notorious whorehouse known in Washington as the Hopkins Institute, run by George Francis Whitehead and his madam, Diane Carter.

The "Institute" was doing a land-office business in the 1940s until warrants were issued, under the White Slave Traffic Act, for Whitehead, Miss Carter, and more than a dozen of the girls working there. Unfortunately for some of Washington's politicians, the heads of various upper-crust families, and certain business leaders, who had favored the "Institute" with their presence, the FBI confiscated lengthy records on the Institute's clients, records so specific that the smallest sexual preference and perversion of each client were listed.

The worth of such sex-oriented records can only be estimated by their keeper, J. Edgar Hoover. It would appear that material of this nature, however, has nothing to do with national security, and can serve only the Director's political needs.

Those affected by this raid were in the usual hopeless position. As one source stated: "Hundreds of men still tremble when they remember the Hopkins Institute. Some still attempt pressure to try to get their names blacked out. They have no success with the FBI."

Hoover insists that these, along with all other records on file in Bureau offices, should never be released. "It is vitally necessary that these files remain inviolate," he once stated, "for to release them to public view would cause irreparable damage and injustice."

If that is the case, one might ask, why then are such files maintained and what kind of information do they contain? A fair answer is that many of them are based on alley gossip from those who stand to profit highly from the establishment of just such files.

The FBI has files on some of the highest-ranking politicians in the country. San Francisco mayor, Joseph Allioto, was linked to reported Mafia members by the appearance of an FBI "intelligence" file.

One of the Bureau's most highly coveted intelligence reports is the many-paged dossier covering the political and personal life of Chicago's popular and powerful mayor, Richard Joseph Daley, who was overwhelmingly elected to an unprecedented fifth term in 1971 by the citizens he serves.

A Chicago-based researcher was recently shown this "intelligence" file on Mayor Daley. First, he was led by the FBI through a ritual of information-letting in a style reminiscent of Eric Ambler. The well-checked researcher met an FBI agent and paid informer for lunch at a lavish Mexican restaurant on Chicago's North Side (the restaurant is a hangout for FBI agents, who consider the place "safe"). This lunch was finally taking place after six weeks of canceled appointments and unanswered phone messages.

The FBI informer cautiously explained that the cancellations were a delaying tactic used by agents who were trying to determine whether or not the researcher worked for "liberal publications."

After a heady repast of Mexican fare, the researcher was instructed to appear the following day in front of the federal building, 219 South Dearborn Street in Chicago's Loop, where, he was told, he would receive information about Mayor Daley. (At the time, the researcher was at work compiling background material for a special project on Chicago politicians.)

The next day, the researcher sat in the informant's car and waited until an FBI agent appeared lugging a heavy briefcase. The agent got in, sat alone in the back seat, and then read from the intelligence files dealing with Mayor Daley as the informer drove through the city, while sheets of rain drummed relentlessly (and dramatically) on the windshield. After each page was solemnly read by the FBI agent, the sheet was handed to the researcher in the front seat. At the top of each page of the intelligence report was the austere letterhead of the FBI proclaiming "bravery, fidelity, integrity."

Typical of many of the Bureau's files, the Daley intelligence reports were rooted in venomous gossip and unsubstantiated allegations.

One of the so-called intelligence items concerned a

$450,000 bribe to Mayor Daley from the city's Mafia. The bribe, according to the FBI's report, was paid to Daley from Mafia chieftains over eighteen years ago when he first campaigned for the mayoralty. This report was given to the FBI by a disgruntled hoodlum. His statements, copied faithfully by the Bureau, alleged that Mayor Daley spent only $200,000 of the reported syndicate campaign donation of $450,000.

The account went on to state that Mafia members visited Mayor Daley and demanded the return of their unspent monies, and Daley made a deal: If he were allowed to keep the $250,000, he would give the "boys" the right to approve the next Chicago police superintendent. That police superintendent would be O. W. Wilson, a man internationally credited with updating and modernizing the Chicago Police Department.

It might be noted here that throughout the long and prestigious term of O. W. Wilson, not one Chicago policeman attended the FBI's National Police Academy.

The report then quoted a Chicago hoodlum who complained that "the only guy making money in this town is the mayor. He's making millions!"

Another portion of the report concerned itself with the youth of Mayor Richard Daley. The federal document, based on the mouthings of an unnamed stoolie, accused Daley of "pulling a couple of jobs when he was a kid and hiding a wanted criminal from the FBI."

A later-dated item in Daley's dossier stated that the Mayor had broken with the Chicago mob in 1960, and that he had been forced to abandon his hoodlum friends under severe pressure from President John F. Kennedy and his brother, Attorney General Robert Kennedy.

The personal and political life of Mayor Daley was not the only subject of unproven and unsubstantiated charges.

According to another FBI-paid informant, a private phone in Mayor Daley's office was tapped by the Chicago office of the FBI. The tap remained on the Mayor's private phone in his office until one afternoon when an FBI agent, who had enjoyed a martini lunch, dialed the Mayor's private number through the tap and asked if he could leave a message for Murray "The Camel" Humphreys. (Before his death, Humphreys was one of the top members of the Chicago syndicate.)

After the call, Daley immediately ordered his private phone removed, and shortly thereafter Hoover ordered the whimsical FBI agent transferred far from the Chicago office.

The FBI's compilation of the so-called evidence that goes to make up the intelligence file on Richard J. Daley testifies as to the overall unreliability of its sources. That the FBI would hand out such shoddy reports to a researcher associated with the press is even more revealing in that this act exposed the sniping techniques—for whatever political reasons—the Bureau has adopted under the leadership of J. Edgar Hoover.

When it comes to civil rights, however, the FBI takes a wholly different approach—more like a frontal attack.

# 12

# Hoover and Civil Rights

The Director's frontal assault on civil rights was not in the area of violations; rather, it was against those leading the fight for integration. As a corollary the Bureau attacked those budding campus political groups that were against the Vietnam war and expressed views on other issues disturbing to the bureaucratic mind of J. Edgar Hoover.

Hoover's head-on confrontation with Dr. Martin Luther King did not leave him with the smug victory he later advertised. The mere thought of the aggressive civil rights leader irritated him. In pointing out that Dr. King had become an obsession with Hoover, one writer quoted a former Justice Department official as saying: "You couldn't spend thirty minutes with Mr. Hoover without his bringing up the sex thing about Dr. King." (He was referring to Hoover's disclosures, gathered via taps and bugs, of Dr. King's alleged sexual promiscuity.)

Hoover's concerted efforts to "get King" became an exclusive FBI job. When the whole shoddy story of the Bureau's snooping into Dr. King's private life was revealed, the public finally became aware of Hoover's attitude about the civil rights movement and its leaders. The public also became increasingly alarmed at the Bureau's awesome power to defame those Hoover chose not to endorse. As one newspaper editorialized: "The King case is a frightening example of how political police can misuse their powers with the help of electronic gadgetry and huge files."

Attorney General Robert Kennedy's insistence that Hoover order his Bureau into action over civil rights infractions accented the Director's decades-long negligence in this area. He was made fully aware of his duties in this area of responsibility as early as 1939, when Attorney General Frank Murphy, under the Order of the Attorney General No. 3204, established a Civil Liberties Unit (now the Civil Rights Division) within the Bureau's Criminal Division. Murphy did not have to seek legislation for this order. The attorney general's directive under the Department of Justice Act of 1870, Section 8, empowered him to "make all necessary rules and regulations for the government of said Department of Justice, and for the management and distribution of its business."

The Bureau at that time rarely employed this unit other than in cases specifically ordered investigated by the attorney general. But Hoover could hide behind his superior's position when it came to civil rights. He could investigate only that which he was ordered to investigate. He never stood on this chain-of-command ceremony, however, when he arbitrarily entered criminal cases that would get him easy and complimentary headlines. The Director could also excuse his agency's inactivity in civil rights investigations by stating that the civil rights acts that did remain in effect through his tenure up to the 1960s were not explicit in respect to his duties. The welter of civil rights acts in the 1960s did not change Hoover's attitude, but Robert Kennedy, Martin Luther King, and others did.

The fact that the Bureau all but ignored civil rights violations was all too clear when one realizes that the number of agents and offices the FBI maintained in the South was small if not nonexistent until Robert Kennedy became attorney general.

Prior to that, Hoover's civil rights investigations consisted of mere dabbling, and that only at the order of the attorney general. In November 1952, Attorney General Herbert Brownell, Jr. ordered Hoover to investigate the brutal death of Robert Byers, a Black inmate at Pennhurst State School in Pennsylvania. The conditions under which Byers met his death suggested gross violations of civil rights.

Upon receiving the order, the FBI did investigate (its findings were inconclusive) and this drew the fire of certain states' rights advocates, particularly Governors John S. Fine of Pennsylvania and John Stewart Battle of Virginia. Thomas E. Dewey, governor of New York, also joined with Battle and Fine in attacking Hoover for trespassing upon states' rights in the Byers investigation.

The NAACP and the Civil Liberties Union sided openly with the FBI, a rare occurrence.

Hoover, ever sensitive to criticism, immediately replied to Governors Dewey, Fine, and Battle in a letter to the *New York Times.* He said, in part, "The FBI over a period of years has experienced difficulty in investigating alleged violations of civil rights. It has not been uncommon, in such investigations which do not meet with the public sentiment of the community wherein the act occurred, for the FBI to be singled out for attack. . . .

"The record, I think, is clear and convincing. More progress has been accomplished in developing consciousness, understanding, and respect for civil rights since 1940 than in any other period in our national history." No doubt, Hoover selected this year because Murphy's 1939 order was in effect and certain statistics could be brought to bear which proved the Bureau's alertness in civil rights matters.

The statistics Hoover chose to sling about in 1953 dealt with the Bureau's possible effect on lynchings in the United States. "In the last thirteen years, for example, a total of 36 lynchings have occurred. . . . In the thirteen years preceding 1940, however, a total of 157 lynchings occurred.

"The fact that the FBI investigates lynchings no doubt causes many would-be lynchers to stop and consider the consequences before engaging in mob violence. In such cases, or in others of the type which the governors [Dewey et al.] had in mind, it makes little difference whether the victim is the most lecherous type of criminal [obviously meaning those Blacks accused of rape]. He still is entitled to be treated as a human being. No one has the right in common decency or under our constitutional republic of taking unto himself the responsibility of inflicting punishment.

"We of the FBI have no other choice but to do our duty as best we can. This we shall continue to do. . . ."

In 1961, this "duty" consisted of idly standing by while freedom riders were threatened and government officials were knocked senseless. In May of that year, while helping a Black freedom-rider escape from howling white mobs in Montgomery, Alabama, a special assistant to the attorney general, John Seigenthaler, was knocked to the ground unconscious by rednecks (he was also President Kennedy's personal representative to the integration marches there).

For twenty-five minutes, as Seigenthaler lay unconscious in a Montgomery gutter, an FBI agent stood across the street taking notes; he did not go to Seigenthaler's aid.

Later, Seigenthaler remarked, "It galls me to think that the FBI stood there and watched me get clubbed and was close enough so that they could positively identify my assailant."

Hoover found refuge, however, in his oft-repeated tenet that the FBI is only a fact-finding agency. His agents, when he so wished it, were to observe only, and report their observations to him; they were never to become personally involved, for this "would be deserting his [the agent's] assigned task and [he] would be unable to fulfill his primary responsibility of making objective observations." And, it might be added, fulfilling his quota of memos for the day.

When Byron "Whizzer" White, then deputy attorney general, went to Montgomery to direct orderly civil rights demonstrations, he found little cooperation from the resident FBI agents. He had to call Robert Kennedy for help in establishing communications with the Bureau, and then the attorney general had to get Hoover to okay, albeit reluctantly, FBI communication relays to White. But the situation between White and the resident agents in Montgomery didn't improve, so Hoover sent his assistant director, Alex Rosen, to Montgomery to personally handle the job.

Later, Assistant Attorney General William Orrick placed a call to Robert Kennedy to explain that another snag had developed in Montgomery. He told Kennedy that Carl Eardley of the Justice Department's Civil Division, who was preparing a motion for a mandatory injunction that would order local police to maintain order, couldn't get any cooperation from the local Bureau. "I can't do a thing," Eardley had told Orrick. "I can't get any help at all. The FBI won't do a thing."

Upon hearing Orrick's report, Kennedy called his brother, and the president called Hoover. A little more than an hour later, three agents and the commanding general of

Maxwell Air Force Base confronted Orrick at his desk. He was asked if he had complained about the Bureau. Orrick said yes. "Please don't do it again," he was told. *Then* the FBI offered its services to him.

Hoover balked every step of the way at the FBI's further involvement in civil rights matters in the 1960s. In 1964 he reluctantly opened his Mississippi offices to handle the large number of civil rights violation claims. In the same year he ordered FBI informants to infiltrate the NAACP, which had supported him in his fight against the governors in 1953 over the Byers affair.

Also in 1964, Hoover himself traveled to Jackson, Mississippi, where he held conferences with Governor Paul Johnson, Mayor Allen C. Tompason, and the local police chief, all of whom civil rights workers had branded as the suppressors of their movement. One writer described the crowning event of the conferences: "He [Hoover] then proceeded to march across the street from the governor's mansion to the post office, where he held a press conference, asserted in no uncertain terms that the responsibility for protection of civil rights workers rested with local Mississippi police, and disavowed any intent to protect civil rights workers."

Following these conferences, Clarksdale (Mississippi) Police Chief Collins stated: "The FBI comes in here every day and we have coffee every day. We're good friends." Collins had been reported by SNCC members as one of the major roadblocks to integration in Mississippi; they charged him in affidavits with brutality and intimidation.

An unsigned affidavit by a SNCC member stated that the FBI had cooperated with the local police in Clarksdale in helping to frighten civil rights workers there. The affidavit read, in part: "When the movement came to Clarksdale, we encouraged the local people to talk to the FBI.

We discovered that everything we told the FBI was told to the local police the next day. Our local people would be picked up by the police after they had spoken to the FBI, and the police would tell them everything they had said."

In Selma, Alabama, on Freedom Day, October 7, 1963, the Bureau went further than leaking confidential information to local police. On that day, four FBI agents watched without comment as three Blacks, attempting to register to vote at the Selma courthouse, were arrested by local police and state troopers, a flagrant violation of federal law.

Incredible as it may seem, J. Edgar Hoover has never admitted to such blatant and well-documented FBI negligence. On the contrary. He has consistently maintained that he and his agency have always operated on noble principles, as he demonstrated in 1952 when he wrote: "Law enforcement, however, in defeating the criminal, must maintain inviolate the historic liberties of the individual. To turn back the criminal, yet, by so doing, destroy the dignity of the individual, would be a hollow victory."

Hoover's concepts of integration were and are as old fashioned as his policy of keeping Black "agents" on the FBI payroll as domestic servants. His patronizing view of Blacks no doubt led him to sum up in his 1964 report to the president that all riots occurring in the Black ghettos were "senseless."

Hoover finds the civil rights movement and the New Left movement synonymous. While sending his paid spies into the activities of the NAACP, he has also, according to charges, ordered the infiltration of any suspicious left-leaning or Black liberal group. An indictment of such infiltration was made by Black delegates attending the United Methodist General Conference in St. Louis in the spring of 1970.

Black delegates to this meeting charged that "FBI agents

were on the conference floor and that some delegates' rooms had been bugged." Conference leaders in effect admitted that these charges had foundation by their ambiguous statement that they had not "invited the agents, but did not deny their presence."

According to the Reverend Robert Moon, a white delegate from Sacramento, California, the Council of Bishops had received reports of an FBI investigation of the conference. This, Rev. Moon said, was "unnecessary intimidation."

Senator Edmund Muskie (D., Maine) was later to charge that in the same month, April of 1970, FBI agents had monitored "Earth Day" rallies across the nation. Muskie's charge, which occurred a year later, was backed by Senator Mike Mansfield (D., Mont.), who demanded a congressional inquiry into claims of improper Bureau surveillance.

As usual, though promises of a full-scale investigation were made, these charges came to nothing. Hoover's agency remained impervious to review, and his order to spy on civil rights organizations, peace groups, and New Left campus movements continued to be carried out for reasons of "national security."

In January of 1970, Hoover reported that there was "a marked change in the New Left movement—particularly among student-oriented groups . . . to a far more militant stand," and that "extremist, all-Negro hate-type organizations such as the Black Panther party continued to fan the flames of riot and revolution."

To illustrate that the various menaces were closing in from all sides, the Director emphasized that the Ku Klux Klan was experiencing "an upsurge in recruiting activity," when, in fact, the Klan as a cohesive nationwide organization had all but crumbled.

But fear not, Hoover's 1970 message implied, "FBI operations during the year 1969 soared to new heights in practically all aspects."

In December of 1970, Hoover informed *Time:* "A lot has been said in the press about the FBI swarming onto the campuses. The FBI is not on any campuses. A Princeton professor blamed me for having agents on the campus, and he even called me a bastard. I wrote him that the FBI never goes on a campus except to investigate bombings of federally funded buildings, and while I do not indulge in vulgarity, I called him a liar. It's an absolute lie.

"Of course most students think we shouldn't go on [campuses] unless they invite us. They can have as many demonstrations, sit-ins, lay-ins as they want, and we will never look into it. I think students have a perfect right to dissent and to express their views through proper channels. But they ought not to resolve their differences by throwing bricks and bottles on the street."

These tolerant statements to the press were completely opposite to Hoover's stand concerning student unrest the previous year, when he told Congress: "What is needed is more guts on the part of many presidents of the universities and colleges. . . . Many of the school administrators appear unable to distinguish between legitimate protest and unlawful acts and there are far too many bleeding hearts among them whose palliative attitude has served only to magnify the problem by encouraging the escalation of demands and further disorders."

The Director's denial that the FBI was on campuses was, of course, an outright lie, unless he also denies any association with the Bureau's paid informants upon whose statements the FBI builds most of its "documentation."

According to one ex-FBI agent, who worked specifically in the areas of the peace groups and New Left movement, the Bureau dispatched to college campuses across the country many informants who infiltrated antiwar organizations and other groups of the New Left. "All one of our FBI informants needed to do," he stated, "was walk into the office [of a peace group] and state briefly that he was opposed to the war and wished to volunteer his services."

Since such organizations are desperate for workers, these informants were almost always accepted without question as volunteers. Once in the group, the FBI informant would acquire copies of handbills, leaflets, mailing lists, and names of contributors, and these would find their way into FBI files as "intelligence" gathered on "subversives."

The ex-FBI agent involved in working on such New Left operations stated that "during my three years working on radical groups I never found any evidence that would lead to a conviction for criminal violence." He concluded: "The FBI claims to be a nonpolitical organization and asserts that it is not a national police force. But in its intelligence and counterintelligence work on the New Left it was engaging in activity that clearly was political. Moreover, in trying to suppress and discourage a broad-based national political movement, it acted as a national political police."

That political police force operated not only on the campus but in the American home as well. When members of Congress began to hear about FBI men visiting people in their homes and instructing them not to have dealings with peace groups, they contacted the Director. At such times, Hoover became solicitous.

Congressman Jonathan Bingham of New York received a quick reply from Hoover when he demanded to know why an FBI agent was allegedly advising the parents of missing Vietnam soldiers not to deal with a peace group known as the Committee of Liaison.

Mrs. George Clarke of Hampton, Virginia, told the Subcommittee on National Security Policy of the House Foreign

Affairs Committee that she was visited in October 1970 by a man who identified himself as an FBI agent and told her to have nothing to do with the Committee of Liaison.

The agent told Mrs. Clarke that the group was a far-left organization and she was better off not dealing with them.

Bingham fired off an angry telegram to Hoover which read:

"Mrs. George Clarke of Hampton, Virginia, mother of a serviceman missing in action in Vietnam, testified today before the House Subcommittee on National Security Policy that she was visited at her home in October 1970 by a man who identified himself as an FBI agent and displayed credentials and who warned her and her husband not to have anything to do with the Committee of Liaison. As a result of this warning, Mrs. Clarke told the Subcommittee, she refrained from attempting through the Committee of Liaison to obtain information as to whether her son is alive and a prisoner. I am shocked and outraged by this report. If it proves accurate, the agent involved should be disciplined and you as Director should make clear to all FBI personnel that any such action exceeds their authority and is an improper and unwarranted infringement on the freedom of action of American citizens. I trust I may have an early response to this wire."

Bingham did receive an early response. Hoover told him that the FBI was investigating the Committee of Liaison to see if it should register as an agent of a foreign government. Hoover said that this investigation was ordered by the attorney general. (The results of the FBI investigation indicated that this peace group should not be required to register as an agent of a foreign government.)

The Director told Bingham that an FBI agent did visit Mrs. Clarke, but the agent denied warning her to stay away from the committee. Other families with missing Vietnam servicemen were also visited by this same agent. None of the other families reported conversations similar to Mrs. Clarke's. An aide to Bingham said that he believed that Mrs. Clarke was telling the truth, but since no other complaints were being made, the matter was at a standstill.

The Bingham aide said that he did not know if the fact that the Clarke family was Black and the other families were white had anything to do with how the FBI agent conducted his interview. "The agent was from the Deep South," Bingham reported, "and maybe he let something slip. Both the Clarkes have master's degrees and are very bright. We believe them."

It is safe to assume that the FBI agent involved in the Clarke case was never reprimanded by the Director for his actions. Since his identity has not been made public, he remains a shadowy figure, only an agent of the FBI. This kind of nameless identification does Hoover no harm. But when an FBI man is identified in connection with someone unpopular with J. Edgar Hoover, no matter what the situation, he is guaranteed a doomsday future in the Bureau.

Such was the case of one hapless FBI agent who made the mistake of being photographed in the presence of Mayor Richard Hatcher of Gary, Indiana.

Hoover (and, incidentally, Mayor Richard J. Daley) was keenly interested in the election of Richard Hatcher as the first Black mayor of Gary, Indiana. (And both Hoover and Daley were disappointed by Hatcher's success.)

Hoover's interest in Richard Hatcher, according to Gary FBI agents, was classic. The Director believed the liberal Black candidate to be under the influence of Communist ideology. (Mayor Daley's interest, on the other hand, was an ordinary political one. According to an FBI informant, Daley had channeled over two hundred thousand dollars in political donations to Hatcher's campaign. However,

Hatcher took a portion of the Daley-donated funds and used it to support independent Black candidates running against Daley's hand-picked candidates in Chicago elections.)

Shortly after being elected, Mayor Hatcher appointed James Hilton as chief of the Gary Police Department. Then Hatcher and Hilton requested an FBI agent in the Gary office to instruct their local police department in modern crime-fighting techniques.

Special Agent Watts, in charge of the Gary FBI office at that time, appeared reluctant, but okayed the request. An agent went immediately to work helping the Gary police. Then one Saturday, the FBI instructor received a call at his home from Chief Hilton. The police chief invited the FBI agent to a luncheon in downtown Gary. At this affair, a surprise award—the Golden Key to the City—was presented to the agent by Mayor Hatcher for service to the Gary police force.

Completely shocked, the agent accepted the award from Mayor Hatcher and was photographed by the local press. Shortly after the publication of that photograph, J. Edgar Hoover ordered the agent transferred to Buffalo, New York, which is on a par with Siberia-like Butte, Montana.

The punishment transfer remained in effect even after the FBI agent pleaded with the Director to reconsider, stating that he was ignorant of Hatcher's plans for presenting the award.

Though a minor incident, this clearly illustrates Hoover's reaction to anything he construes as bad press about FBI relationships with those labeled by him as undesirables.

This is understandable for a man who considers favorable press coverage as the "Oscar" of law enforcement—and who will perform just about any role to win it.

# 13

# See What the Boys
# in the Press Room Will Have

J. Edgar Hoover's talent for politics is exceeded only by his genius as a publicist. He is, however, in a unique, almost unassailable position which allows him to speak out *ex cathedra* in unending press releases without being seriously challenged.

Hoover's credo is cranked out methodically by the Bureau's Crime Records Division. FBI officials have informed newsmen that the Bureau "has no public relations office," yet the Crime Records Division performs the ubiquitous tasks of preparing press releases and crime reports, handling press inquiries (which are invariably turned down or answered so vaguely as to be useless should the inquisitor represent a publication not on Hoover's approved list), and publishing the FBI's annual report and, in slick magazine format, the *FBI Law Enforcement Bulletin,* which is issued nationwide to police.

Hoover writes a regular editorial for this magazine. It was from these writings, according to one reporter, that Republicans culled a great deal of propaganda for their 1968 campaign. One GOP campaigner admitted that "we'll

211

quote him [Hoover]. We'll say he has been saying it for years [demands for the Republican law-and-order slogans]. We'll say that the present administration has been ignoring him for years and we won't ignore him."

Useful political statements have flowed freely from Hoover to Republican politicians over the years, but the Director has never been so generous with the press. He has retained his high-priest-of-law-enforcement mystique by treating the general press with practiced disdain and, at times, utter contempt, favoring only those in whose editorial policy he delights, chiefly the *Chicago Tribune,* and, to a lesser degree, the *New York Daily News* and the *Washington Star.* He has never appeared on TV to mouth generalities, let alone to answer questions. Hoover has consistently refused to address the National Press Club. And he is never in to the *Wall Street Journal,* the *Washington Post,* the *National Observer,* and the *New York Times.* Hoover considers these publications "anti-Bureau" and treats them accordingly.

Though he has granted a few closely-guarded interviews with such publications as *Time* in recent years, Hoover prefers to channel his good news from the Bureau through press release procedures and, when possible, through trustworthy newsmen, considered in the trade to be "leak men." Some of these "writers" are broadly classified as "investigative reporters," and it is into their hands that the FBI places unsubstantiated "intelligence" material (which cannot be attributed to the Bureau). The "leak men" then filter the Bureau's message (sometimes unknown to the editors) into their respective newspapers.

Sandy Smith, late of the *Chicago Tribune* and now an investigative reporter with *Life* has fallen heir to a tremendous amount of material, particularly tape recordings made by agents, funneled to him by the FBI.

Another way the Bureau leaks information it deems

important is to bring along on raids that are assured of success in advance certain approved reporters who will tell the FBI story the "right way." This is especially important if an individual FBI office is drying up—that is, not getting enough publicity to sustain Hoover's image and blessing.

One such raid occurred recently in northern Indiana. The Gary office of the FBI desperately needed publicity. It also needed help in smashing syndicate-controlled gambling operations in Lake County, Indiana (which had, at that time, more federal gambling licenses than any other area of the United States except Las Vegas, Nevada).

Special Agent Watts of the Gary Bureau contacted Elmer Jacobson of the Northwest Indiana Crime Commission, a small, privately-financed organization that had been effectively battling the syndicate for years. Watts offered Jacobson a fifty-fifty deal in an investigation of the gambling operations in East Chicago, Indiana. Jacobson and one of his agents would handle all undercover operations, while the combined forces of the Indiana and Chicago FBI offices would supply the money. There was also an agreement between Jacobson and Watts that the sure-to-come good publicity resulting from their combined efforts and the credit for their success would be shared equally.

For months Jacobson's undercover man sat shoulder-to-shoulder with syndicate hoods, gathering vital information for criminal indictments. He would leave the Indiana casinos at dawn, and usually find the FBI man assigned to guard him asleep in his car.

Though Watts had promised Jacobson that he would receive a three-day notice from the Bureau prior to the time the FBI would carry out its raids on the gambling casinos, the agent ignored the Crime Commission chief and directly contacted the undercover man. The man was told he must attend an important FBI conclave that evening in Gary and that the Indiana raids would take place that night. Watts also told him not to tell his boss about it. The undercover agent hung up and called Jacobson who told him to go along with Watt's order.

Jacobson, who sensed that the Bureau's promise of equal publicity was not to be trusted, called Pulitizer Prize winning reporter George Bliss at the *Chicago Tribune,* who then drove him down to Indiana to cover the raid. Bliss stood by with Jacobson waiting to hear from the FBI.

The undercover man, meanwhile, attended a highly dramatic meeting of Bureau personnel in Gary. Calvin Howard, head of the Bureau's Indianapolis office, an old-timer, surrounded himself with thirty FBI men and announced in the melodramatic voice of a 1930s radio actor: "We're going in at 8:25 P.M. tonight!"

The undercover man explained to Howard that raiding the places at such a time would preclude snaring syndicate hoodlums. The crime commission man explained that the hoods seldom arrived in any of the casinos before 11:00 P.M. But Howard insisted that the raids be made at exactly 8:25.

"I knew why they wanted to crack those places at that time," Jacobson later reported. "If they pulled the raids off that early, they could make the deadlines for the home edition of the *Chicago Tribune.*"

Once inside the syndicate gambling casino in East Chicago, the undercover man noticed that there were only three people at the tables, none of them syndicate hoodlums. He called the Bureau offices and begged them to postpone the raids until a later hour. Reluctantly, Howard agreed to unleash the raid at 9:00 P.M. The undercover man arranged to have the casino's doors unbolted and the guard in front distracted. The FBI agents arrived late, marching down a long corridor and into the casino.

A young, well-dressed agent announced to everyone: "All right, everybody. We're FBI and this is a pinch. Everybody up against the wall."

The undercover man resisted rolling his eyes at the G-man cliché as he and the others were lined up against the wall to be searched. Suddenly, everyone was ushered out to the street. Except for a few nonentities, including the undercover man, the agents took everyone into custody.

After months of work, the undercover man was left standing alone on the East Chicago street with the remaining hoodlums, who eyed him suspiciously. The agents were supposed to pick up the Crime Commission man some blocks away and he waited for an hour. His own car was parked in Gary next to the Bureau offices. Finally, the undercover agent was forced to call a friend to come pick him up.

Just as the FBI left the undercover man without a ride, they left Elmer Jacobson without publicity and George Bliss without a story. Bliss and Jacobson waited for a phone call from the Gary agents that the raid had been completed. It never came.

Robert Wiedrich, another *Chicago Tribune* reporter, personally viewed the FBI raid in East Chicago, handpicked by the FBI to get the story. Weidrich, now a *Tribune* gossip columnist, had long been favored by the Bureau with such treatment because of his colorful writing style and the abundant admiration he had displayed in print for the FBI.

The press release the FBI promised Jacobson, which was to give proper credit to the Crime Commission for its role in this raid, was never issued by the Bureau. The considerable contribution of the Northwest Indiana Crime Commission in doing undercover work (Hoover almost never has his agents perform any undercover work for fear of corruption) appeared as a minor fact in Weidrich's lengthy account which was published the next day in the *Chicago Tribune.*

Later, George Bliss carefully wrote a series of articles on the same raids in which he casually mentioned the FBI. Even though the Crime Commission was approached and promised equal publicity treatment by the FBI, the agents could not break Hoover's credo: The FBI *first* in peace and war . . . and in the press.

When the FBI issues its press releases, J. Edgar Hoover's name is always prominent. Although the attorney general, whoever he happens to be at the time, is credited with some innocuous statements, the Director is always associated with the "hard facts" of any FBI raid. A perfect example is the press announcement the Bureau issued in May of 1970 after agents arrested fifty-eight persons in Detroit and Flint (Michigan) raids of several numbers operations.

Attorney General John Mitchell was credited with statements about the raids resulting in the largest federal gambling arrest in history. "Through operations such as this," Mitchell was quoted as saying, "this administration is convinced it can dry up the biggest source of funds for organized crime in this country."

Hoover, on the other hand, was accorded all the statements which described the heroic actions of his agents. "Agents seized bundles of currency, numbers slips, water soluble paper, and gambling records in the raids, according to FBI Director J. Edgar Hoover." Though the attorney general's name precedes that of the Director in such releases (a practice Robert Kennedy insisted upon), Hoover is generally accorded the lion's share of the release and his name linked with the most dramatic aspects of the FBI action.

In this particular FBI raid, in which the efforts of the Department of Justice's organized "strike forces" were minimized, Hoover was careful to allow U.S. Attorney James Brickley to be the spokesman in confirming the Bureau's release. He was also careful, unlike his handling of the Berrigan case, to state through Brickley that "the raids were not involved with the probe of the sports betting ring" then under investigation. Any premature announcement of action might result in a failure to get mandatory indictments. Hoover would only risk such premature announcements, as he did in the Berrigan case, when he was up against the proverbial fund-raising wall. In the Berrigan case, Hoover's announcement of the alleged plot to destroy government buildings and kidnap federal officials before the indictments were returned coincided with his need for additional congressional funds with which to add a thousand new agents to his roster.

The Director would never risk having his press balloons punctured unless, by posing a new threat to national security, he could get what he wanted on the spot. This is known as Hoover expediency.

Many problem situations arise daily in Hoover's stilted relationship with the American press.

A particularly embarrassing one in 1964 involved President Johnson's closest adviser, Walter Jenkins, who had been exposed as a homosexual by Washington police who had been peeping into a men's room in the Capitol. The publicity wrecked Jenkins' career as well as his personal life. The Director, however, was concerned only with the image the public might affix to the Johnson administration, so he prepared "a special report" stating "that there was no violation of security" in the Jenkins affair.

Hoover's press announcements are connected umbilically to his self-promoting statistics. When the President's Commission on Crime made its recommendations in 1966-67, Hoover bristled with invective responses. He issued a public statement condemning "the shallow pronouncements of that 'select' group of impractical theorists who would 'define away' and reduce the crime problem by wielding a heavy eraser on [crime] statistics."

In the past, few have challenged Hoover's use of statistics (he has been organizing crime statistics since 1930). These crime statistics are released to the press annually, and are designed not only to prove the Bureau's ability to chart crime rates but to publicize the agency's street work in combating the menace entailed in these rising figures.

In recent years, independent criminal experts have attacked Hoover's statistics. One stated that the Director's figures "are not worth the paper they're printed on." Police officials have come to emphatically disagree with the FBI Chief on his statistics. Captain James Parsons of the Birmingham (Alabama) Police Department stated that the FBI's uniform crime reports are misleading. The captain felt this was the result of poor police department reporting procedures of known crimes and the fact that a large number of crimes are never reported to the police.

Hoover's annual crime statistics are compiled twice a year from monthly reports submitted voluntarily by police departments across the country. Parsons insisted that these reports do not represent the actual picture of crime in the United States. Yet Hoover uses these fluid statistics to impress Congress and the press with the keen ability of the FBI as a fact-finding agency.

Whenever possible, the Director has tried to ingratiate himself with people of the press, and these friendships have often brought favorable publicity for the Bureau. In addition to Walter Winchell, Hoover has cultivated warm relationships with columnist Ed Sullivan, the *National Review*'s Ralph de Toledano, and *This Week* chief, William Nichols.

Should a czar of publishing pass away, someone like

Eleanor M. "Cissy" Patterson of the *Washington Times-Herald,* whose wealthy newspaper clan spawned the *Chicago Tribune* and *New York Daily News,* Hoover sends condolences. At Miss Patterson's death, Hoover remarked, "During the decade that she headed the *Washington Times-Herald,* I knew and respected her as a tough executive who made no attempt to follow the conventional, and as a gracious hostess whose charm and courtesy warmed many a social evening. . . .

"I recall with pleasure the parties I attended in Washington at which Miss Patterson was present. She was possessed of tremendous energy and wit which enlivened even the most staid affair. But most of all, I remember her friendship and support which made my job a little easier in the hectic days before and during World War II."

Films and all the potent propaganda entailed in their production were not overlooked by the Director. From the gangster days of James Cagney's heroic portrayal of an FBI agent in the 1935 film *G-Men,* to the present, Hoover has been ever-mindful of this medium. The Director has emphasized certain FBI activities in each decade, such as his war with gangsters in the 1930s as publicized in *G-Men.* The FBI has been heroically featured in films through subsequent decades combating other mortal enemies of America.

In the 1940s, Twentieth-Century Fox produced *The House on 92nd Street,* which glorified the Bureau's counterespionage battle against the Nazis. In 1952, the FBI was honored again for its struggle against communism in *Walk East on Beacon,* which featured George Murphy and was also made by Twentieth-Century Fox. In both movies, FBI-backer Louis de Rochemont was the producer. A few years later, Warner Brothers brought to the screen a synopsis of Don Whitehead's Hoover-approved book, *The FBI Story,* starring James Stewart.

One FBI agent who viewed this picture commented: "It was so mawkish and overripe that I felt like hiding under my seat, a reaction shared by other agents. But Hoover reportedly was greatly moved, exclaiming that it represented a crowning moment in his career."

The steady flow of these and other FBI-sanctioned productions through the years has kept the Bureau's public image of miracle worker against crime and subversives fresh in the public's memory. To date, there has not been one full-length Hollywood production even slightly critical of the FBI. A lawyer for Universal Pictures remarked in 1970 that "any studio in Hollywood that would produce an anti-Hoover [FBI] movie would be insane. We need the Bureau. We work with them and have on a lot of productions. It's the FBI's cooperation we need, not its wrath. Hollywood will never produce an anti-Hoover [FBI] movie, never!"

For those book writers who have nothing but praise for the Director and the FBI, Hoover reserves fond sentiments and reciprocates with honors. When Courtney Ryley Cooper published his hosanna to the Bureau, *Ten Thousand Public Enemies,* and Herbert Corey wrote another praise-filled tome on the FBI, *Farewell, Mr. Gangster,* Hoover blessed them with introductions. Brain truster Raymond Moley's efforts to keep FDR from firing Hoover in 1933 did not go unrewarded either. When Moley's book, *The American Legion Story,* appeared, it too carried a kudos-crammed introduction by J. Edgar Hoover.

Three of Hoover's own books, according to one source, were actually written and researched by FBI personnel in the Crime Records Division of the Bureau (agent Charles Moore is credited as being the real author of Hoover's *Masters of Deceit*). These books have reportedly brought the Director more than $250,000 in royalties, and were "produced . . . at taxpayer's expense." No royalty checks, the source carefully stated, were ever made out to Hoover personally.

Hoover's plagiaristic habits have not always gone undisputed. On May 19, 1965, when addressing a House Appropriations subcommittee, Hoover delivered a six-hundred-word summarization of the activities of the Minutemen in the United States. Newsman and author, J. Harry Jones, Jr., was aghast when he read the Director's report.

"I found in reading it," Jones later wrote, "that it seemed somehow familiar. So familiar, in fact, that it slowly dawned on me I had written essentially the same analysis in an article the *Washington Post* had asked me to write six months earlier—on November 19, 1964."

There exists an almost word-for-word lift from the Jones article in the Hoover report. Of course, Hoover never acknowledged Jones' article or his investigative work in digging up material on the Minutemen.

Statistics on the Minutemen, however, vary between Jones' in-depth analysis of that organization and Hoover's estimation. In 1968, Jones alleged that between one thousand to two thousand people belonged to this extreme right-wing organization, but Hoover reported the membership in that year figured less than five hundred. In light of the Director's sweeping lift job, it is safe to assume he knew considerably less about the organization than Jones, and that his statistics regarding this group were merely more ball park figures deftly fielded by Hoover's famous backhand stop.

Such maneuvering with the press is standard procedure for Hoover and the Bureau. A magazine that I edited for a number of years published an article which exposed financial links between Las Vegas and a Chicago bank whose stockholders included some of the town's most powerful politicians.

Five advance copies of the magazine were requested by an FBI informer. These copies were hand-delivered to the Chicago FBI office, and one was forwarded to Hoover in Washington. A little over fifteen months later, several hoodlums were indicted by the federal government, the same hoods exposed in the magazine.

Hoover, Inc. is not above following the press for headlines. When the magazine I was editing exposed wide-open gambling in a nearby steel town, the article was placed in the *Congressional Record* by Senator John McClellan. The Bureau then sent an investigative squad to the steel town, where they tarried for but a moment. A report reached Hoover that *Life* was investigating a vice ring in St. Louis, so the flying squad was yanked from the steel town and dispatched to St. Louis posthaste. Such actions may be fickle, but Hoover knows that it's headlines that keep him in business.

Certain FBI informers are used exclusively as press contacts. Their jobs consist of having clandestine meetings with reporters from major metropolitan newspapers and giving them snippets of information, based on gossip, which are of little or no editorial use. In these conversations, the Bureau informant casually grills the reporter about what might be happening in his city room. The reporter, to keep on the good side of the informant in the event the Bureau does have something concrete to pass along, will invariably tell the informant about a few of the hot items his paper is checking on.

The informant immediately passes this information along to the Bureau for possible investigative development.

Sometimes, though the occasion is rare, the newsman himself becomes the FBI informant. This was the case with the hapless Louis Saltzberg, who began spying on leftist and activist groups for the Bureau in 1967. Saltzberg was photographing a leftist demonstration at the time and working for the Spanish-language publication *El Tiempo.* FBI agents approached the photographer after the demonstration and asked for the negatives of the photos he had shot.

Saltzberg readily turned over the negatives and from that day forward was an active FBI informant. He attended demonstrations regularly at the request of the Bureau. Each time, he took dozens of photographs of the demonstrators and turned the negatives over to FBI agents.

The photographer's income was so slim that he asked the Bureau for support money, especially since most of his assignments were coming from the FBI. The Bureau began to pay him regularly. Later he was to say, "I couldn't live without the FBI, unless I took another job."

Saltzberg, over a period of approximately three years, was paid ten thousand dollars by the FBI for his spying activities, all of which were unknown to anyone outside the Bureau. "No one knew about what I was doing," he later admitted, "including my own wife."

"Winston" was the cover name the Bureau assigned to Saltzberg. Using this name as a whispered code, Saltzberg met with agents regularly in "secluded parking lots" at the Bronx Zoo, where he delivered his negatives and other tidbits of information on political activists.

When Saltzberg lost his job at *El Tiempo* in January of 1969, the FBI, he reported, helped him to set up his New York Press Service at 41 Union Square West. Beneath the glaring photograph of leftist hero Che Guevarra on his office wall, Saltzberg aggressively went about the Bureau's spy business. He hired three left-leaning photographers as assistants and sent out letters to radical groups.

One letter read: "The next time your organization schedules a demonstration, let us know in advance. We'll cover it like a blanket. . . . No obligation to purchase, naturally."

The New York photographer eventually became so well known to the radicals that he began to sell photos to their publications. He was also asked to attend radical meetings of a closed-door type, which he did. Saltzberg made special attempts to get close to the leaders of the Veterans for Peace and the Veterans and Reservists to End the War.

After several months, Saltzberg was "in" with almost all well-known eastern radical leaders. "I made almost all the demonstrations," he said later, ticking off the sites of protest as a war veteran would battles, "Union Square, Central Park, Madison Square Garden. Even Washington and Chicago."

But Chicago was to be Saltzberg's undoing as an FBI spy. He took part in all the major melees that occurred in Chicago during the 1968 Democratic Convention. He was even knocked down and his camera smashed in one wild stampede.

As a result of his close association with leaders of the radical left in the Chicago demonstrations, Saltzberg was asked by the Bureau to testify in the trial of the Chicago Seven. "Winston" took the stand on October 23, 1969.

Saltzberg's testimony implicated defendant Tom Hayden as a conspirator in the plot to disrupt the convention in Chicago. Defendant David Dellinger took one look at Saltzberg and muttered, "It's quite a let-down, Louis."

The press spy's testimony against the Chicago Seven was anemic at best. During one recess, defendant Abbie Hoffman shook his head and said, "He [Saltzberg] knew us so well. I can't understand why he blew his cover for just that little testimony."

Perhaps Saltzberg didn't understand either. Suddenly, after his testimony, the forty-year-old Bronx newsman was no longer on the FBI payroll. Returning to New York,

Saltzberg found out that he was not employable. He applied for dozens of jobs, but the answer was always no. "One editor said that if he hired me," Saltzberg later stated, "he was afraid his reporters would walk out within an hour."

Saltzberg was reduced to attending conservative political functions where he told his story and received heaps of praise from well-fixed diners. A hat was passed around at one dinner meeting and Saltzberg was given the collection, less than one hundred dollars. No one ever offered to help him find a job.

Whereas Hoover could easily forget an informant who was no longer of use to the Bureau, he would never forget or forgive any writer who dared to attack him or his beloved FBI.

"Let me reiterate my oft-stated position," Hoover once remarked, "that as long as I am Director of this Bureau, any attack upon an FBI employee who is conscientiously carrying out his official duties will be considered an attack on me personally."

Hoover took the profile on him published by the *National Observer* in 1971 personally. He retorted in a vituperative barrage that the article was "slanted, unfair, distorted, fantasy, sensationalized, an outright lie, a malicious lie, an absolute and unqualified lie, designed to undermine confidence," and "a blatant attempt to set forth a string of innuendoes, inaccuracies and plain, outright distortions in such a manner [that] they give the appearance of representing true facts . . . which they do not."

When the *New York Daily News* criticized the FBI for not communicating with the Secret Service, Hoover took that personally, too. He fired off a letter which began, "Knowing the *News'* reputation for objectivity, I felt you would want me to bring to your attention a glaring inaccuracy in your . . . editorial. . . ." That Hoover directed a lesser degree of bombast at the *News* is understandable since he likes this newspaper.

Many times, the Director has allowed right-wing publications to answer for him. A good example was *America's Future*, fanatically partisan where Hoover is concerned, taking issue with the *New York Times* for its opposition to Hoover's reappointment at the advent of the Nixon administration.

This publication approached the subject using the typical sniper tactic.

In part, *America's Future* stated: "It was interesting to note that perhaps the greatest tribute to Mr. Hoover's retention as head of the FBI came not necessarily from those who properly praised the choice but from the *Daily World,* the official New York paper of the Communist party in the United States. It was, of course, horrified at Mr. Hoover's reappointment, which was to be expected. The sad part of its horror was that it was able to quote the illustrious *New York Times* in support of its position. But no doubt the majority of Americans are happy in the knowledge that the official Communist party newspaper opposes Mr. Hoover, even if it has the concurrence of the *Times*."

Such snide snickers from Hoover-backers in the press immediately classify any publications critical of the Director as being aligned, in theory at least, with the Communists.

When Beacon Press published the *Pentagon Papers,* its parent organization, the Unitarian Universalist Association, was investigated by the Bureau. The FBI examined the association's donor lists and bank records. The association charged the Bureau with conducting a "punitive" investigation. But that is Hoover's way of safeguarding national security, and the association should have known better.

Columnists Drew Pearson and Jack Anderson should have known better, too, when they picked one of Hoover's congressional friends as an editorial target. "When we began exposing the chicanery in Dodd's [Senator Thomas Dodd, D., Conn.] office," Pearson and Anderson wrote in 1969, "FBI agents photostated all the documents in our possession, then turned the investigation around and began snooping into our news sources."

Another report has it that if a president wanted to know if one of his cabinet members was leaking information to a columnist, Hoover "might arrange for surveillance of the columnist."

In 1950, when lawyer Max Lowenthal published his attack on Hoover, *The Federal Bureau of Investigation,* the Director's press pals went to work smearing the author. Invectives and unsubstantiated charges were lavished on Lowenthal, including this sample from two pro-Hooverites:

"He [Lowenthal] wrote the unwieldy book purporting to pulverize the FBI which sold only six thousand copies. Almost as many were given away. Yet no one knows much about him. He is a shadowy figure who thrives on obscurity. . . . His name does not appear in *Who's Who.* . . . Born in Minneapolis in 1888, he attended Harvard Law School, like many other parlor pinks, fellow-travelers, Communists, and convicted perjurers. . . ."

Fred J. Cook had no sooner published his *The FBI Nobody Knows* than the Hoover partisans were at his throat in print. Since Cook had interviewed many people whose positions would be in jeopardy should their names be mentioned, he naturally kept these sources anonymous. For this reason he was attacked and discredited by two Hoover backers with: "We recognize that the press has an established right to protect its sources. But in this age of the anonymous smear, it does well to use this right sparingly." Perhaps the two writers might have been thinking about the uses of intelligence reports in J. Edgar Hoover's files.

William W. Turner's *Hoover's FBI* caused the author, an ex-FBI man, to be investigated at every turn. Magazine editors considering Turner's material for publication were approached by FBI agents who convinced them not to publish it. That he was tailed from talk show to talk show was evidenced by Tom Snyder's (host of a KYW-TV talk show in Philadelphia) greeting to him: "We even knew the color suit you'd be wearing."

For other members of the press, the Bureau reserves the cold shoulder; they are on the FBI's "No Contact" list and are therefore not privy to the Bureau's gossipy "leaks." They are, as one news source stated, "the persons who have spoken critically of the Bureau and are in a position to spread public word of any direct contact with the Bureau."

According to this report, some of those on this "No Contact" list include columnist Carl Rowan, investigative reporter for the *Miami Herald,* Gene Miller, Amherst University historian, Henry Steele Commager, and Robert M. Hutchins, president of the Center for the Study of Democratic Institutions. The entire staff of the *Washington Post* is also on the list.

But Hoover's "No Contact" roster does not confine itself to the press. Notably, politicians, with Senator McGovern and former Senator Eugene McCarthy at the top, have been placed on this list.

These are the men who, in recent years, have dulled Hoover's clout with Congress and therefore are considered perhaps more dangerous to the Director's reign than any member of the press.

In the case of Capitol Hill, it is not what is said about Hoover but what is done for him. It is in this arena that the Director, in order to stay in office, must be awarded annually two ears, a tail, and all the hooves.

# 14

# Hoover's Power Elite

The lights in the FBI building used to burn bright on the eve of a congressional election. Hoover's employees were kept busy typing letters of congratulation to those engaged in congressional battles. There was a letter for each candidate signed by the Director's own hand. The finished letters resting on desk tops, FBI personnel awaited the final results with impatience. Once the election was over, the weary employees mailed letters to all the winners, and dumped the losers' mail into trash cans.

Recently, Hoover changed that system of ingratiation. Now, no one waits all night for the election results. The Director's letters of congratulation are mailed several days after the elections are concluded. In these practical days, Hoover no longer has time for losers.

The Director's relations with Congress are personal and intense; they go far beyond staff-written letters to election victors. Hoover actively courts the friendships of the most influential national leaders on Capitol Hill. These selected officials, along with phalanxes of ex-FBI agents, are the Director's wellspring of permanent power.

Leading the congressional Hoover-backers is Vice-President Spiro T. Agnew. Following the charge by Hale Boggs that Hoover had been tapping the phones of congressmen, Agnew, in an address, praised the Director and flatly dismissed the possibility of any FBI wrongdoing. "The Bureau does not have the time or the manpower for the surveillance that it is accused of maintaining on innocent people," Agnew stated.

The vice-president also grouped most of Hoover's critics into the un-American camp of "subversives, mobsters, extremists and anarchists—enemies of the American system, who quite naturally detest an agency [the FBI] that stands between them and the accomplishment of their objectives —the perversion or destruction of our institutions."

Agnew did concede that recent criticism of Hoover stemmed from other typically political sources, singling out Senators Muskie and McGovern. "These opportunists," the vice-president charged, "are being aided and abetted by certain of their friends in the liberal news media who automatically shout 'Right on!' every time someone claims his civil liberties have been threatened, regardless of the transparency of such charges."

The defense of the Director by Agnew was obviously another way in which he could direct his attacks against what he thinks to be an antagonistic press. Answering critics who charged that Hoover was getting too old for his job as the FBI chief, Agnew stated, "I have complete confidence in this dedicated, steel-willed public servant with the twenty-twenty vision. . . ."

And even if Hoover was getting on, Agnew explained, so were a lot of the newsmen who were insisting that Hoover retire because of his advanced years. "And just the other night, the commentator, Eric Sevareid, in a mild disparagement, described the FBI Director as 'surrounded by old cronies.' One would assume that Mr. Sevareid isn't surrounded by old cronies. Yet, with silver hair and silken voice, he has appeared before us nightly for years in tandem with the familiar countenance of Walter Cronkite."

Next to the vice-president, Hoover's staunchest supporters in Congress appear to be those who control the flow of funds to the Bureau from the Senate and House. Senator John McClellan (D., Ark.) and Congressman John J. Rooney (D., N.Y.), chairmen of the companion appropriations committees, are close, personal friends of Hoover. It has been their habit to always allow Hoover more than ample time to make his case when testifying before their committees each year.

Rooney is the one who okays the expenditure for Hoover's new bullet-proof car each year. The congressman's feelings for Hoover run deep and have caused him to utter sharp statements against the elected officials who have criticized the Director in recent years. Rooney called McGovern "a lightweight," and declared he would write Muskie a letter telling him "I will not support you for anything."

Long-time FBI admirer Rooney does not consider the Bureau faultless, however. "They're entitled to a few boners once in a while," he insists.

While some congressmen demand Hoover answer for his activities and those of his agents, others, whenever the Director is criticized, rush to his defense, using their free-mail privilege to aid their cause.

Congressman John T. Myers of Indiana, in the wake of Boggs' tidal wave, mailed out a two-page release entitled "In Defense of the FBI." In part, the letter read: "My contact with Mr. Hoover, and those of my colleagues, confirm that the Director is just as sharp, just as alert as he has been throughout the entire forty-one [*sic*] years of service to his nation. I consider it an outrage and a shame as he approaches the time when he might retire, that this dedicated public servant should be subjected to these kind of irresponsible, unsubstantiated charges raised in recent days.

"The baseless allegations raised to date are an insult to every member of the FBI and to the integrity and intelligence of every American. Until hard evidence is produced, my faith in the FBI and its leadership remains unshaken."

Senator John Sparkman of Alabama, a strong voice in the U.S. Senate, also wanted to make sure that his intense and positive feeling for Hoover and the FBI reached his voters via the free government mail privilege he enjoys. Sparkman said: "J. Edgar Hoover has guided and shaped the FBI in such a way that his department has the overwhelming respect and admiration of professional officers throughout the country and of the American people. There are those in American society today who seem to feed on disrespect for law enforcement. It seems to me that attention should be called from time to time to the vital stake that our citizens have in effective law enforcement. I congratulate Mr. Hoover on a job well done."

Other congressmen have felt a need to do more than inform their voters on how strongly they felt about the Director. Congressman William L. Dickinson of California wrote President Nixon: "Mr. Hoover has my utmost confidence, and I hope you will not be swayed by scurrilous attacks upon him personally and upon the Federal Bureau of Investigation. Our enemies—both foreign and domestic —would like nothing better than an ever-increasing criticism of the FBI. I hope you will remain firm."

President Nixon, though he has publicly supported Hoover, remains somewhat undecided on the question of keeping the Director in his position. As one member of the White House staff observed, "It's axiomatic that in a law-and-order administration, you don't fire your top policeman. . . ." The aide went on to add, "There has been talk about how do you get rid of Hoover gracefully without hurting him. Because of his age, if nothing else, he has become a problem. But how do you get rid of a national institution?"

Others, particularly many congressmen, do not consider the Director the totemic being his friends deem him to be. In addition to Senators Muskie and McGovern, and former Senator Eugene McCarthy, Senators Edward Kennedy, Birch Bayh, and Harold Hughes have demanded that Hoover step down and out.

Other members of Congress have approached the problem of getting rid of Hoover differently. Bella S. Abzug (D., N.Y.) recently introduced a resolution calling for a House Judiciary Committee study of the FBI. But this has been attempted before, and such attempts have always foundered because of the abysmal haggling by pro-Hoover congressmen on the committees.

Congressman William R. Anderson (D., Tenn.) was one of the first to publicly risk taking on Hoover by telling him to put up or shut up regarding the Director's premature announcement of the alleged Berrigan plot. Anderson summed up the general attitude of his peers when he commented, "Many members of Congress have a great fear of Mr. Hoover."

Anderson could have added that this situation is no different now than it was in 1924. There were rumors then that the FBI had been gathering incriminating information on Washington politicians who were against Coolidge administration policies, in order to destroy their political careers.

Shortly after Hoover took office, Senator Jones of Washington asked him if he had issued orders to have these investigations halted. The Director replied, "Most certainly.

Instructions have been sent to officers in the field to limit their investigations in the field to violations of the statutes." The irony of such a statement on Hoover's part is that though he denied such practices were taking place, he nevertheless ordered them stopped.

Then again, Hoover's double-talk brings to mind his odd dealings with certain members of Congress. Whereas he emphatically denies having investigated any Capitol Hill politician, he reportedly has investigated persons pointed out by congressional friends of the FBI. According to one source, Senator Thomas Dodd (D., Conn.) asked the Bureau for surveillance of "an office employee" to "report back on his romantic activities." This the FBI did.

Dodd is a former FBI agent and one of those who took part in the abortive raid to capture Dillinger at Little Bohemia, Wisconsin, in 1934. This loyal Hoover supporter has had a rather spectacular career himself since he left the Bureau after approximately one year's service.

Elected in 1952 as a congressman, Dodd ran for his Senate seat in 1958. After this win, the senator entrenched himself in the powerful Foreign Relations and Judiciary committees. It was Dodd who helped to soundly quash two bills in 1963 and 1965 that would have made it mandatory for the Senate to confirm the appointment of the head of the FBI rather than his being arbitrarily selected by the attorney general.

Senator Dodd's voting habits were also peculiar. When the Senate was deciding whether or not to confirm President Nixon's nominee, Judge Clement F. Haynsworth, for a Supreme Court post, Dodd entered the Senate chamber late. This tardiness caused him to be the ninety-ninth senator called on the roll. By that time, the Senate had already decided against Haynsworth, and Dodd voiced a quick nay when called. Yet when Vice-President Agnew left the

Hoover in 1954, ready for business and the Reds. The Director helped Senator Joseph Mc-Carthy in every way during the witch hunts. (Wide World)

Senator Joseph McCarthy (right), Hoover's close friend, conducted the Communist conspiracy investigations of the early 1950s. He rests here while his chief counsel, Roy Cohn, another Hoover favorite, does the grilling. (Wide World)

Lewis Rosensteil of Schenley Industries; he donated over $1 million to the Hoover Foundation and bought up all of Hoover's books for friends. (Wide World)

Soviet master spy Colonel Rudolf Abel (left) was captured through CIA operatives, but Hoover took the credit. (Wide World)

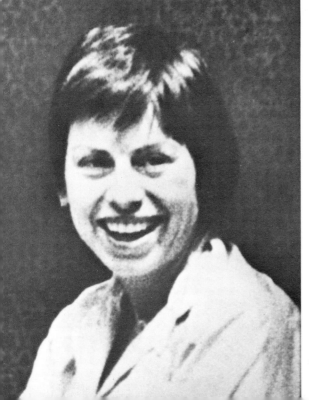

Judith Coplon spied on the FBI for the Russians and never served a day in jail, thanks to FBI inefficiency. (Wide World)

Raymond Moley, one of FDR's brain trusters, saved Hoover's job when the president wanted to fire the FBI Chief. The Director showed his gratitude years later. (UPI)

Hoover has a drink with Attorney General Homer Cummings, who never interfered with the Director's doings. (UPI)

Hoover with Attorney General J. Howard McGrath in 1951. They split over slot machines. (Wide World)

Assistant director of the FBI and long time Hoover booster, Lou Nichols, went to work for Rosensteil and labored long for Richard Nixon's election. (UPI)

Dr. Martin Luther King criticized the Bureau; Hoover called him a liar and bugged the civil rights leader's phone. (Wide World)

Both Hoover and his friend Clyde Tolson are beyond retirement age, but the Director got around that easily enough. (Wide World)

Senator Thomas J. Dodd, an ex-FBI man and staunch Hooverite, was censured by the Senate for spending political contributions for his personal needs. (UPI)

The Director attending a recent party for Martha Mitchell at which time he stated that criticism of the FBI "doesn't bother me at all." (UPI)

J. Edgar Hoover walking toward the president's plane on his way to Florida to celebrate his seventy-seventh birthday. Plans for the future? "None of them includes retirement." (UPI)

chamber, one source stated, his tally sheet listing possible votes was inspected and Dodd's name was listed in the "Yea" column.

More serious was the charge that Senator Dodd spent campaign funds raised at "Dodd Day" dinners in 1963-64 for his personal use.

The Senate was informed that Dodd had written then Vice-President Johnson on August 5, 1963, requesting him to attend a "Dodd Day" fund-raising event in Connecticut on October 26, 1963. The ever-wary Johnson wanted a signed letter from Dodd which guaranteed the fact that the funds raised were to be strictly applied to the senator's campaign. Dodd sent a letter affirming this fact.

Yet, after a lengthy investigation, the Senate censured Dodd on June 23, 1967, by a vote of ninety-two to five on the grounds that he had spent $116,083 to repair his house, pay liquor and personal travel bills, cancel personal loans, and pay delinquent federal taxes, though these funds were campaign donations given for political use.

Even more interesting is the Department of Justice's handling of the Dodd affair and Attorney General Mitchell's quick dismissal of any criminal prosecution against Dodd on income-tax charges. The ex-FBI agent's lawyer, Edward Bennett Williams, was told in a letter by Mitchell: "This is to inform you that the United States will institute no criminal prosecution against your client."

It is interesting to note that the U.S. attorney most energetically opposed to Dodd's prosecution was Richard Crane, who had worked in Senator Dodd's offices prior to the Department of Justice appointment.

Hoover's ties with Congress are strengthened by administrative appointees who are close to him and his thinking. In 1969, the Director recommended Major General Carl C. Turner for the post of chief U.S. marshal in the Nixon administration. Supposedly cleared for this position by the Bureau, Turner unexpectedly quit this post in September of 1969. This was followed by a Senate probe of army graft involving General Turner, who was charged with covering up kickbacks to sergeants running service clubs. General Turner was also accused of using his post to obtain guns from two police departments—Kansas City and Chicago—guns that he sold or kept in his private collection.

In May of 1967, Hoover had given General Turner a special award "in appreciation of his valuable assistance to the FBI."

Hoover's idea of "valuable assistance" from police departments across the country is homage to the Director. Many police chiefs know that to earn such credit from the Bureau necessitates allowing the FBI to take over any case it enters, particularly the kind of cases that will win the Bureau flashy headlines.

Hoover's propaganda-type infiltration of police departments has been offending chiefs for years. In 1948, Hugh Clegg, an assistant director of the FBI, addressed the International Association of Chiefs of Police, telling the law enforcement officers that the best police chief "cooperates with the FBI in such a generous manner that he has earned our undying gratitude." Clegg was referring to those chiefs who sent their officers to the FBI police academy school, sent in fingerprints to the FBI, and sent laboratory problems to the Bureau in Washington.

The IACP has praised the "Honorable J. Edgar Hoover" in florid resolutions each year. The resolutions praising the Director, however, not only were written by FBI officials but were approved by Hoover before being delivered.

When O. W. Wilson of the Chicago Police Department and William Parker of the Los Angeles Police Department began to emerge in the late 1950s as recognized authorities in law enforcement, Hoover's reaction was one of suspicion if not envy. These men, showing exceptional organizational abilities and revolutionary techniques that achieved quicker results, became recognized law enforcement leaders whose prestige surpassed that of the Director.

The showdown between Hoover and the IACP came in 1959 when Chief Parker was nominated for sixth vice-president at the association's annual convention. On the following day, when Parker's nomination came to a vote, someone on the floor nominated the Newton (Massachusetts) police chief, Philip Purcell, in opposition to Parker. Purcell won the vice-presidency by a three-to-one vote.

Almost ten years later, Chief Purcell was asked if the FBI had anything to do with keeping Parker from the IACP post. Retired, Purcell openly admitted, "Oh, yes. Hoover poisoned Parker."

This kind of behind-the-scenes intriguing by the FBI angered IACP members and, moreover, convinced them that their organization should grow independent of Bureau control and become the rightful leader in American law enforcement. When ex-FBI official Quinn Tamm was interviewed for the job of the organization's executive director, he was asked bluntly if his former job would prompt him to interfere in IACP operations. Tamm gave a vigorous no.

Tamm, now recognized as one of the guiding spirits and honored experts of modern law enforcement, emphasized his nonallegiance to Hoover in the 1962 IACP convention in St. Louis. He insisted in his address to members that the IACP should remain "the dominant voice in law enforcement." As an added criticism of the Director, Tamm added that in the past "this . . . has not been true."

Under Tamm's leadership the association, within six years, increased its budget from $272,800 to $2,300,000 in order to accelerate and enlarge training, management consultant, and other much needed police services.

Police Chief Purcell's criticism of Hoover earned him the swift vengeance of the Director. When the FBI's annual National Academy Associates booklet was issued January 1, 1967, Purcell's name was missing. Purcell had graduated from the FBI academy in 1946, and this was the first time he was not mentioned in more than twenty years. An ex-Bureau official stated that this omission was deliberate on the part of the Director. "Mr. Hoover struck the name," according to a news source, "and cut off the Newton Police Department from FBI training and some other services.

"The incident is significant because it confirms what many police chiefs fear: that they also could be cut off if they incur Mr. Hoover's displeasure."

Parker, Wilson, and Purcell were not the only police chiefs who had trouble with Hoover because they refused to allow the Bureau to dominate their operations. Those chiefs who will not be ramrodded by the FBI usually wind up in FBI files with critical notations attached to their names. A file in the New Haven (Connecticut) office of the FBI has a notation about the local police force under the command of James Ahern.

When Ahern was appointed chief of police, he was visited by an FBI agent, who identified himself as the liaison between the FBI and the New Haven police. Ahern welcomed the agent and told him that if a criminal case involving FBI authority developed, his department would certainly call the Bureau. Pointing out that Ahern apparently did not understand, the agent went on to explain that his "liaison" job was to review daily active police cases and the intelligence reports of the New Haven Police Department.

Ahern said he would agree to that procedure only if one of his men could review daily the FBI's active cases. The

FBI agent was shocked and replied that such an agreement was impossible.

Chief Ahern then told the agent that the FBI plan was not acceptable. Later, a memo was attached to the FBI's file on the New Haven Police Department (the Bureau maintains a file on almost every police department in the country), a memo ordering no cooperation with Ahern and his police force because it was "anti-Bureau."

Hoover continually attempts to direct police thinking from on high. A special method he employs to achieve this end is issuing monthly bulletins "To All Law Enforcement Officials." In one of these bulletins, Hoover took pains to retaliate against the President's Crime Commission for stressing the necessity of rehabilitating criminals. This was definitely against the Hoover credo. The Director's bulletin read:

"Actually, the American public is seeking, and sorely needs, a proven formula to deter crime. The people are growing tired of substitutes. Swift detection and apprehension, prompt prosecution, and proper and certain punishment are tested crime deterrents. Coddling of criminals and soft justice increase crime; denials to the contrary have no valid support. Yet, these truths are still lost in the maze of sympathy and leniency heaped upon the criminal. Lame excuses and apologies offered for the lawbreaker are exceeded only by the amount of violence he commits."

Such archaic and rigid "the law is the law" pronouncements by Hoover were echoed by his chief "axe-man," Cartha "Deke" DeLoach, who always considered himself the Director's heir apparent. DeLoach, according to a former Department of Justice official, "pointed to a common denominator between real criminals and peace and civil rights demonstrators. 'All these people believe they are above the law,' he said."

Cartha DeLoach, it will be remembered, was the man whose hospital bills were paid by J. Edgar Hoover. He was also the man who showed up as the FBI's new liaison agent to the White House, replacing Courtney Evans almost immediately after President Kennedy's assassination; DeLoach was a long-time friend of Lyndon Johnson. As one Hoover critic put it, "This small detail of promptly substituting DeLoach for Evans is the sort of thing—duplicated thousands of times—that has been crucial to Hoover's remarkable longevity."

Assistant Director DeLoach showed up again as the Bureau's representative on President Johnson's National Crime Commission. In this capacity, DeLoach defended Hoover to the nth degree and refused to discuss anything that even remotely criticized the Bureau's crime statistics or Hoover's theories on crime.

The Department of Justice press secretary, Edwin Guthman, called DeLoach and some other FBI men to a special meeting about Joseph Valachi. Guthman told the agents that allowing Joseph Valachi to tell his *Cosa Nostra* story publicly would be a good combative tactic against the syndicate. Guthman wanted to know Hoover's thinking. He was stalled off by the FBI agents for two days. Finally, DeLoach reportedly told Guthman to "go ahead and do it."

After Valachi "went public," DeLoach and the other FBI men who met with Guthman "leaked the word that they had done it against their will." Guthman added that "we [the Justice Department] made the mistake of dealing with them [the FBI] like we dealt with everybody else. . . . We didn't understand that they never really said what they were thinking. Dealing with the Bureau was a different deal."

Dealing with Hoover's emissary, Cartha DeLoach, was also risky business. It was DeLoach, one source has it, who leaked the scandalous reports of Dr. Martin Luther King's alleged promiscuity. He played tapes on the matter for journalists, but then told them that if they credited him with the information he would deny it.

When the rumor that Bobby Kennedy was thinking of replacing Hoover reached him, Cartha DeLoach, who was head of the press-servicing Criminal Records Division, questioned Kennedy's press secretary, Guthman, repeatedly seeking to verify such rumors.

Cartha DeLoach left the Bureau in 1970 at the age of fifty to become an executive of the Pepsico Company. This firm is run by Donald M. Kendall, a close associate of President Nixon. DeLoach himself became friendly with Nixon while handling the Bureau's public relations. (His having left the FBI does not rule him out as a possible replacement for Hoover.)

FBI agents who leave the Bureau almost always continue to support the Director unquestioningly. From influential positions in American business and law enforcement, these agents, for the most part, energetically come to Hoover's defense whenever he is challenged or criticized.

The list of those ex-agents is almost endless; a few now or at one time in prominent positions are: Robert E. Lee, federal communications commissioner; Harvey G. Foster, vice-president of American Airlines; John Bugas, once vice-president of Ford Motor Company; Harold M. Perry, president of the CIT Financial Corporation; Edwin Foltz, president of the international division of Campbell Soup Company; George Myers, executive vice-president of Standard Oil Company of Indiana; William J. Quinn, president of the Chicago, Milwaukee, St. Paul, and Pacific Railroad.

Hoover's power stems not only from these ex-FBI agents, who exercise considerable economic influence, but also from former agents who are active in Congress. Ten former agents have become members of the House: Omar Burleson

(D., Tex.), Robert V. Denney (R., Nebr.), Samuel L. Devine (R., Ohio), Ed Edmonson (D., Okla.), Donald Edwards (D., Calif.), Lawrence J. Hogan (R., Md.), Wiley Mayne (R., Iowa), H. Allen Smith (R., Calif.), and Wendell Wyatt (R., Oreg.). William T. Cahill, another former agent, was a Republican congressman from New Jersey until he was elected that state's governor in 1969.

Aside from Congressman Edwards, who is a liberal, these representatives toe the Hoover line at all levels. Congressman Smith, for instance, has regularly fought for legislation that would guarantee Hoover's successor to be an FBI agent who has had seven years of experience with the Bureau (and who is, therefore, the Director's hand-picked candidate).

Police departments throughout the country are saturated with former FBI agents, but these men generally have a weaker political bent than those in business and on Capitol Hill, and also are less inclined to nod agreement at Hoover's every announcement.

The Society of Former Agents of the FBI, to which most ex-agents belong, however, wields enormous power on local levels, where the Bureau is more feared. When the Boggs controversy raged in 1971, several chapters of this society loudly rallied to Hoover's support.

For example, the north-central chapter of the society, in its annual meeting, April 17, 1971, adopted a resolution which praised the Director's record and deplored allegations by his critics. This resolution was formally drawn up, and, in the best Bureau tradition, released to the press. It was given wide coverage, as were similar resolutions elsewhere.

The north-central chapter's resolution said, in part, that there was no basis "to the criticism by some" that "the FBI has become oppressive in its investigative activities and is becoming a threat to the civil liberties of citizens. . . . We know without any question that the FBI, under the most explicit direction of Mr. Hoover, has jealously protected the nation against any invasion of these liberties."

William O. Gray, national president of the society (which boasts a membership of fifty-five hundred), stated that "the attack on Mr. Hoover is very much unjustified, for he and the FBI have done a fine job in performing the duties imposed on them by Congress."

Regional president of the society, Duane Traynor, went further in the society's orgiastic eulogy for the Director. He said that there was "no fairer man who ever lived or was more attuned to the needs of the nation than Mr. Hoover."

Rooted in Congress, in executive levels of American business, in local law enforcement agencies, and in the legal-judicial areas of small communities throughout the country, former FBI agents actually function as a massive secret society which stands stoically behind every move made by J. Edgar Hoover; a society constantly at the ready to initiate public outcries against any criticism leveled at him. The reason why these men are so unswerving in their loyalty to the Director is one of simple survival, since many of them have obtained their positions purely on the basis of having been agents of the FBI.

It is this right-wing force in America, coupled with the conservative element of Congress, that makes up the Director's private power elite, a force that is activated like flame to powder every time a new threat arises against Hoover; many shouting like one voice that "no fairer man ever lived."

# 15

# The Inner Directives

The thinking and words of J. Edgar Hoover are, and always have been, harsh and uncompromising. To Hoover's supporters, his philosophy—ranging from theories of crime to concepts of the Communist threat—merely reflects his hard-pressed, lonely position as America's law enforcement leader; they believe he is a man forced to pedestal pronouncements because of his intimate knowledge of our society's state of affairs.

To the Director's detractors, he is an archaic symbol of ruthless authoritarianism, who mumbles jingoistic and illogical phrases to further his pet crusades and wishes to arbitrate American ethics and morality.

Even a casual study of his writings and reports reveals Hoover to be paradoxical, vituperative, and monotonously repetitive. His thinking, like his tactics, hasn't changed since he took office. Change itself is anathema to Hoover; he undoubtedly views change as a threat to his authority and corrosive of a system that has perpetuated his stoic image for close to fifty years.

The Director's attitude toward communism, for example,

has not altered since he first envisioned it, in 1919, as a worldwide menace. Communism haunts Hoover; perhaps fear of its existence goads him on, making him cling to his office long after he should have settled into introspective retirement.

Yet to retire would appear to signal some sort of concession by Hoover, perhaps even a denial of everything he has stood for. To the Director, retirement is more than vacating an office. It is abandoning ideals and discarding methods; it is desertion and defeat. Therefore, any measure that retains the Bureau under his direction is essential, whether it be promoting fear of the Red dagger at our throat or warning of the criminal hand in our pocket.

Hoover has never tired of reminding us of the Communist threat. In 1959, the Director said, "The international Communist conspiracy is clearly the greatest menace free civilization has ever known." In *Masters of Deceit,* Hoover exhorted the public to be ever watchful for Communist conspirators. He asked: "What can one do in the fight against communism?

"I repeat: a lot. Always remember that this fight is something which must be carried on soberly, seriously, and, above all, *responsibly.* Our best weapons are facts and the truth. 'And ye shall know the truth, and the truth shall make you free.' "

Beyond his spiritual advocations, Hoover explicitly told the American public how to spot a Communist who was trying to avoid detection on the road. According to Hoover, Communists resort to:

1. Driving alternately at high and low rates of speed.
2. Entering a heavily traveled intersection on a yellow light, hoping to lose any follower or cause an accident.

3. Turning corners at high rates of speed and stopping abruptly.
4. Suddenly leaving a car and walking hurriedly down a one-way street in the direction in which vehicle traffic is prohibited.
5. Entering a dark street in a residential area at night, making a sharp U turn, cutting into a side alley, and extinguishing the car's lights.
6. Driving in rural areas, taking a long walk in a field, then having another car meet them.
7. Waiting until the last minute, then making a sharp left turn in front of on-coming traffic.
8. Stopping at every filling station on the highway, walking around the car, always looking, then going on.

Heaven help the motorists who have such driving habits. The public can take great comfort in knowing that any driver running a yellow light is probably a Red, or at least a pinko.

In 1947, Hoover stymied critics who challenged his theories on communism. "Anyone who opposes the American Communist," he stated, "is at once branded as a disrupter, a Fascist, a Red baiter, or a Hitlerite, and becomes the object of a systematic campaign of character assassination. This is easily understood because the basic tactics of the Communist party are deceit and trickery."

Thus to be anti-Hoover was to be branded a Communist.

The Director never seemed to exhaust this theme. Seven years later he stated, "It is an established fact that whenever one has dared to expose the Communist threat, he has invited upon himself the adroit and skilled talents of experts of character assassination."

But when it came to Communists and communism,

Hoover was *the* expert and he knew whereof he spoke. Hadn't he been battling the Reds for years? It was his long experience with the evils of communism and with the stealthy infiltration of radical thought in America which, no doubt, prompted him to state in 1937, "Youth is unable to evaluate such theories [radical ideas] properly."

More than thirty years later, Hoover was moved to say that "we do not give sufficient attention and credit to the responsible youth of our country." But this contradictory statement served only to preface Hoover's reaffirmation that "too many in America today are blinded by the permissiveness of the New Left and the communist conspiracy. These influences instigate, nurture, and foment discontent so as to bewilder, terrify, and undermine a constructive society."

The meat of Hoover's philosophy was then served up in this 1968 statement: "Unless we stand united with a free society *ruled by supremacy of law* [italics mine]—we shall fall prey to the forces which seek to enslave the world."

Hoover's black-and-white code demands only one kind of decision from the American public: "To my mind the big question for every American is whether he wants to support and defend our free society or let it be overrun and destroyed by visionary agitators, whether he wants to promote the cause of justice and order or give in to crime and chaos, and whether he wants to hold the line on decency and morality or let depravity and degeneracy corrupt our populace. . . . Freedom for all citizens cannot exist without order and self-discipline."

Hoover has never believed that a society should be directed by an intellectual elite. His attitude toward intellectuals is, at best, a grudging tolerance. The Director is suspicious of any college professor who steps forth from his classroom to pass comment on political events. These are "the false liberals who would subvert our Constitution and undermine our democratic processes in furtherance of their selfish ends."

To counter these disruptive voices in our society, Hoover advocates more ministers of the caliber of Dr. Norman Vincent Peale and Bishop Fulton J. Sheen "to preach sermons that are understood by all people."

The New Left poses the greatest threat to our way of life today, Hoover insists. "They are the Communists and other subversive elements who wave false banners of legitimacy and patriotism while relentlessly plotting to destroy our heritage of freedom."

Black groups play no small part in this new conspiracy. The Director pointed out in 1969 that "the growing number of Black extremist organizations throughout the United States represents a potential threat to the internal security of the nation."

A year later he painstakingly detailed a complex plot being developed by one of these groups, the Republic of New Africa (RNA), to aid foreign invaders. "RNA was established for the purpose of forming a Black nation inside the United States. Its structure was designed to be revolutionary in nature, and its founders proposed that efforts be made for international recognition with assistance from Fidel Castro's Cuba, Red China, Tanzania, and other nations.

"Steps have been taken to buy land in Mississippi where RNA proposes to build a landing strip long enough for 'Chinese jets to land.'

"The group's plans call for the establishment of a Black army to be known as the Black Legion. A training program has been formulated and a complete uniform has been designed, including leopard-skin epaulets."

Hoover has not overlooked the press. He has labeled American news media as the willing tool of demonstrators:

"Professional demagogues, extremists, and revolutionaries have learned that the news media—television in particular —are their most effective weapon to gain notoriety and to discredit law enforcement."

Just as the political revolutionary endangers the American way, his evil twin, the criminal, "reaches into every community of our land."

"Were I to list what I believe to be one of the greatest present-day contributors to our growing crime annals," Hoover wrote in 1938, "I am afraid that I should be forced to lay the blame squarely at the door of parental over-indulgence." It is this permissiveness along with a general relaxation of total authority that creates the American criminal, according to Hoover.

Such conditions give rise to disobedience, delinquency, promiscuity, and habitual criminality. Hoover, therefore, has forever advocated the hard line with juvenile offenders. In 1961 he stated, "There are still among us muddle-headed sentimentalists who would wrap teenage brigands in the protective cocoon of the term 'juvenile delinquency' with emphasis upon all its connotations of youthful prankishness. . . . As a representative of law enforcement, I would like to see the term 'juvenile delinquency' banished forever from our language as a description for vicious acts. Such teenager gangsterism should be labeled for exactly what it is—'youthful criminality.' "

The Director added, in 1962, that teenage delinquents were "beastly punks."

Hoover has saved his most vitriolic statements for adult criminals. To him they have always been "fungus . . . human vermin . . . rodents." Big name gangsters such as Dillinger deserve the best of Hoover's lexicon. The Indiana bandit was a "super rodent . . . low and vile . . . public rat number one . . . a cheap, selfish, tightfisted plug-ugly." Any woman ever associated with a criminal was a "cheap, deluded, silly little moll."

In 1938, Hoover separated these females into two classes —dominating mothers and fast women. For the Director, the epitome of the fast woman was the notorious wife of "Machine Gun" Kelly, Kathryn Thorne Kelly. "She was attractive to look upon," he wrote, "of good carriage, and pleasing mannerism. She was excellently and expensively dressed, especially when driving about in her big, sixteen-cylinder automobile, with silver fox furs floating from her smooth shoulders. . . . Kathryn Kelly [was] sleek, well-dressed, alluring of face and body. . . . Her good appearance, her mannerisms of innocence, and a certain queer quality which almost could be called charm, permitted her an entree [into the inner sanctums of the underworld] denied most gun molls. . . ."

Devastating though she was, Hoover knew the real Kathryn Kelly to be a "cunning, shrewd criminal-actress. . . . Here was a woman who could conceive a kidnapping, and force it through to a conclusion largely through her domination over her husband, who, in spite of his terrorizing name, could only bow before her tirades—and do as she bade him.

"If ever there was a henpecked man, it was George 'Machine Gun' Kelly."

Eve, the serpent, and "Machine Gun" Kelly formed the triangle which to Hoover's mind brought about the damnation of the gullible, susceptible, and "impure" apprentice gangster.

While the "alluring" Kathryn Kelly epitomized Hoover's idea of the spider woman of crime, the "mother lode of crime" was Arizona Kate Clark "Ma" Barker, mother of the four Barker brothers and mentor to Alvin "Old Creepy" Karpis, whose downfall was Hoover's white plume of achievement.

Hoover has always taken motherhood and its responsibilities seriously. In a 1944 article, the FBI chief stated that the problem in America was "not juvenile delinquency but adult delinquency" under the headline, "Mothers . . . Our Only Hope."

He condemned a criminal for "using your mother's home as a hideout." He damned criminals who abused their mothers by being "maudlin concerning yourself and cynical about the feelings of others. Believe yourself fine and noble if you indulge in cheap sentimentalities about sweethearts, parents, babies, or animals, thus building a psychology by which you can condone murder if 'you have always been a good boy to your mother.' "

Ma Barker was the symbol of warped motherhood. "In her sixty or so years," Hoover stated, "this woman became a monument to the evils of parental indulgence." She was "an animal mother of the she-wolf type" who had turned into "a veritable beast of prey."

Hoover relished telling of this evil woman's end in a wild shootout (in 1935 at a remote Florida resort), which resulted in the death of Ma Barker and her son Fred. FBI agents had called on them to surrender, Hoover recalled, "but there was no surrender in the heart of Ma Barker or that of her dominated son."

FBI justice prevailed. Both were shot to pieces. "Freddie had been pierced by eleven bullets, Ma Barker by three. One had gone through her heart. In her pocketbook was found $10,200, in bills of large denominations. Crime had paid Kate Barker extremely well, except in the things which really count."

Ma Barker and Kathryn Kelly had violated the cardinal virtues of womankind. They had forsaken family and God, and they had paid the price. Their sons and husbands had been dominated sheep, and that contributed to their fall.

It was this kind of prosaic and hortative thinking that undoubtedly led Hoover to ignore any possible salvation for the convicted criminal. Regarding the paroling of prisoners, Hoover once bombastically stated, "I'm going to tell the truth about . . . the slimy, silly or sob-sister convict lovers who let them out on sentimental or ill-advised paroles."

Another time he urged that "a criminal should be regarded with utter revulsion; such a viewpoint is the best insurance against temptation." The Director's philosophy regarding convicts is simple. They broke the law, they must pay the penalty. Those who oppose a criminal's execution by the state are "misguided do-gooders," "maudlin viewers of the death penalty," and "Bible quoters who object to capital punishment."

The Director believes that parole for prisoners is too great a risk for society to take. Criminals who have broken their word once will do it again. "Sentimentalists tell us," he once wrote, "that we must not hold any type of offender in prison for the full length of his term 'because it will embitter him.' . . . Suppose they do become disheartened? Suppose they even become angry about it? To my mind, it is far better for a man to be angry in prison than to be a predatory animal outside of it."

Eight years later, Hoover had not relinquished his point of view: "Many of us become discouraged at times because of soft-hearted judges who grant unwarranted clemency to vicious criminals who tell tear-jerking stories. We grow tired of risking our lives time after time to apprehend dangerous men who are allowed new opportunities to prey upon society because of almost criminal laxity in granting paroles, prison 'vacations,' and pardons. Culpable neglect on the part of those charged with keeping dangerous convicts in confinement is another source of the law enforcement headache. . . . We have become soft in such matters."

One of those embittered men who came to Hoover's mind—in fact the criminal foremost in his mind—was John Dillinger (who was paroled in 1933 because his stepmother was dying). Of Dillinger, Hoover said, "Many trusting souls came to his defense on the basis that he had been embittered by a long sentence for burglary while his companion in the crime was given a shorter one. This was not true and I speak from the evidence of the voluminous reports turned in on this criminal by hard-working crews of special agents who followed his trail, day and night, for many months."

Dillinger's first crime was committed in 1924 when, following the lead of an older man, Edgar Singleton, he attempted to rob a grocer, B. F. Morgan, of his Saturday night receipts (it was not a burglary). After his apprehension Dillinger was given two to fourteen years and ten to twenty years (concurrent sentences) for the attempted robbery.

Edgar Singleton was given a much lighter sentence. Singleton was paroled in 1926; Dillinger spent seven more years behind bars than did the man who initiated the crime. Had Hoover's agents followed the trail leading back to the courtroom of Judge Joseph W. Williams, the Bible-quoting man who sentenced Dillinger, and examined his court records in Martinsville, Indiana, the Director might have learned why the Indiana outlaw became "embittered."

Hoover has never proposed methods of rehabilitation of criminals to any great extent. Yet he is most definite in knowing what convicts shouldn't do while incarcerated. One of the most important things a convict must not do while in prison, according to Hoover, is pursue a writing career.

In 1966, the Director said, "My feeling is that no person who is incarcerated in a penitentiary, particularly a federal penitentiary, should be allowed to write and have published any book, whether for money or not, while he is incarcerated. I think this is highly improper."

Apparently, such thinking extends to those outside of prison walls also. "By all means," Hoover stated in 1938, "let us extend education; but while we are doing so, we should remember that mere sharpening of the intellect will not produce a respect for law and order."

Law and order to J. Edgar Hoover means that the public should be alert and on the lookout for evildoers twenty-four hours a day. "Frankly," he once commented, "my purpose is to create apprehension—if someone could only teach the American citizen to look about him constantly, to be less bland and more suspicious, our crime taxes might start downward instead of constantly increasing. . . . Again I must remind you that crime is ever at your elbow, vicious crime, dangerous crime, against which you cannot relax your vigilance for an instant."

It is for these reasons the Director feels his FBI has been created and his leadership in law enforcement justified. He is the "watch that ends the night." Hoover extends these convictions to all policemen everywhere. Any deviation from this end Hoover considers to be a threat to law enforcement.

In 1970, Hoover took exception to those policemen on the Los Angeles Police Department who wanted to unionize. This appeared to be a definite threat to his code of eternal vigilance. "Under our system of government, most employees and workers have a lawful right to highlight their grievances through concerted action," he stated. However, Hoover felt that policemen did not have this "lawful right" if it involved the right to strike. "No matter how unfair or unjust conditions may be or may appear to be, those who voluntarily accept the sacred trust of enforcing the law and protecting the public should have serious misgivings about taking or supporting any action which leaves their community unprotected."

Hoover did not argue the right of policemen to bargain for better wages, hours, and benefits. But, to him, unions apparently signify two overriding threats—the possibility of a strike, and perhaps the even more fearful threat of losing control. To the Director, control of law enforcement personnel is at the top of the list of any administrator's responsibilities. And that would explain why he has so adamantly resisted all efforts to bring the Bureau under the jurisdiction of the Civil Service Commission.

In 1940, the Director reported to a House appropriations committee: "I want very definitely to indicate that I am as strong a champion of the merit system as, I believe, any official of the government. But the work of the Bureau is of such a character that I think the selection of its personnel is most vital to its proper and efficient and economical functioning."

In short, such conditions didn't apply to the Bureau. Undaunted, the Civil Service Commission applied pressure and sent Hoover the names of potential employees for the FBI's fingerprint division. The Director declared that these candidates were "physically deformed, psychotics, criminals, persons with radical tendencies, believers in Communist principles, and sufferers from hypertension and cardiac enlargement."

The FBI has managed to get along under its own system since 1924; Hoover has had the authority to hire and fire any Bureau employee at will.

This authoritarianism is probably the single most compelling reason why many of Hoover's ex-agents and Department of Justice officials have turned against him in recent years. Though still reluctant to publicize their names, they are increasingly determined that the Director step down.

Those who dare to use their names when criticizing Hoover face banishment, economic ruin, and the kind of smear-type labeling critic John P. Roche received. "From the time I first began advocating Mr. Hoover's retirement," Roche wrote in 1971, "I received two distinct varieties of advice. The first: That I was a Red, or at least a 'Comsymp' who was out to destroy America's major bulwark against Communist infiltration and takeover. . . .

"The second line of criticism from my advisers . . . indicated that I should learn a little about the realities of American politics, that Hoover had congressional protection which made him invulnerable, which gave him autonomy from both the attorney general and the president."

President Johnson, for one, certainly agreed with this viewpoint. Johnson wanted Hoover to remain in his job. He told a senator, "Until I get out of here myself, *I* don't want to be the one that has to pick his successor."

Neither does J. Edgar Hoover. One report has it that the Director intends to remain in office until January 1, 1975, in celebration of his eightieth birthday. He insists that he is in excellent health and that his advanced age of seventy-seven should be of no concern to anyone.

"We have employees in the Bureau who are in their eighties," he told *Time* in 1970. "I've always been against retiring a man my age; the longer a man is with us, the more valuable he becomes. To keep fit, I walk several blocks almost daily to the office."

At home, Hoover's only companions are his dogs. "My two dogs are among the smartest and most affectionate dogs I've ever seen. Anybody would think twice before they'd commit murder because of the way those dogs bark. They're great company for me. The less I think of some people, the more I think of my dogs."

Hoover pays for the maintenance of seven little graves in

an exclusive pet cemetery in Washington. One of the graves is marked: "In memory of Spee Dee Bozo, Born 1922, Died 1934."

Hoover's own decision concerning a possible step-down from his office is firm and unyielding. "I have many plans and aspirations for the future," he stated last year. "None of them includes retirement. As long as God grants me the health and stamina to continue, I have no ambition other than to remain in my post as director of the FBI."

The American public, however, feels differently. Pollster George Gallup, in a broad canvas of opinion on Hoover, stated that most of the country felt he should retire. A Louis Harris survey gave pretty much the same story.

Perhaps this reaction today from the man-in-the-street should be expected. Hoover has become unreal. He is a man of the past, as often as not confused with President Herbert Hoover or irrevocably linked to the Dillinger era, a time gone by—a period as distant as the days of Devil's Island or the Chateau d'If.

And those who would defend Hoover are presented with the perplexing problem of explaining why he should remain in office. When embarking upon this book, I was confronted by an acquaintance who had learned of my intent. He shook his head sadly. "I don't see how you can do a thing like that. For all that man Hoover has done for this country, well, they ought let him die in office. Hoover. Why, he's the man who . . . who . . ."

# Notes

CHAPTER 1: The Man Nobody Knows

*Pages 1, 2, and 3:*

The new FBI building currently under construction will cost $102.5 million; it will be the most expensive federal edifice in Washington. Hoover personally helped to design it (*Newsweek,* April 12, 1971). The Bureau's new home will have 550,000 square feet of floor space, roughly the size of twelve football fields (Tom Wicker, *Life,* April 9, 1971).

"Seat of government" quote (Victor S. Navasky, "His Majesty's Secret Society: Another Problem of Ethnicity," *Antioch Review,* Number 3, 1971).

Hoover's conversation with Harlan Fiske Stone (Don Whitehead, *The FBI Story,* New York: Random House, 1956).

Hoover's limousines (Jack Nelson and Ronald J. Ostrow, *Los Angeles Times,* April 4, 1971). There are *five* cars available to Hoover—two in Washington, one each in New York, Los Angeles, and Miami, which, at the present estimate of $30,000 each brings the total car expenditure each year to $150,000. When questioned, the House Appropriations subcommittee chairman, Congressman John J. Rooney, reported that President Johnson used these cars occasionally when visiting the various cities in which they were located (Ken W. Clawson, *Washington Post,* April 11, 1971).

*Page 4:*

Hoover's handwriting was analyzed specifically for this book by Eleanor L. Vivian, Dean, International Graphoanalysis Society, a Master Certified Graphoanalyst. Information was based on two signatures of J. Edgar Hoover, one appearing in: Jay R. Nash and R. Offen, *Dillinger: Dead or Alive,* Chicago: Regnery, 1970, and the other in "Signatures of Famous Americans," IGAS pamphlet G351.

Hoover's present salary (Associated Press, May 1, 1969).

Hoover's raise in salary and quote by Congressman John J. McCormack (*Congressional Record,* May 3, 1946).

Hoover's favorite movie stars (Nina Totenberg, "Hoover: Life and Times of a 76-Year-Old Cop," *National Observer,* April 12, 1971).

Hoover's eating and drinking habits (Louis Cassels, UPI, Published in *The State* [Columbia, S.C.], April 11, 1971; Victor Navasky, *Antioch Review,* Number 3, 1971).

Hoover as a sports spectator (Associated Press, May 1, 1969).

*Pages 5 and 6:*

Hoover is reported to be a Mason, both Royal Arch and Scottish Rite, 33rd degree, and a Shriner (*Who's Who in America,* Vol. 36, Chicago: Marquis Who's Who Incorporated, 1970).

The Director's use of ultra-violet lamps (Nina Totenberg, *National Observer,* April 12, 1971).

Bishop quote (Judy Klemesrud, "How the Famous Prepare for a Good Night's Sleep," *New York Times,* November 28, 1971).

Attendance at the FBI museum in Washington, D.C. *(FBI Annual Report,* 1968). The report shows that in one year, from 1967 to 1968, attendance dropped from 659,692 to 570,097, the lowest number in a span of five years since 1964. Aside from being able to view the Dillinger and Karpis displays, visitors are treated at the end of their tour of the museum to a small fireworks display: an FBI man stands behind a glass partition and fires off twenty rounds from a submachine gun (Louis M. Kohlmeier, "Focus on the FBI," *Wall Street Journal,* October 10, 1968).

*Pages 7, 8, and 9:*

Nixon's application for a job with the FBI (Earl Mazo and Stephen Hess, *Nixon,* New York: Harper and Row, 1967).

FBI's budget for 1937 (Congressional Appropriations Committee Hearings, 1936-1937).

President Nixon's friendship with Hoover (*Detroit News,* December 28, 1969).

Nixon's role in breaking the Hiss case (Meyer A. Zeligs, M.D., *Friendship and Fratricide,* New York: The Viking Press, 1967).

Nixon's plan to fire Hoover (Roland Evans and Robert Novak, *Providence Journal,* January 1, 1972). According to Evans-Novak, Assistant Attorney General Robert Mardian, an avowed anti-Communist and law-and-order advocate, is one of the prime movers in the Department of Justice working to have Hoover replaced. Mardian's discontent with Hoover reportedly began last spring when "Hoover, running from responsibility for dealing with the May Day demonstrations in Washington, barred FBI officials from all the department's strategy meetings."

Nixon dines in Hoover's home (*Detroit News,* December 28, 1969).

Hoover's titular role of "chairman of the board" (Glen Elsasser, *Chicago Tribune,* January 27, 1972).

Boggs' quote and charge that the FBI bugged his phone (*Washington Post,* April 6, 1971).

Nixon quote on Hoover, "to be fair" (*New York Times,* April 17, 1971).

Lawrence quote on Hoover (*U.S. News and World Report,* April 19, 1971).

*Page 10:*

Clawson quote on Hoover (*Washington Post,* April 5, 1971).

Hogan quote on Hoover (*Congressional Record,* May 5, 1971).

Biddle quote on Hoover (Francis Biddle, *In Brief Authority,* Garden City, New York: Doubleday and Company, 1962). It was not made clear by Biddle whether the information came to him at cocktail parties or was included in the secret reports that crossed his desk daily. If this information was FBI-based, who assigned Hoover to watch members of the president's cabinet?

*Pages 11 and 12:*

Scott quote on the FBI (*Washington Post,* April 12, 1971). An aide to Scott said that the senator was referring to Robert Kennedy. Scott was a member of the Senate Rules Committee during the investigation of Bobby Baker, the former secretary to the Senate Democratic leadership, who is presently serving a prison term for income tax evasion. Appearing on ABC's "Issues and Answers," April 11, 1971, Scott, who is held in high esteem by Hoover, termed the Boggs charges of congressional wiretapping a "new form of reverse McCarthyism. They [Congressmen] are developing psychomatic tendencies, and it makes you sort of a hero in the eyes of some unthinking people if you imply that the FBI is somehow menacing you or your friends." Scott, however, was not very clear about the role Hoover's FBI played in his tax problem. Was the FBI planning an investigation to show that Scott did not have a tax problem? If so, under what authority was Hoover going to investigate a tax case, which is the business of the Internal Revenue Service? It is known that Hoover and the late Robert Kennedy did not speak to each other during the last six months of Kennedy's job as attorney general. Scott's statements show that Hoover was ready to assist Scott, who allegedly was a target of his boss, Kennedy. How much help Hoover was to Scott is explained by the Senator: "I not only didn't end up paying a penalty, I ended up demanding a review and getting $3,000 of my income taxes back."

McGovern and Muskie plans to fire Hoover if elected (*Chicago Tribune,* January 27, 1962).

McGovern reads an anonymous letter from ten FBI agents (Louis

Cassels, UPI, April 11, 1971). The letter, written on Bureau stationery, stated that the FBI was failing in its fight against crime because of Hoover's obsession with "the Director's image and the preservation thereof. At present, that is all we exist for."

McGovern's relating of the incident of TWA Captain Donald J. Cook and the FBI (*Chicago Daily News,* April 19, 1971).

CHAPTER 2: The Young Years

*Pages 14, 15, and 16:*

Hoover's early personal background (Walter Trohan, "Chief of the G-Men—Record of His Career," *Chicago Tribune,* June 21, 1936).

Hoover quote, "Many Communist fronts. . . ." (Unmarked pro-FBI pamphlet issued circa June 1971 under the title, "National Council on Churches, Are They Promoting Christ or Anti-Christ?").

Hoover quote about his Bible (Associated Press, May 1, 1969).

Hoover's school years and home life (Walter Trohan, *Chicago Tribune,* June 21, 1936).

*Pages 17 and 18:*

The "Hun Scare"; Hoover's appointment to the Department of Justice; Hoover's study of and briefs on communism (Don Whitehead, *The FBI Story,* New York: Random House, 1956). According to *The National Cyclopaedia* (Vol. 33, New York: James T. White and Company, 1937), Harry Daugherty, later attorney general (1921-24) was the man responsible for bringing J. Edgar Hoover into the Department of Justice.

*Pages 20, 21, and 22:*

Hoover poses for photographers on the gangplank of the *Buford* (Drew Pearson and Jack Anderson, *True,* January, 1969).

Background and quotes by Louis F. Post, Attorney General Palmer, and Harlan Fiske Stone concerning the "Palmer Red Raids" (Don Whitehead, *The FBI Story*). Historian Robert K. Murray wrote: "In fact, there are indications that both Flynn and Hoover purposely played on the attorney general's [Palmer's] fears and exploited the whole issue of radicalism in order to enhance the Bureau of Investigation's power and prestige" (Robert K. Murray, *Red Scare, A Study in National Hysteria,* Minneapolis: University of Minnesota Press, 1955).

CHAPTER 3: Takeover

*Pages 24 and 25:*

Hoover's transfer to the Bureau of Investigation (Don Whitehead, *The FBI Story,* New York: Random House, 1956).

Hoover changes his name; Hoover's relationships with his family (Drew Pearson and Jack Anderson, *True Magazine,* January 1969).

Hoover's distrust of women and his early male friendships (Walter Trohan, "Chief of the G-Men—Record of His Career," *Chicago Tribune,* June 21, 1936). According to Don Whitehead in *The FBI Story,* T. Frank Baughman entered the Bureau in 1919 and remained one of the Director's closest friends until his retirement in 1948. Baughman was chief of the physics and chemistry section of the Bureau's technical laboratory, and was a leading expert in firearms. Clyde Tolson, who told Senator McGovern that his attacks on Hoover were made to "buoy your political career" (Louis Cassels, UPI, April 11, 1971), is associate director of the FBI. Tolson joined Hoover in 1928 and has seldom been away from the Director's side. Though seventy-two and past the mandatory retirement age, Tolson has been kept on in the Bureau by Hoover, who, according to Jack Anderson, "used a legal provision which allows the employment of retired personnel temporarily to complete a project they were working on at the time of their mandatory retirement."

Hoover quote on female associates of criminals (J. Edgar Hoover, *Persons in Hiding,* Boston: Little, Brown and Company, 1938).

*Pages 26 and 27:*

Bonaparte quote (*Century Magazine,* March 1910).

Corruption in the Harding administration (Gene Caesar, *Incredible Detective: The Biography of William J. Burns,* Englewood Cliffs: Prentice-Hall, 1968).

"Goon squad" quote (Joseph Kraft, "J. Edgar Hoover, The Compleat Bureaucrat," *Commentary,* February 1965).

"Private secret service" quote (Alpheus Thomas Mason, *Harlan Fiske Stone: Pillar of the Law,* New York: The Viking Press, 1966).

*Pages 28 through 31:*

Background on Gaston Bullock Means (Don Whitehead, *The FBI Story*).

Means' Senate hearing testimony (*Congressional Record,* 1924).

Herbert Hoover and Larry Richey quotes (Don Whitehead, *The FBI Story*).

Burns quote (Gene Caesar, *Incredible Detective, The Biography of William J. Burns*).

Hoover's firing of agents for political reasons (Walter Trohan, *Chicago Tribune,* June 21, 1936). Trohan reported that Hoover "had some fears that the New Deal might presume existence of relationship of the Director to Herbert Hoover, the departing Republican president, and sweep him out with other vestiges of the old order, but careful political stepping saved his post."

*Pages 32 and 33:*
Purvis hired through political connections (Melvin Purvis, *American Agent,* Doubleday, Doran and Co., 1936).

Hoover memo on drinking (Don Whitehead, *The FBI Story*).

Hoover's files on Washington politicians (Walter Trohan, *Chicago Tribune,* June 21, 1936).

CHAPTER 4: The 'Gangbuster'

*Pages 34 through 38:*
Hoover's behavior in the early 1930s (Walter Trohan, *Chicago Tribune,* June 21, 1936).

Hoover quote on "Machine Gun" Kelly capture (*Tennessee Law Review,* June 1946).

Account of Kelly's capture by Memphis Police Detective W. J. Raney (Lew Louderback, *The Bad Ones,* New York: Fawcett Publications, 1968).

Purvis' background and the War Eagle episode (Melvin Purvis, *American Agent,* New York: Doubleday, Doran and Co., 1936).

*Pages 39 through 45:*
Purvis-Touhy information and quotes in the Hamm and Factor kidnapping cases (Roger Touhy with Ray Brennan, *The Stolen Years,* Fremont, Mo.: Pennington Press, 1959).

The Dillinger case (Jay Robert Nash and Ron Offen, *Dillinger: Dead or Alive,* Chicago: Henry Regnery Co., 1970). Pro-Hoover writers Harry and Bonaro Overstreet wrote in *The FBI in Our Open Society* (New York: W. W. Norton and Company, 1969) that "no reason had been found to charge the FBI agents with trigger-happiness [in the raid against the Little Bohemia lodge in 1934] . . . . They were under fire from machine guns which the Dillinger gang had mounted on the roof of the roadhouse when the citizen-victim [Boiseneau]—one of three men from a nearby CCC camp, who had emerged from the house a few minutes earlier—was caught in the cross fire." Nothing could be further from the truth. I have personally inspected almost every inch of the facade of the Little Bohemia resort. All of the bullets fired during the raid against the main lodge ("Baby Face" Nelson traded shots with Melvin Purvis from a cabin off in the woods) came out of FBI guns. All of the bullet holes, still preserved under glass, are in the first-floor area of the lodge. Dillinger, John Hamilton, Homer Van Meter, and Tommy Carroll never fired a shot, according to the eyewitnesses I questioned. There was no time. They slipped out a back window and escaped. I attempted to climb up to the top of the roof, and found that it would be impossible to mount a machine gun there. Boiseneau was not caught in cross fire; he and his two companions were in their car trying to start the engine when agents opened up on them. Purvis, the man who led the raid, admits in his book, *American Agent*, that Boiseneau died from bullet wounds inflicted by the FBI. A film was taken of the bullet-ridden car a day after the raid. The Overstreet claim is typical of the false and shoddy reporting which Hoover sanctions, and which built the sterling image of the Bureau.

Information about and quotes of Charles Arthur "Pretty Boy" Floyd; statements by Melvin Purvis and other FBI agents (Lew Louderback, *The Bad Ones*).

*Pages 46 and 47:*
Audett quotes (Blackie Audett, *Rap Sheet*, New York: William Sloane, 1954).

Rudensky's escape from Leavenworth (Morris "Red" Rudensky, *The Gonif*, Blue Earth, Minn.: The Piper Company, 1970).

*Pages 48 and 49:*
Means' involvement in the Lindbergh case (Don Whitehead, *The FBI Story*, New York: Random House, 1956; J. Edgar Hoover, *Persons in Hiding*, Boston: Little, Brown and Company, 1938).

Hoover's statements on the apprehension of Hauptmann (*Congressional Record*, 1936).

*Pages 51 and 52:*
Involvement of and statements by Treasury Agent Thomas H. Sisk and NYPD Lieutenant James J. Finn in the Lindbergh case, (James P. Horan, *The Desperate Years*, New York: Crown Publications, 1962).

Information on Victor "The Count" Lustig case (Walter Trohan, *Chicago Tribune*, June 21, 1936).

*Pages 53, 54, and 55:*
Hoover-McKellar exchanges on FBI publicity (*Congressional Record*, 1936).

Hoover's screening of G-men films; information on Courtney Ryley Cooper, Washington newspaperman, and cartoonists promoting the FBI (Walter Trohan, *Chicago Tribune*, June 21, 1936).

Henry Soudam's PR job for the FBI (Drew Pearson and Jack Anderson, *True Magazine*, January 1969). Another personal friend of Hoover's, Rex Collier of the *Washington Star*, published a series under the head "War on Crime." This series was based almost solely on information Collier received from FBI files via the Director. (William W. Turner, *Hoover's FBI: The Men and the Myth*, Los Angeles: Sherbourne Press, 1970).

Hoover-McKellar exchanges on Stoll and Weyerhaeuser kidnapping cases (*Congressional Record*, 1936).

Turreau quote (William W. Turner, *Hoover's FBI: The Men and the Myth*).

Hoover-McKellar exchanges concerning citizen aid to the FBI (*Congressional Record*, 1936).

*Page 56:*

Stone's desire for an FBI chief with police experience (Alpheus Thomas Mason, *Harlan Fiske Stone: Pillar of the Law*, New York: Viking Press, 1966).

Hoover as a "criminologist" (*Who's Who in America*, Vol. 19, 1936-37, Chicago: The A. N. Marquis Company, 1936).

Hoover-McKellar exchanges on Hoover's arrest record (*Congressional Record*, 1936).

Information and Hoover quotes on the capture of Alvin "Old Creepy" Karpis (Alvin Karpis with Bill Trent, *The Alvin Karpis Story*, New York: Coward, McCann and Geoghegan, 1971). Karpis states in his book that "the FBI story of my arrest is totally false. Just as false as the one that Hoover put out in 1935 to the effect that I had sent him a note threatening to kill him. . . . That May Day in 1936, I made Hoover's reputation as a fearless lawman. It's a reputation he doesn't deserve. . . . I have nothing but contempt for J. Edgar Hoover."

*Pages 57 through 60:*

Brunette capture and Valentine quote (Associated Press, May 1, 1969).

Lepke capture and quotes (Don Whitehead, *The FBI Story*). Don Whitehead reported that "Director Hoover walked along through New York City's streets to the corner of Twenty-eighth and Fifth Avenue. And there the hunted man, Buchalter, surrendered to him. The FBI got Buchalter, and Winchell got an exclusive story." Years later, Winchell denied this story, claiming that he, not the Director, really arrested Lepke on the night of August 24, 1939. "I was not waiting in G-man Hoover's car for Lepke to surrender," Winchell said in his syndicated column. "Mr. Hoover was waiting at Twenty-eighth and Fifth [in his car] where I brought Mr. Murder, Inc., after he [Buchalter] kept a rendezvous with me four blocks south." Technically, Lepke was arrested illegally by Hoover, who assumed he had fled across state lines to avoid prosecution. The bantam killer, however, had never left New York City; he had remained there while evading federal narcotics and state murder charges.

Background of Sherman Billingsley, and the incident at the Stork Club (Bob Thomas, *Winchell*, New York: Doubleday and Company, 1971; Lyle Stuart, *The Secret Life of Walter Winchell*, New York: Boar's Head Books, 1954).

CHAPTER 5: The Spyhunter

*Pages 61 and 62:*

Hoover met with President Roosevelt on August 24, 1936, at which time FDR appointed the Director head of U.S. counterespionage (Don Whitehead, *The FBI Story*, New York: Random House, 1956).

Quote on Hoover welcoming counterespionage responsibilities (H. Montgomery Hyde, *Room 3603*, New York: Farrar, Straus, 1963).

Hoover statement on lack of foreign espionage in the United States. (Testimony before the House Committee on Un-American Activities, March 26, 1947, *Congressional Record*).

Of the eight German saboteurs who landed in Florida, June 13, 1942, two were violently opposed to the Hitler regime. These two men, George John Dasch and Ernest P. Burger, contacted Hoover personally in Washington and told him the complete story of the Nazi plot. Their six confederates were then apprehended and executed within sixty days. Dasch and Burger, for their cooperation, went to prison, Dasch for thirty years, Burger for life. Hoover never admitted that the capture of the Nazi agents was affected by Dasch and Burger. Dasch was promised that though he would have to stand trial with the others, his would be a sham conviction to fool the Germans, and he would be set free within six months. At trial's end, Dasch was stunned when he received thirty years. He saw Hoover in the hallway after the trial. The German pleaded with the Director: "He continued on, ignoring me. Again I cried out, this time louder than before: 'Mr. Hoover, aren't you really ashamed of yourself?' An FBI agent walking nearby struck me on the face, sending me sprawling to the floor. One of the army guards helped me to my feet, and through the tears brought on by the hot sting of the agent's hand, I saw the Chief disappear down the hall, seemingly surrounded by an impregnable wall of justice and strength." ("Eight Spies Against America," reprinted in William W. Turner, *Hoover's FBI: The Men and the Myth*, Los Angeles: Sherbourne Press, 1970).

Quote on the conduct of Nazi spies (Nathaneal Weyl, *Treason, The Battle Against Disloyalty*, Washington: Public Affairs Press, 1950).

*Pages 63 through 70:*

Background for the Spanish Civil War recruiter raids; quotes by suspect, FBI agent, and Attorney General Robert H. Jackson (Don Whitehead, *The FBI Story*).

National magazine quote, "In foreign countries . . . ." (*The New Republic,* February 19, 1940).

Hoover-Hull-FDR conversation; Hoover's staff memorandum; Norris, Schweinhaut, and Boas quotes (Don Whitehead, *The FBI Story*). Professor Boas was the chairman of the American Committee for Democracy and Intellectual Freedom, and an anthropologist of worldwide fame. Though Boas initiated this letter, Whitehead wrote that "Professor Boas' name was being used to rally intellectuals against the FBI."

German infiltration into government plants; the operations of Nazi agent William Lonkowski; types of secrets stolen by Abwehr agents (Ladislas Farago, *The Game of the Foxes*, New York: David McKay Company, 1972).

Operations by Japanese espionage agents Harry Thompson and John S. Farnsworth (Ronald Seth, *Secret Servants*, New York: Farrar, Straus and Giroux, 1957). Yamaki was a naval attaché assigned to the Japanese Embassy in Washington. Sato was a correspondent for the Japanese news agency, *Domei*.

Information on the Norden bombsight and its plans being stolen by German agents (Ladislas Farago, *The Game of the Foxes;* Richard Wilmer Rowan with Robert G. Deindorfer, *Secret Service, Thirty-Three Centuries of Espionage*, New York: Hawthorn Books, 1967). Farago states that the spy, Ritter, assumed the name "Alfred Landing." Rowan and Deindorfer say Ritter's cover name was "Dr. Ranken."

*Pages 71 through 74:*
Background on the Kuehn family operations in Hawaii (Ronald Seth, *Secret Servants*).

Quote, "And it was no secret. . . ." (Whitehead, *The FBI Story*).

Operations of and quote about Takeo Yoshikawa (Richard Wilmer Rowan with Robert G. Deindorfer, *Secret Service, Thirty-Three Centuries of Espionage*).

*Pages 75 through 78:*
Statements of FBI Agent Shivers; Hoover's reaction to Pearl Harbor; background of and quote on the SIS in South America; quote of FBI agent in Mexico (Don Whitehead, *The FBI Story*).

German colonization in South America (Richard Tannenberg, *Greater Germany: Work of the Twentieth Century*, English edition, Leipsig-Gohlis: B. Udger, 1911).

Information and quotes concerning the espionage activities of Nazi agent, Walter Koehler (Ladislas Farago, *The Game of the Foxes*).

Hoover quote on "Albert van Loop" (J. Edgar Hoover, "The Spy Who Doublecrossed Hitler," *American Magazine*, May 1946).

Espionage successes of Axis agents (Ladislas Farago, *The Game of the Foxes*).

*Page 79:*

Hoover's opposition to Nisei internment (Nina Totenberg, *National Observer*, April 12, 1971). According to Ronald Seth, six Nisei worked as FBI agents, doing undercover work in Los Angeles prior to World War II. Just after they unearthed the Japanese master plan for sabotage on the West Coast, two of them were murdered. The FBI knew the Nisei agents had been found out, but warned them too late.

Hoover action and quote on the arrest of Nisei (Don Whitehead, *The FBI Story*).

Quote from Japanese internee in an American internment camp during the war (Personal interview).

Los Angeles police arrests of Nisei (Jack Webb, *The Badge*, New York: Prentice-Hall, 1958).

Nisei at Del Mar racetrack; Del Webb background (Personal interviews).

*Pages 80 and 81:*

Hoover quote on Las Vegas casinos (Nina Totenberg, *National Observer*, April 12, 1971).

Hoover quote on Benjamin "Bugsy" Siegel and Siegel's association with Del Webb (Dean Jennings, *We Only Kill Each Other*, Englewood Cliffs, New Jersey: Prentice-Hall, 1968).

CHAPTER 6: The Organization That Didn't Exist

*Pages 82 through 85:*

Hoover quote on organized crime (Associated Press, May 1, 1969).

Hoover-Karpis conversation (Lew Louderback, *The Bad Ones*, New York: Fawcett, 1968).

The Black Hand: their background, techniques, bombings, and sentences (Herbert Asbury, *The Chicago Underworld*, originally published as *Gem of the Prairie*, New York: Alfred Knopf, 1940).

Background for Mafia killings and lynchings in New Orleans (Ed Reid, *Mafia*, New York: Random House, 1952). Reid has also documented the rise of the Mafia in Sicily and its subsequent development in the United States, particularly its merger after 1920 with its Italian counterpart, the Camorra, in *The Grim Reapers: The Anatomy of Organized Crime in America* (Chicago: Henry Regnery Company, 1969). In 1938, J. Edgar Hoover seemed to be faintly aware of the Mafia when he said, "It is true that certain foreign nations possess a crime stratum with which American law enforcement must come to grips when it reaches these shores" (J. Edgar Hoover, *Persons in Hiding*, Boston: Little, Brown and Co., 1938). The Mafia in force had reached "these shores" well over half century before the Director wrote those words. Investigative reporter Hank Messick reports that a disillusioned Mafioso, Nicola Gentile, wrote out a long "confession" detailing the operations of the Mafia for the FBI in the 1960s. Messick claims that Gentile's manuscript was written in Italian and that a Sicilian-born agent translated it. "It was read by J. Edgar Hoover. . . . Gentile's story finally convinced Hoover there was a Mafia." (Hank Messick, *Lansky,* New York: G. P. Putnam's Sons, 1971).

Detective Frank Dimaio's pentration of a Mafia enclave in the New Orleans prison (James D. Horan, *The Pinkertons: The Detective Dynasty That Made History,* Crown Publishers, 1967).

Baron Fava's demands (Ed Reid, *Mafia*).

Quote on "murder breeds" (*Review of Reviews,* No. 111, 1891).

The killing of NYPD Lieutenant Joseph Petrosino (Ed Reid, *Mafia*).

*Page 86:*

Tony Notaro's description of an initiation into the brotherhood (Ed Reid, *Mafia;* Nicholas Gage, *The Mafia Is Not an Equal Opportunity Employer,* New York: McGraw-Hill Book Company, 1971). Reid points out that the sensational revelations made by Notaro applied to the Camorra, but its oath of allegiance is essentially the same as that of the Mafia. At the murder trial of Pelligrino Morano, Notaro testified: "Tony the Shoemaker said to me, 'Now we are going to make a Camorrista and give you that title.' He said, 'The leader of the society, the boss, is Pelligrino Morano, and Vincenzo Paragallo is the second boss.' Then Pelligrino Morano said to me, 'Do you consent to become a Camorrista and receive the title that we give you?' I answered, 'Yes.' He then said to me, 'Whatever is done between us, not a word should be breathed on the outside. You have to respect the bosses. When you are ordered to do a job or kill anybody, or whatever it is, even if you are arrested, never say a word and do not talk at all. And do not be afraid and do not speak to the police. . . . In whatever town you might find yourself—Boston, Philadelphia, Pittsburgh, Chicago, Buffalo—in any town, simply mention my name and you will be respected, because they all know me everywhere.' I said, 'Yes' " (*NYC Trial Records,* May 14, 1918).

Hoover quote on "American" criminals (J. Edgar Hoover, *Persons in Hiding*).

*Pages 87 and 88:*

Quotes about and general background of Murder, Inc.; fight over Lepke's jurisdiction; Lepke's "secret" information (Burton B. Turkus and Sid Feder, *Murder Inc.: The Story of the Syndicate,* New York: Farrar, Straus and Young Co., 1951).

*Pages 89 through 95:*

Quote on Fischetti's promise to Lepke (Jack Lait and Lee Mortimer, *Chicago Confidential,* New York: Crown Publishers, 1950).

Bugsy Siegel's migration to California and his criminal activities with Jack Dragna (Dean Jennings, *We Only Kill Each Other,* Englewood Cliffs, New Jersey: Prentice-Hall, 1968; David Mazroff "Get In Line—Or Die!," *The Racketeers,* New York, Pyramid Books, 1970).

Hoover statistics (FBI annual reports, 1968-70). In 1968, for example, Hoover reported that there were only eight convictions in antiracketeering cases involving the FBI, where there were 1,527 convictions in government and Indian reservation matters involving the Bureau. In this same year, the Bureau had 4,622 convictions in interstate transportation of stolen motor vehicles or aircraft cases, and could claim that, through its efforts, savings and recoveries amounted to a staggering $36,024,307. This isn't quite so impressive as it seems when one realizes that Hoover lists the top retail price when new of each returned car.

Ex-FBI agents serve on the Nevada Gaming Control Board during the 1950s; background of Desert Inn employees; the Frank Costello shooting; Accardo-Lansky ties in Las Vegas (Lester Velie, *Reader's Digest,* October 1959).

Background of Howard Hughes' move into Las Vegas; Mayheu quote; Hughes employees with criminal histories and connections (Steven M. Lovelady, *Wall Street Journal,* May 23, 1969).

Quote on Hoover concentrating on routine police work and car theft statistics (Anthony Lewis, *New York Times,* December 6, 1964).

Wicker quote,"Hoover resisted taking jurisdiction. . . ."; Hoover's stingy cooperation with the Senate Labor Rackets Committee (Tom Wicker, *Life,* April 9, 1971).

Kennedy quote on the FBI's failure to investigate organized crime (Ovid Demaris, *America the Violent,* New York: Cowles Book Company, 1970).

Quote and background on New York FBI agents' neglect of the syndicate in 1959 (Peter Maas, *The Valachi Papers,* New York: G. P. Putnam's Sons, 1968).

Warnings of syndicate activities by Federal Bureau of Narcotics director, Harry Anslinger, and the Kefauver committee; Mafia Apalachin meeting (Donald R. Cressey, *Theft of the Nation,* New York: Harper and Row, 1969).

FBI's 1958 Mafia memo retrieved by Hoover (Victor S. Navasky, *Kennedy Justice,* New York: Atheneum, 1971).

Hoover quote, "No single individual. . . ." (J. Edgar Hoover, *FBI Law Enforcement Bulletin,* January 1962).

Kennedy quote on the Dillinger display in the FBI museum (Nina Totenberg, *National Observer,* April 12, 1971).

Kennedy's order to Hoover on the Kilpatrick killing in Chicago and the subsequent investigation (Ovid Demaris, *Captive City,* New York, Lyle Stuart, 1969). Syndicate hit men, William Triplett and Dana Horton Nash, were convicted of Kilpatrick's murder in Chicago's Superior Court, October 9, 1962. Nash received ninety-nine years, and Triplett, for turning state's evidence, fourteen years. In 1934, Sam Bruno was sentenced to serve fourteen years in the Illinois State Penitentiary after being convicted as an accessory in the murder of Joseph Adduci.

Quote on Kennedy-Hoover differences in approach on combating organized crime; Hoover quote on mass arrests of syndicate gangsters (Nina Totenberg quoting a former Justice Department official, *National Observer,* April 12, 1971).

*Pages 96 and 97:*

Valachi quote and writing of manuscript (Peter Maas, *The Valachi Papers*).

Background on Abe "Kid Twist" Reles (Burton B. Turkus and Sid Feder, *Murder, Inc.: The Story of the Syndicate*). Reles was being guarded by six policemen when he fell from the sixth-floor window of the Half Moon Hotel, Coney Island, November 12, 1941.

Valachi first captured by and revealed information on the *Cosa Nostra* to Federal Bureau of Narcotics officials (Personal interviews with informants who wish to remain anonymous because of their position relative to the FBI).

Hoover quote on La Cosa Nostra (J. Edgar Hoover, Testimony before the House Committee on Appropriations, 1966). On July 23, 1970, Attorney General Mitchell sent Hoover a memo stating that the FBI and the Department of Justice would no longer use the term *Cosa Nostra* since "there is nothing to be gained by using these terms except to give gratuitous offense." Mitchell had been under heavy pressure, as had the Bureau, from the Italian Anti-Defamation League and the Italian American Civil Rights League. Ten days before Mitchell issued his order, Hoover had used the term *La Cosa Nostra* eleven times in a report on organized crime (Jack Nelson, *Los Angeles Times,* July 24, 1970).

*Pages 98 and 99:*

Information on the Mafia meeting at the Edgewater Beach Hotel (Personal interviews with informants who wish to remain anonymous because of their position relative to the FBI).

Information and quotes by a syndicate hit man on the FBI's payroll as an informant (Personal interviews with informants who wish to remain anonymous because of their position relative to the FBI).

CHAPTER 7: Netting the 'Red Herring'

*Pages 101 and 102:*

Hoover's practical jokes on Julius Lully (Jack Lait and Lee Mortimer, *Washington Confidential,* New York: Crown Pub., 1951).

Quotes and background on Hoover's naivete in posing with notorious hoods (Hank Messick, *Lansky,* New York: G. P. Putnam's Sons, 1971).

Senator Joseph McCarthy's West Virginia speech (*Wheeling Intelligencer,* February 9, 1950). McCarthy later denied making this speech; however, it was recorded by Wheeling's WWVA radio station.

*Pages 103 and 104:*

Hoover quote on his counterintelligence work against foreign powers (1945 IACP Convention in Miami).

Atomic spies and their operations (Ronald Seth, *Unmasked!: The Story of Soviet Espionage,* New York, Hawthorn Books, 1965).

Espionage laws of 1917 under which the Rosenbergs were convicted (William W. Turner, *Hoover's FBI: The Men and the Myth,* Los Angeles: Sherbourne Press, 1970).

Senator McCarthy's activities (Gustavus Myers, Edited and revised by Henry M. Christman, *History of Bigotry in the United States,* New York: Capricorn Books, 1960).

McCarthy quote on the backing of Communists in his 1946 senatorial campaign (Jack Anderson and Ronald W. May, *McCarthy: The Man, The Senator, The "Ism,"* Boston: Beacon Press, 1952).

McCarthy as Communist dupe in the Malmedy Massacre hearings (James Rorty and Moshe Dector, *McCarthyism and the Communists,* Boston: Beacon Press, 1954).

*Pages 105 and 106:*

Hoover quote on the FBI as a "fact-finding" agency (Don Whitehead, *The FBI Story,* Foreword, New York: Random House, 1956).

FBI information funneled to McCarthy's committee; quote (Nina Totenberg, *National Observer,* April 12, 1971).

McCarthy's charge of "complicity," and subsequent fistfight with columnist Drew Pearson (Frank Kluckhorn and Jay Franklin [John Franklin Carter], *The Drew-Pearson Story,* Chicago: Charles Hallberg and Company, 1967).

*Pages 107 and 108:*

Hoover quote on McCarthy (William V. Shannon, *Commonweal,* December 1964; First published by the *New York Post* in 1953).

Thomas quote (Victor S. Navasky, *Kennedy Justice,* New York: Atheneum, 1971).

Senator Benton versus McCarthy; Hoover quote denying he had given McCarthy photostats on Communists in the State Department (Myers-Christman, *History of Bigotry in the United States*).

Eisenhower quote (Dwight David Eisenhower, *Mandate for Change, 1953-1956, The White House Years*, Garden City, New York: Doubleday and Company, 1963).

Hoover "false accusation" quote (J. Edgar Hoover, "The Communists Are After Our Minds," *American Magazine,* October 1954).

Hoover quote, "Anybody who will allege. . . ." (J. Edgar Hoover testimony before the Warren Commission, May 14, 1964).

Hoover quote on McCarthy, "I've come to know him. . . ." (William W. Turner, *Hoover's FBI*).

*Pages 109 through 113:*

Quote on Hoover's admiration for Roy Cohn (Maxine Cheshire, *Washington Post,* March 21, 1969).

Donations by Cohn, Rosensteil, and Nichols to the Hoover Foundation; the function of the foundation; Morganthau prosecution of Roy Cohn (Hank Messick, *Lansky;* William W. Turner, *Hoover's FBI*; Maxine Cheshire, *Washington Post,* March 21, 1969). It was through Roy Cohn's connections that Nichols got his job with Schenley, at an annual salary of $200,000 (William W. Turner, *Hoover's FBI*).

Hoover's friendship with Rosensteil, Alfred Hart, and Arthur Samish, and their syndicate connections (Hank Messick, *Lansky*; William W. Turner, *Hoover's FBI*).

Hoover's association with the note to Clint Murchison (Jack Anderson, April 7, 1971; William W. Turner, *Hoover's FBI*).

Background and quote on Davidson-Licavoli connections and donation to the Hoover Foundation (*Life,* May 2, 1969).

*Pages 114 through 117:*

Agents watch suspected Communists in Washington, D.C. (Robert Wall, "The Confessions of an FBI Agent," *New York Review of Books,* January 27, 1972).

Background and quote of FBI agent watching suspected Communists in Chicago (Personal interview with informant who wishes to remain anonymous for reason of his position relative to the FBI).

Background and quotes regarding the Berrigan case (Mark Arnold, *National Observer,* April 5, 1971).

Communists existing in Washington in 1967; functions of the "Red squads"; march on the Pentagon (Robert Wall, *New York Review of Books*). Hoover blamed the idle rich for supporting the New Left. According to *Reader's Digest,* Oct. 1969, "J. Edgar Hoover told Congress, four individuals—a Cleveland industrialist, the wife of a millionaire Chicago attorney, a New England heiress, and a wealthy New York lecturer and writer—have contributed a total of more than $100,000 to New Left activities."

CHAPTER 8: The International Hoover and the CIA

*Pages 118, 119, and 120:*
Background and quotes on William J. Donovan's visit with President Roosevelt; achievements of the OSS in Burma and Africa (Richard Wilmer Rowan with Robert G. Deindorfer, *Secret Service, Thirty-Three Centuries of Espionage*, New York: Hawthorn Books, 1967).

OSS achievements in Europe (Charles B. MacDonald, *The Mighty Endeavor*, New York: Oxford University Press, 1969).

Hoover's memo to Donovan (Don Whitehead, *The FBI Story*, New York: Random House, 1956). Senator Burton K. Wheeler, who had brought charges of corruption against Attorney General Harry Daugherty, was himself being investigated by the Department of Justice for allegedly taking bribes from oil interests in Montana. FBI agents, as was and is the custom, were working on the case for U.S. attorneys.

Donovan's penetration of KGB headquarters and Hoover's veto of his plan to plant agents there (David Wise and Thomas B. Ross, *The Espionage Establishment*, New York: Random House, 1967).

*Pages 121, 122, and 123:*
Hoover demands that the OSS be abolished and Truman complies (Andrew Tully, *CIA: The Inside Story*, New York: Morrow, 1962).

OSS budget during World War II (Richard Wilmer Rowan with Robert G. Deindorfer, *Secret Service, Thirty-Three Centuries of Espionage*).

FBI's budget during World War II (*Congressional Record*, 1941-45).

Truman quote; creation of the CIA (Andrew Tully, *CIA: The Inside Story*).

Allen Dulles deals with Nazi generals (Charles B. MacDonald, *The Mighty Endeavor*).

Hoover places agents in espionage assignments abroad (David Wise and Thomas B. Ross, *The Invisible Government*, New York: Random House, 1964).

McCarthy charge of CIA infiltration by Communists; Dulles denies charge; CIA must put in writing all requests for information from the FBI (Andrew Tully, *CIA: The Inside Story*).

The FBI's failure to inform the Secret Service of Oswald's activities and associations (Michael Dorman, *The Secret Service Story*, New York: Delacorte Press, 1967).

Hoover quotes before Warren Commission (Warren Commission hearings, 1964).

*Pages 124 through 128:*
Warning of Oswald's killer (Michael Dorman, *The Secret Service Story*).

Hoover quote on "total security" (Associated Press, May 1, 1969).

Hoover quote on Puerto Ricans and Mexicans (*Time,* December 14, 1970).

Information on Hoover's 1923 brief on Communist Russia (Victor S. Navasky, *Kennedy Justice,* New York: Atheneum, 1971; Don Whitehead, *The FBI Story*).

Hoover quote on recognition of Soviet Russia in 1933 (FBI report, May 1960).

Hoover's delaying of U.S.-Russian consular treaty and subsequent denial quote (Louis M. Kohlmeier, *Wall Street Journal,* October 10, 1968).

Background information on Ch'ien Hseuh-shen (David Wise and Thomas Ross, *The Espionage Establishment*).

Hoover's warning of Chinese Communist espionage activities (J. Edgar Hoover, Testimony before the House Appropriations subcommittee, March 4, 1965).

Hoover's statement on the FBI's workload being increased by the Chinese espionage threat (J. Edgar Hoover, Testimony before the House Appropriations subcommittee, February 10, 1966).

Chinese seamen jump ship; quote on espionage risks (*London Sunday Express,* November 28, 1971).

*Pages 129 through 135:*
FBI budget and staff for 1964 (*Congressional Record,* 1964).

Background and Hoover quote on KGB budget (J. Edgar Hoover, Testimony before House subcommittee, January 1964).

Philby quote in *Izvestia* (Reprinted by George Morgenstern, *Chicago Tribune,* October 3, 1971).

Lonsdale quote on Hoover (Gordon Lonsdale, *Spy: Twenty Years in the Soviet Secret Service,* London: Neville Spearman Limited, 1965).

Background on Colonel Rudolph Abel (Richard Wilmer Rowan with Robert G. Deindorfer, *Secret Service, Thirty-Three Centuries of Espionage*).

Discovery of Abel's coin containing microfilm; FBI's failure to crack the code; CIA's turncoat, Hayhanen, breaks the case (Andrew Tully, *CIA: The Inside Story*).

Hoover quote on "incarceration" (*Time,* December 14, 1970).

Abel's arrest, beatings, and detention by FBI (James B. Donovan,

*Strangers on a Bridge,* New York: Atheneum, 1964; Louis Berni-kow, *Abel,* New York: Trident Press, 1970).

Background of and quotes by and about Colonel Michael Gole-niewski (Guy Richards, *The Hunt for the Czar,* New York: Double-day and Company, 1970). Goleniewski was identified as the heir ap-parent by several important persons who had been in the Czar's court before the revolution; his leg is crippled just as Alexei's was, and he suffers from after-effects of hemophilia, which plagued the Czar's son. Goleniewski lives in Long Island still waiting for rec-ognition and to see Hoover. Alger Hiss, when under suspicion of being a Communist, was also advised to talk directly with Hoover, but the Director refused to see him (Meyer A. Zeligs, *Friendships and Fratricide,* New York: Viking Press, 1967).

Background and quotes on Hoover's move into foreign espionage, backed by President Nixon (Evans-Novak, *Chicago Sun-Times,* January 21, 1972).

*Pages 136 through 139:*
Charge that German master spy, Reinard von Gehlen, had an operative in the FBI (Gordon Lonsdale, *Spy: Twenty Years in the Soviet Secret Service*).

Bedell-Smith quote, and background on Judith Coplon case (Ronald Seth, *Unmasked!: The Story of Soviet Espionage,* New York: Hawthorn Books, 1965). Ex-G.I. Robert Glenn Thompson, resentful of serving his time in the army, successfully spied on the FBI for seven years, penetrating, for one, the FBI residence agency in Babylon, Long Island, where he cased the premises for Soviet agents to enable them to bug the office (*Saturday Evening Post,* May 22, 1965).

Quote on "voluminous documents" (*Washington Post,* June 12, 1949).

FBI files revealed in Coplon case (Turner, *Hoover's FBI: The Men and the Myth,* Los Angeles: Sherbourne Press, 1970).

Quote, "If the FBI accepts. . . ." (John Griffin, *Boston Sunday Post,* June 12, 1949).

FBI's failure to obtain arrest warrant for Judith Coplon (Ronald Seth, *Unmasked!: The Story of Soviet Espionage.*)

CHAPTER 9: Hoover and His 'Bosses'

*Pages 140, 141, and 142:*
Background and Moley quote on FDR's plans to fire Hoover (Raymond Moley, *After Seven Years,* New York: Harper and Bros., 1939; Charles Hurd, *When the New Deal Was Young and Gay: F.D.R. and His Circle,* New York: Hawthorn Books, 1965; R. G. Tugwell, *The Brains Trust,* New York: The Viking Press, 1968).

According to Victor S. Navasky, FDR's attorney general designate, Senator Thomas Walsh, had planned to fire Hoover, but died before taking his cabinet post (Victor S. Navasky, *Kennedy Justice,* New York: Atheneum, 1791).

Wheeler quote on Cummings (Victor S. Navasky, *Kennedy Justice*).

FDR-Supreme Court battle; Hoover's note to Hughes (Leonard Baker, *Back to Back: The Duel Between FDR and the Supreme Court,* New York: Macmillan, 1967).

*Pages 143 through 146:*

Hoover's order to tail Farley (Guy Richards, "The FBI Spied on Farley," *New York Star,* September 28, 1948).

Quote on Hoover's checking for wiretaps on FBI lines (Jack Lait and Lee Mortimer, *Washington Confidential,* New York: Crown Pub., 1951).

Harry Bridges affair and FDR quote (Francis Biddle, *In Brief Authority,* New York: Doubleday and Company, 1962). Biddle took pains to have Hoover attend top-level policy meetings of the Department of Justice heads in the early 1940s. Though he thought Hoover was an asset to the department, Biddle also knew the Director's "weaknesses—his passion for the limelight, his obsession with the Communists . . . his hypersensitiveness to any criticism of his beloved bureau."

Hoover-Truman relationship (Clinton Rossiter, *The American Presidency,* New York: Harcourt, Brace and Company, 1956).

McGrath-Hoover slot-machine background and quote (Jack Lait and Lee Mortimer, *Washington Confidential*).

Illegal wiretapping episode in Rhode Island; Harry Dexter White background and Hoover quote (Don Whitehead, *The FBI Story,* New York: Random House, 1956).

*Pages 147 through 150:*

Rogers-Hoover relationship and quote (*Newsweek,* March 3, 1969).

Hoover's "independence" quote (Anthony Lewis, *New York Times,* December 5, 1964).

John Kennedy-Hoover background and proclamation quote (Drew Pearson and Jack Anderson, *True,* January 1969).

Robert Kennedy-Hoover relationship and quotes (Victor S. Navasky, *Kennedy Justice*). Kennedy thought nothing of issuing direct orders to agents. When planning a conference in New York which was to deal with organized crime, Kennedy stated, "I want Harvey Foster to attend." Foster was the agent in charge of the Bureau's New York office. Assistant attorney generals fared no better with Hoover than did Kennedy. One assistant attorney general, whose office was on the same corridor as Hoover's, arrived at the Department of Justice building at 8:30 every morning. He got in the habit of switching on the lights in the corridor since he was the first to arrive. After some time, an FBI agent came into his office and asked him not to turn on the lights. "Why?" the assistant attorney general asked. "Because the Director likes to turn them on," the agent said.

Kennedy's statement on hearing about his brother's death from Hoover (Drew Pearson and Jack Anderson, *True,* January 1969).

Hoover quote on Robert Kennedy (*Time,* December 14, 1970).

*Pages 151 through 155:*

Background on and quote about James Amos (Don Whitehead, *The FBI Story*).

Black agents serve as Hoover's chauffeur and receptionist in Washington (William W. Turner, *Hoover's FBI: The Men and the Myth,* Los Angeles: Sherbourne Press, 1970).

Black agent hired in the FBI Chicago offices (Personal interviews with informants who wish to remain anonymous for reason of their position relative to the FBI).

Aubrey Lewis background and Hoover quotes (*Ebony,* September 1962).

Statistics on white and Black agents in the FBI (*Congressional Record,* 1964, 1970; Victor S. Navasky, *Kennedy Justice*).

Hoover-Kennedy claims of wiretapping Dr. King's phone; Hoover delaying civil rights violations investigations in the Deep South (Victor S. Navasky, *Kennedy Justice*).

Quote, "Long record of hostility. . . ." (*The Nation,* July 1943).

Hoover's liking for "Amos 'n' Andy" (Louise Tanner, *All the Things We Were,* Garden City: Doubleday and Co., 1968).

Hoover's memo on Dr. King and other civil rights leaders (Drew Pearson and Jack Anderson, *True,* January 1969).

Quote on FBI's increasing anti-King memoranda (Victor S. Navasky, *Kennedy Justice*).

Hoover quote on Dr. King (*Time,* December 14, 1970).

Johnson-Hoover beagle story (Drew Pearson and Jack Anderson, *True,* January 1969).

Johnson privy to top secrets (David Wise and Thomas B. Ross, *The Invisible Government,* New York: Random House, 1964).

Hoover turns over political files to Johnson (William W. Turner, *Hoover's FBI*).

*Pages 156 through 158:*

Johnson quote on Hoover; Hoover quote on "zealots"; quote on finding a new FBI chief (Anthony Lewis, *New York Times,* December 6, 1964).

Background and quotes on FBI agents investigating students, union pickets, Poor People's March, Smithsonian exhibits, and Stokely Carmichael (Robert Wall, *New York Review of Books,* January 27, 1972).

Katzenbach-Hoover feud and quote (Louis Kohlmeier, *Wall Street Journal,* October 10, 1968; Drew Pearson and Jack Anderson, *True,* January 1969). Tom Wicker reported that Katzenbach "used to ask the FBI to stamp a notice on the many items it sent directly to the president" that had not been seen by him (*Life,* April 9, 1971).

Ramsey Clark's opposition to wiretapping; Hoover's replacement; the creation of "strike forces" (Louis Kohlmeier, *Wall Street Journal,* October 10, 1968).

Clark's report and quote on Ballistreri wiretapping (Ramsey Clark, *Crime in America,* New York: Simon and Schuster, 1970).

Clark-Hoover quotes on Chicago riots ("Clash Over Violence," *New York Times,* September 26, 1968).

*Page 159:*

Clark quote on Dr. King wiretap; call for Hoover's resignation; Nixon's support of Hoover in the King controversy (John Herbers, *New York Times,* June 21, 1969).

Clark's investigation of Nixon's campaign fund sources (*Wall Street Journal,* November 11, 1968).

Clark quote about Hoover and the FBI (Ramsey Clark, *Crime in America*).

*Pages 160 and 161:*

Hoover quotes about Clark (Mark Brown, Associated Press, April 11, 1971; Louis Cassels, UPI, April 11, 1971).

Hoover quote on Nixon, "one of my boys" (Ralph De Toledano, *Nixon,* New York: Duell, 1960).

Hoover assigns agents to protect Nixon and Humphrey during 1968 conventions (Drew Pearson and Jack Anderson, *True,* January 1969).

Nixon sends birthday greetings to Hoover (*Newsweek,* January 12, 1970).

Lou Nichol's support for Nixon (Maxine Cheshire, *Washington Post,* March 21, 1969).

Mitchell quote on American justice ("Observations," *National Observer,* July 5, 1971).

Mitchell quote on Boggs (Louis Cassels, UPI, April 4, 1971).

Mitchell background and quote about keeping data on protestors (*Chicago Daily News,* July 20, 1970).

Mitchell's "no-arrest" bill (*Jet,* May 7, 1970). Mitchell's bill provided that police have the authority to compel suspects to submit to fingerprinting, blood sampling, and other tests without arrest. Mitchell said that the new bill would apply to all those who were within "reasonable grounds not amounting to cause to arrest." He didn't explain what "reasonable grounds" meant.

Mitchell quotes on educators and America going right-wing (*Los Angeles Times*, September 19, 1970).

*Pages 162 and 163:*

Martha Mitchell's attack on Fulbright (Brooks Jackson, Associated Press, Report printed in the *Los Angeles Herald Examiner*, April 10, 1970).

Mitchell not ordering an FBI check on Carswell and Haynesworth (*New York Daily News*, April 21, 1970).

*Life* calls for Mitchell's resignation (*Life*, April 12, 1970).

Kleindienst quotes (Jack Nelson and Ronald Ostrow, *Los Angeles Times*, April 8, 1971).

Hoover quote on presidents and attorney generals (Associated Press, May 1, 1969).

CHAPTER 10: Hoover's 'Boys'

*Pages 164 through 166:*

Background and quote on the war hero who was dropped from the FBI (Drew Pearson and Jack Anderson, *True*, January 1969). On another occasion, Hoover, while visiting an FBI office, spotted an agent who he thought looked like a "truck driver." Hoover told the agent-in-charge to work him out of the Bureau. Upon returning to the same office, Hoover discovered the man still at work. "I thought I told you to get rid of that truck driver," he exploded at the agent in charge. The man was eased out of the FBI.

Hoover quote relating to actor Zimbalist (J. Edgar Hoover, Testimony before a House subcommittee, February 10, 1966). Zimbalist became, for a while, honorary chairman of the Friends of the FBI, organized by Lee Edwards and Luis Kutner. More than fifty thousand letters asking for support and contributions to combat the "vicious smear campaign" against Hoover were mailed out over the actor's signature. (William W. Turner, *Hoover's FBI: The Men and the Myth*, Los Angeles, Sherbourne Press, 1970).

Hoover quotes on the appearance of FBI agents (*Time*, December 12, 1970; *Congressional Record*, February 10, 1966).

Hoover-Tolson-Martin relationship; FBI agents work for the TV show; Bishop quote on benefits from the TV program (Jack Nelson and Ronald J. Ostrow, *Los Angeles Times*, April 4, 1971).

Hoover quote on agents selling themselves (*Congressional Record*, 1966).

Hoover quote on "youth's hero" (*Congressional Record*, 1960).

*Pages 167, 168, and 169:*

Dillinger and Nelson photos on FBI target dummies (Jay Robert Nash and Ron Offen, *Dillinger: Dead or Alive*, Chicago: Henry Regnery Co., 1970).

Agents chosen from ex-Viet Nam line officers and Hoover quote (*Time*, December 14, 1970).

Hoover quote on requirements for FBI agents ("Federal Bureau of Investigation," *Encyclopaedia Britannica*, 1970).

Wages and pensions for FBI agents; estimate of Courtney Evans' pension (Victor S. Navasky, *Kennedy Justice*, New York: Atheneum, 1971).

Agents fired for indiscretions (Personal interviews with informants who desire to remain anonymous because of their position relative to the FBI). One agent quit the Bureau outright for purely political reasons. Walter Sheridan, now an investigative reporter for NBC News, stated: "I was a cut liberal, and the FBI is a right-wing organization" (*Newsweek*, October 23, 1967).

Background and quotes on Hoover firing FBI clerk, Thomas H. Carter (Louis Kohlmeier, *Wall Street Journal*, October 10, 1968). Victor S. Navasky reported that "one FBI man, who contested the matter in court, was summarily dismissed for spending the night with a girl in his room" (*Antioch Review*, Number 3, 1971).

*Pages 170, 171, and 172:*

Janca-Hoomes background and quotes (Jack Nelson and Ronald J. Ostrow, *Los Angeles Times*, April 8, 1971).

Quote on Hoover's FBI reports (Personal interview with an informant who wishes to remain anonymous for reasons of his position relative to the FBI).

Information on one Chicago-based agent turning in another over a forgotten briefcase (Personal interview with informant who wishes to remain anonymous because of his position relative to the FBI).

An agent is fired because he didn't lose weight (Nina Totenberg, *National Observer*, April 12, 1971).

Smoking and drinking coffee in FBI offices (Louis Kohlmeier, *Wall Street Journal*, October 15, 1968).

*Pages 173 through 177:*

Turner reprimand (William W. Turner, *Hoover's FBI*).

Background and quotes on the dismissal of FBI Agent Jack Shaw (*Life*, April 9, 1971).

McGovern's defense of Jack Shaw (Louis Cassels, UPI, April 11, 1971).

Kansas City agent and his superior fired by Hoover over handling of an FBI informant (Personal interview with informant who wishes to remain anonymous because of his position relative to the FBI).

Information and quotes on an announcement by assistant director of the FBI, William Sullivan, of the Weatherman plot in 1970 (*Newsweek,* April 12, 1971).

Background and quotes on Hoover forcing Sullivan's retirement (*Washington Post,* March 2, 1971).

Sullivan statements on being appointed assistant director of the Insurance Crime Prevention Institute (*St. Louis Post-Dispatch,* January 11, 1972).

Information on Melvin Purvis leaving the Bureau in 1935; Purvis quote (Jay Robert Nash and Ron Offen, *Dillinger: Dead or Alive*).

CHAPTER 11: Your FBI in Action

*Pages 178, 179, and 180:*

Hoover quote on "the rubber hose" (Associated Press, May 1, 1969). In an article entitled "Third Degree," Hoover had previously said, "Are we to give the criminal an even break? Does the criminal give the law-abiding public an even break?" (*American Magazine,* May 1940).

Lockerman quote (Doris Lockerman, "A Girl Among Manhunters," *Chicago Tribune,* October 7, 1935).

Agents attend G-man pictures in the 1930s (Jay Robert Nash and Ray Offen, *Dillinger: Dead or Alive,* Chicago: Regnery, 1970).

Purvis quote (Melvin Purvis, *American Agent,* Doubleday, Doran and Co., 1936).

McLaughlin's complaint of FBI abuse; Probasco's death (Jay Robert Nash and Ron Offen, *Dillinger: Dead or Alive*). Another suspect in the Dillinger case was Dr. Wilhelm Loesser. He was held incommunicado by the FBI for thirty days. The Bureau kept Loesser in various places until he was ready to talk their way; Loesser was compelled to sleep on floors, and newsmen reported that when he did appear in court, there were noticeable cigarette burns on his hands and face.

Information on and quotes of Anthony Polisi (William W. Turner, *Hoover's FBI: The Men and the Myth,* Los Angeles: Sherbourne Press, 1970).

Background and quotes on FBI Agent David O. Hale in Tucson, Ariz. (Adam Clymer, *Baltimore Sun;* Lyle Denniston, *Washington Sunday Star,* June 6, 1971). The attacks were reportedly made against Mafia czar Joseph "Joe Bananas" Bonnano.

*Pages 181 through 185:*

Background and quotes on FBI agents in Powelton Village, Pa. (Sarah Shapley, *Lancaster Independent Press* [Leola,˜ Pa.], Reprinted by *Los Angeles Free Press,* December 24, 1971).

FBI agents apprehend archdeacon Robert Kimball of the Church of Lord Jesus Christ in San Francisco (William Cooney, *San Francisco Chronicle,* February 13, 1970).

Washington executive is quizzed by the FBI over a derogatory remark about Hoover (Drew Pearson and Jack Anderson, *True,* January 1969).

The FBI pays janitors to turn over garbage for inspection (Victor S. Navasky, *Antioch Review,* Number 3, 1971).

FBI surveillance of Giancana; Judge Austin's remarks (Ovid Demaris, *Captive City,* New York: Lyle Stuart, 1969).

Information on and quote by a call girl grilled by the FBI (Dr. Harold Greenwald, *Call Girl: A Social and Psychoanalytical Study,* New York: Ballantine Books, 1958).

*Pages 186 through 191:*

The FBI acquires computerized data on individuals from business firms (Arthur R. Miller, *Assault on Privacy: Computers, Data Banks and Dossiers,* Ann Arbor: University of Michigan Press, 1971).

Background and quotes on FBI informant working with a credit reporting firm (Personal interviews with informant who wishes to remain anonymous because of his position relative to the FBI).

Information and quotes on the D'Autremont case (Eugene B. Block, *The Wizard of Berkeley,* New York: Coward-McCann, 1958; E. B. Block, *Great Train Robberies of the West,* New York: Coward-McCann, 1959).

Apprehension of Melvin Rees by the FBI through an informant (Brad Steiger, *The Mass Murderer,* New York: Award Books, 1967).

Statement of FBI spokesman on Bureau informers breaking the law (*Washington Sunday Star,* June 6, 1971).

David Sannes quotes (CBS interview, June 1, 1971).

Background and quote on FBI informant, Herbert Itkin (*Washington Sunday Star,* June 6, 1971).

*Pages 192 through 197:*

Information on and quotes by FBI informer, Alfred R. Burnett (*Los Angeles Times,* May 2, 1971).

FBI recruitment of Black informants; FBI infiltration of veterans' organizations; quotes (*New York Times,* April 8, 1971. The source of information was FBI records taken from the Bureau's office in Media, Pa.).

Police check with Bureau on applications for business permits (Jack Webb, *The Badge,* New York: Prentice-Hall, 1958).

Analysis of Media files (Sarah Shapley, *Lancaster Independent Press* and *Los Angeles Free Press,* December 24, 1971).

Background on and quotes about the Hopkins Institute (Jack Lait and Lee Mortimer, *Washington Confidential,* New York: Crown Pub., 1951).

Hoover quote on FBI files (Louis Kohlmeier, *Wall Street Journal,* October 15, 1968).

Information on San Francisco mayor, Joseph Alioto, leaked from FBI files (*Newsweek,* April 12, 1971).

Background and quotes on Mayor Daley's alleged connection with the Mafia, as revealed by FBI files (Personal interviews with informants who desire to remain anonymous because of their positions relative to the FBI). The FBI dossier also has Mayor Daley secretly renting an apartment in the fashionable Drake Hotel, where, according to the "raw data," he meets with members of Chicago's underworld.

The FBI taps Mayor Daley's private phone (Personal interview with informant who wishes to remain anonymous because of his position relative to the FBI). Daley, this informant claims, continues to have his phone checked for FBI bugs and wiretaps.

## CHAPTER 12: Hoover and Civil Rights

*Pages 198 through 202:*

Quote by a former Justice Department official on the Hoover-King feud (Nina Totenberg, *National Observer,* April 12, 1971).

Quote on the FBI tapping Dr. King's phone (*St. Louis Post-Dispatch,* June 22, 1969).

Background and quotes on Attorney General Frank Murphy's order to the FBI to establish a Civil Liberties Unit; the Byers case (Harry and Bonaro Overstreet, *The FBI in Our Open Society,* New York: W. W. Norton and Co., 1969).

Hoover statement to Dewey et al. on Byers case (J. Edgar Hoover, Letter to the *New York Times,* August 26, 1953).

Information and quotes on John Seigenthaler; Byron White and William Orrick episodes in Montgomery (Victor S. Navasky, *Kennedy Justice,* New York: Atheneum, 1971).

*Pages 203, 204, and 205:*

Hoover orders agents to infiltrate NAACP (Louis Kohlmeier, *Wall Street Journal,* October 15, 1968). One of the reasons Hoover gave for FBI infiltration of Black groups is that the Communist party "is avidly attempting to infiltrate the present civil rights movement in order to manipulate it and control it for the sole benefit of Communist objectives" (Associated Press, May 1, 1969).

Background and quotes on Hoover's conference in Jackson; SNCC affidavit on FBI procedures; Freedom Day arrests in Selma (Victor S. Navasky, *Kennedy Justice*).

Hoover quote on civil liberties (J. Edgar Hoover, "Civil Liberties and Law Enforcement: The Role of the FBI," *Iowa Law Review,* Vol. 37, 1952).

Hoover terms riots "senseless" (FBI annual report, 1964).

Information and quotes on FBI infiltration of the United Methodist General Conference (Charles Lerrigo, *Boston Herald Traveler,* April 21, 1970).

Senator Muskie's charge of FBI monitoring of "Earth Day" demonstrators (*National Journal,* April 24, 1971).

Hoover quotes on the New Left, Black groups, and the KKK (*Newsweek,* January 12, 1970). In his own annual report for 1970, Hoover stated that "membership of the Ku Klux Klan fell sharply from about 6,800 to approximately 4,300. . . . The United Klans of America, Incorporated, Knights of the Ku Klux Klan, headquartered in Tuscaloosa, Ala., continued as the largest Klan group, although its membership showed a decline from 5,400 to 3,200."

*Pages 206 through 210:*
Hoover statement that FBI agents were not on campuses (*Time,* December 14, 1970).

Hoover quote on campus disorders (House committee hearing, *Congressional Record,* April 17, 1969).

Background and quotes on FBI informants infiltrating campus groups (Robert Wall, *New York Review of Books,* Jan. 27, 1972).

Congressman Bingham charges FBI harassment of Mr. and Mrs. George Clarke and Hoover's response (Bingham release and interviews with Bingham aide).

Hoover-Daley interest in the election of Richard Hatcher; FBI agent transferred from Gary office (Personal interviews with informants who wish to remain anonymous because of their positions relative to the FBI).

CHAPTER 13: See What the Boys in the Press Room Will Have

*Pages 211 through 218:*
Functions of the FBI Crime Records Division (Victor S. Navasky, *Kennedy Justice,* New York: Atheneum, 1971; Navasky, *Antioch Review,* Number 3, 1971).

Information and quotes on Republicans using Hoover's editorials (Louis Kohlmeier, *Wall Street Journal,* October 10, 1968).

FBI-Northwest Indiana Crime Commission raids on gambling casinos and subsequent publicity (Personal interviews with informants who wish to remain anonymous because of their positions relative to the FBI).

Hoover's press release on the Detroit and Flint raids; Mitchell and Brickley quotes (UPI, Reprinted in the *Los Angeles Herald Examiner,* May 12, 1970).

Background for Hoover's press release concerning President Johnson's aide, Walter Jenkins; Hoover quote on President's Commission on Crime; quote by independent crime statistics expert (Robert M. Cipes, *The Crime War: The Manufactured Crusade,* New York: New American Library, 1967).

Captain James Parson's comments on FBI statistics (Earl Holland, *Birmingham News,* January 7, 1972).

*Pages 219, 220, and 221:*
Hoover quote on Eleanor Patterson (Paul F. Healy, *Cissy: A Biography of Eleanor M. "Cissy" Patterson,* Garden City, New York: Doubleday and Company, 1966).

FBI agent's quote on *The FBI Story* (William W. Turner, *Hoover's FBI: The Men and the Myth,* Los Angeles, Sherbourne Press, 1970).

Background and quote of the Universal Studio lawyer (Personal interview).

Hoover's introductions (Courtney Ryley Cooper, *Ten Thousand Public Enemies,* Boston: Little, Brown and Company, 1935; Herbert Corey, *Farewell, Mr. Gangster,* Appleton-Century Company, 1936; Raymond Moley, *The American Legion Story,* New York: Duell, Sloan and Pearce, 1966). Cartha DeLoach, long-time assistant director of the FBI, was once national vice-commander of the American Legion and presently serves as the chairman of its public relations division. For Fulton Oursler's epic of popular religion, *The Greatest Story Ever Told,* Hoover was moved to write (his blurb appeared on a cover page): *"The Greatest Story Ever Told* might well serve as a design for human life and a guide to eternity."

Hoover's books authored by others; the amounts earned on these books (Jack Anderson, April 7, 1971).

Agent Charles Moore ghostwrites Hoover's *Masters of Deceit* (William W. Turner, *Hoover's FBI).*

Hoover's use of an analysis of and statistics about the Minutemen movement (J. Harry Jones, Jr., *The Minutemen,* Garden City, New York: Doubleday and Company, 1968).

Las Vegas-Chicago link ("The Morganatic Bank Marriage," *ChicagoLand Magazine,* February 1970).

*Pages 222, 223, and 224:*
Gambling in "steel town" ("Welcome to East Chicago," *Chicago-Land Magazine,* October 1969). The magazine published several short pieces on local hoods with long criminal records who were working for the city government (which was and is illegal). It was not uncommon for the FBI to send an agent to the magazine to obtain information and photos on these hoodlum moonlighters for their files. On one occasion, an agent spotted the prepublication

cover for *Dillinger: Dead or Alive.* "I hear that's an anti-Bureau book," he said. "Could be," I said. "I don't give a damn," he said, "but why don't you tell me about it?" I declined.

Background on Bureau informers grilling newspaper men (Personal interviews with informants who wish to remain anonymous).

Information and quotes on FBI spy Louis Saltzberg (James W. Singer, *Chicago Sun-Times,* October 24, 1969; Judson Hand, *New York Daily News,* March 29, 1970).

*Page 225:*

Hoover quote on attacks against FBI agents (Victory S. Navasky, *Kennedy Justice*). On another occasion Hoover stated, "I have tried for years to avoid public disputes. But I cannot let attacks on the FBI go unchallenged when they are not justified. If I didn't speak out in behalf of my agents, I would have no morale in this organization" (Associated Press, May 1, 1969).

Hoover quotes on criticism (J. Edgar Hoover, Letters to the Editor [dated April 14 and April 13, 1971], *National Observer,* July 5, 1971). The Director finds it abominable that those criticizing him and the Bureau are not identified by the press. "In other arenas," Hoover wrote to the *National Observer,* "such 'sources' have been called 'faceless informers.' Certainly the use of such 'sources' on this scale as the basis for what purports to be factual reporting is pretty poor journalism."

Hoover's letter to the *New York Daily News* (Victor S. Navasky, *Kennedy Justice*). Under the banner of the "New Year's Day's Best News," the *Daily News* (on January 4, 1970) published a gushy tribute to the Director which read in part: "It was the news that John Edgar Hoover had *not* celebrated his seventy-fifth birthday— January 1, 1970—by resigning as director of the Federal Bureau of Investigation. Ill-wishers of Mr. Hoover had been circulating predictions of a resignation for months. There was a general licking of chops in U.S. criminal, foreign-agent and traitor circles in anticipation of such a stepdown. It didn't happen. Mr. Hoover stayed on as FBI Chief, his health excellent, his mind as keen as ever, his devotion to his country's best interests unimpaired. . . . Further cause for congratulations: The failure of Mr. Hoover to take his departure as head of the FBI touched off a nationwide chorus of whinnying and whickering among professional 'liberals,' enraged by this dashing of one of their fondest hopes for the glad New Year. . . ."

*Pages 226, 227, and 228:*

*America's Future* (Vol. 11, January 17, 1969).

FBI investigation of Beacon Press (*Chicago Daily News,* February 5, 1972).

Pearson and Anderson investigated by FBI (Drew Pearson and Jack Anderson, *True,* January 1969).

Quote about Max Lowenthal and his book (Jack Lait and Lee Mortimer, *Washington Confidential,* New York: Crown Pub., 1951).

Quote on Fred J. Cook's book (Harry and Bonaro Overstreet, *The FBI in Our Open Society,* New York: W. W. Norton and Co., 1969).

Background and Snyder quote on the Bureau investigating Turner (William W. Turner, *Hoover's FBI*).

FBI's "No contact" list (*New York Times* News Service, Published in the *St. Louis Post-Dispatch,* January 14, 1972).

CHAPTER 14: Hoover's Power Elite

*Pages 229 through 232:*

Hoover's letters to winners of congressional elections (Louis M. Kohlmeier, *Wall Street Journal,* October 10, 1968).

Agnew statements on Hoover (Speech before the Southern Gas Association Convention in New Orleans, La., April 26, 1971, Reprinted in *Human Events,* May 29, 1971).

Rooney quotes (Ken W. Clawson, *Washington Post,* April 11, 1971).

Myer's quote on Hoover (Release by Congressman John T. Myers, April 1971).

Sparkman quote on Hoover (Release by Senator John Sparkman, April 1971).

Dickinson quote on Hoover (Letter to President Nixon, later released by Congressman William L. Dickinson).

*Pages 233 through 237:*

Anderson quote (Louis Cassels, UPI, April 11, 1971).

Background and Hoover quote on the FBI investigating congressmen in 1924 (Max Lowenthal, *The Federal Bureau of Investigation,* William Sloan Associates, 1950).

Information and quote on Senator Thomas Dodd asking the FBI to investigate an employee in his office (Drew Pearson and Jack Anderson, *True,* 1969).

Dodd and the Haynsworth vote; "Dodd Day" campaign funds; censure by the Senate (E. W. Kenworthy, *New York Times,* December 24, 1969).

Hoover's nomination of and charges against General Carl C. Turner (Morton Kendracke, *Chicago Sun-Times,* Oct. 23, 1969).

Quotes of Hugh M. Clegg, Police Chief Purcell, and IACP director, Quinn Tamm (Louis Kohlmeier, *Wall Street Journal,* October 15, 1968).

*Pages 238 and 239:*

Background on Police Chief James Ahern (Personal interviews with informants who wish to remain anonymous because of their position relative to the FBI).

Hoover quote, "Actually, the American public. . . ." (J. Edgar Hoover, *FBI Law Enforcement Bulletin,* March 1967).

Quote on Cartha DeLoach's attitude toward criminals and demonstrators (Robert M. Cipes, *The Crime War: The Manufactured Crusade,* New York: New American Library, 1967).

*Pages 240 through 243:*

DeLoach replaces Courtney Evans; DeLoach as the FBI representative on President Johnson's National Crime Commission (Tom Wicker, *Life,* April 9, 1971). DeLoach acted as a conduit for Hoover's thinking, and through him, the Director convinced the President's Crime Commission, among other things, to reject any liberalization of marijuana laws (William W. Turner, *Hoover's FBI: The Men and the Myth,* Los Angeles: Sherbourne Press, 1970).

DeLoach's association with Guthman; quotes by Guthman; DeLoach leaks tapes on Dr. King; DeLoach questions Guthman on Robert Kennedy (Victor S. Navasky, *Kennedy Justice,* New York: Atheneum, 1971).

DeLoach leaves the Bureau and joins Pepsico (William W. Turner, *Hoover's FBI*).

Congressman Smith's legislation on Hoover's successor (William W. Turner, *Hoover's FBI*).

Public announcement praising Hoover by members of the Society of Former FBI Agents (Edward S. Kerstein, *Milwaukee Journal,* April 18, 1971).

CHAPTER 15: The Inner Directives

*Pages 245 through 248:*

Hoover quote, "The international Communist conspiracy. . . ." (Statement at a House Appropriations Committee hearing, February 5, 1959).

Hoover quote, "What can one do. . . . ?" (J. Edgar Hoover, *Masters of Deceit,* New York: Henry Holt and Company, 1958).

Hoover quote, "Anyone who opposes. . . ." (Testimony before the House Committee on Un-American Activities, March 26, 1947).

Hoover quote, "It is an established fact. . . ." (Speech before the Daughters of the American Revolution, April 22, 1954).

Hoover quote, "Youth is unable. . . ." (Jack Alexander, *Reader's Digest,* December 1937).

Hoover quotes; "We do not give. . . ," "Too many in America. . . ," and "Unless we stand united. . . ." (Melvin Mann, *Freedom Talk,* Number 46, December 11, 1968).

Hoover quote, "To my mind. . . ." (*Newsweek,* January 12, 1970).

Hoover quote on "false liberals" (Speech before the Catholic Youth Organization, New York City, November 16, 1963).

Hoover quote, "To preach sermons. . . ." (Statement at a House Appropriations hearing, February 8, 1960).

Hoover quote, "They are the Communists. . . ." (Speech before the Catholic Youth Organization, New York City, November 16, 1963). With respect to communism, Hoover considers the nation to be a giant hothouse, and the public to be plants which must be protected from foreign elements. In 1969, he said: "Communism in reality is not a political party. It is a way of life—an evil and malignant way of life. It reveals a condition akin to disease that spreads like an epidemic and, like an epidemic, quarantine is necessary to keep it from infecting the nation" (Associated Press).

Hoover quote, "The growing number of Black extremist organizations. . . ." (A report to Attorney General Ramsey Clark, Reprinted in *Human Events,* January 11, 1969).

Hoover quote on the RNA (FBI annual report, October 30, 1970, Reprinted in *U.S. News and World Report,* November 9, 1970).

*Pages 249 and 250:*

Hoover quote, "Professional demagogues. . . ." (J. Edgar Hoover, Testimony before President Johnson's Commission on Violence, September 18, 1968).

Hoover quote, "Reaches into. . . ." (John H. Lyle, *The Dry and Lawless Years,* Englewood Cliffs, New Jersey: Prentice-Hall, 1960).

Hoover quote, "Were I to list. . . ." (J. Edgar Hoover, *Persons in Hiding,* Boston: Little, Brown and Co., 1938).

Hoover quote, "There are still among us. . . ." (*FBI Law Enforcement Bulletin,* January 1961).

Hoover quote, "Beastly punks" (*FBI Law Enforcement Bulletin,* November 1962).

Hoover quotes on adult criminals, Dillinger, Kathryn Kelly, and Ma Barker (J. Edgar Hoover, *Persons in Hiding*).

*Pages 251 and 252:*

Hoover quote, "Not juvenile delinquency. . . ." (*Woman's Home Companion,* January 1944).

Hoover quote, "I'm going to tell the truth. . . ." (J. Edgar Hoover, *Persons in Hiding*). In an address, "Patriotism and the War Against Crime," to the annual convention of the DAR in Washington (April 23, 1936), Hoover stated: "I warn you to stay unswerving to your task—that of standing by the man on the firing line—the practical, hard-headed, experienced, honest policemen who have shown by their efforts that they, and they alone, know the answer to the crime problem. The answer can be summed up in one sentence—adequate detection, swift apprehension, and certain, unrelenting punishment. That is what the criminal fears. That is what he understands, and nothing else, and that fear is the only thing which will force him into the ranks of the law-abiding. There is no royal road to law enforcement. If we wait upon the medical quacks, the parole panderers, and the misguided sympathizers with habitual criminals to protect our lives and property from the criminal horde, then we must also resign ourselves to increasing violence, robbery, and sudden death." Such moving, if not terrifying, bombast earned for Hoover, no doubt, a prominent position as an available speaker of the International Platform Association. The IPA features his name as one of their most distinguished speakers in their advertisements to this day.

Hoover quote, "Misguided do-gooders" (*FBI Law Enforcement Bulletin,* June 1961).

Hoover quote, "Sentimentalists tell us. . . ." (J. Edgar Hoover, *Persons in Hiding*). Hoover has no tolerance for "those sentimental moo-cows of scant knowledge but loud voices who are forever interfering with businesslike law enforcement by their turn-the-other-cheek theories of crime and eradication" (J. Edgar Hoover, *Persons in Hiding*).

Hoover quote, "Many of us. . . ." (J. Edgar Hoover, "The Crime Wave We Now Face," *New York Times,* April 21, 1946).

Hoover quote, "Many trusting souls. . . ." (J. Edgar Hoover, *Persons in Hiding*).

Background on John Dillinger's sentence (Jay Robert Nash and Ron Offen, *Dillinger: Dead or Alive,* Chicago: Regnery, 1970).

Hoover quote, "My feeling. . . ." (House Appropriations Committee testimony, 1966). The Director was being asked by Congressman Rooney whether or not Hoover thought it would be proper for Joseph Valachi to write a book on the Cosa Nostra while a prisoner in the federal penitentiary at Atlanta.

Hoover quote, "By all means let us extend education. . . ." (J. Edgar Hoover, *Persons in Hiding*). The Director's idea of law enforcement is spartan, and he believes it is everybody's business. In 1959, he felt that the rise of crime "clearly indicates that growing numbers of our citizens have been afflicted by a sickness which I call the 'decadence disease.' Its symptoms are lethargy, self-indulgence, and the principle of pleasure before duty" (Testimony before a House Appropriations subcommittee).

Hoover quotes, "Under our system. . . ." and "No matter how unfair. . . ." (*Los Angeles Herald Examiner,* March 11, 1970).

*Pages 255, 256, and 257:*

Hoover quotes on being a champion of the merit system and on Civil Service applicants to the FBI (Max Lowenthal, *The Federal Bureau of Investigation,* William Sloan Associates, 1950).

"It's almost as if the Director pushed the self-destruct button," a Department of Justice official said after the Boggs controversy flared up (Ken W. Clawson, *Washington Post,* April 11, 1971). When an ex-FBI agent learned of Hoover's backbiting comments on Ramsey Clark he said, "The old man's getting childish. He's old and he should get out. He was good for law enforcement. He'll never retire. He doesn't have any interests. He has no family. What does a fellow do? You get tired of going to the races" (*Life,* April 9, 1971).

Roche quote (John P. Roche, "Hoover Mystique Difficult," *The Birmingham* News, April 13, 1971).

Johnson quote (Tom Wicker, "Nobody Dares to Pick His Successor," *Life,* April 9, 1971).

Hoover quotes on his age and his dogs, (*Time,* December 14, 1970).

Hoover quote, "I have many plans. . . ." (Mark Brown, Associated Press, April 11, 1971).

Gallup, Harris surveys (Associated Press, April 11, 1971).

# Index